Sex Killers

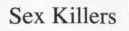

Sex Killers

Nigel Cawthorne

Magpie Books, London

Constable & Robinson Ltd
3 The Lanchesters
162 Fulham Palace Road
London W6 9ER

First published by Boxtree, 1994

This edition published by Magpie Books,
an imprint of Constable & Robinson Ltd 2009

A copy of the British Library Cataloguing in
Publication Data is available from the British Libary

ISBN: 978-1-84901-115-0

Printed and bound in the European Union

1 3 5 7 9 10 8 6 4 2

Contents

Introduction

Sex is our most basic drive. It has been the inspiration for great poetry, art, sacrifice – and murder. Sexual passion lurks a millimetre beneath the surface of the mildest life like a wild animal. Without warning, it can explode into violent action.

Sex plays its part in the slaughter of war, even in recent conflicts. A large number of Vietnamese men joined the Viet Cong, the Communist resistance during the Vietnam war, because American soldiers were coming to their country and taking their women. This caused what was known at the time as 'shrinking bird syndrome'. Vietnamese men believed that the presence of foreigners in their country caused their penises to shrink – a powerful reason to go to war against the military might of the world's most powerful nation. No wonder the Vietnamese won.

The problem with sex is that we are all vulnerable. Every one of us can be caught up in its heady passion. It is not hard for us to sympathise with lovers who have killed an unfaithful partner. Who of us has not suffered the paranoid nightmare of sexual jealousy? If a gun was handy, there are few of us who would not be tempted to pull the trigger and shoot the dirty dog down.

But how far would most of us go in other circumstances? If, say, we found that our particular sexual predilection was considered a little abnormal, would we stray outside the law to satisfy it? And if it demanded violence, cruelty, even death, for its fulfilment, would the hunger building day upon day eventually force us over the edge?

But worse, what are those people around us thinking and feeling? What are the secret desires of our docile partner – could they suddenly erupt in a murderous rage? Most murder victims are killed by people they know intimately. And what about that attractive stranger we have fancied from afar? If we get them back to our place tonight – for coffee – are we putting at risk our very existence?

The truth is that comparatively few people are murdered in the course of muggings, kidnaps or armed robberies. Many more were slain by rapists, sex attackers and jealous lovers.

Since the beginning of the AIDS epidemic in the 1980s, governments around the world have begged us all to think about 'safe sex'. But there is no such thing as safe sex – no matter how many condoms you use. You are far more likely to be killed by your lover than by any HIV virus.

Chapter 1

Rough Sex

At six o'clock on the morning of 26 August 1986, Patricia Reilly was taking an early morning cycle ride in New York's Central Park. She was cycling down the winding East Drive when, barely fifty yards behind the Metropolitan Museum of Art, she saw what she thought was a bag lady sprawled in the grass. She rode on. But about fifty yards past the obelisk – New York's own Cleopatra's Needle – she stopped and turned the bike around. Something was definitely wrong.

From about thirty yards away, at the foot of a large elm tree, she could see a body. It was not moving. As she walked closer, across the grass, she saw it was the body of a young woman, almost naked. Her blouse and bra were pushed up around her throat, exposing her tanned breasts. Her pink miniskirt was hiked up around her waist. Her legs were bare. Her panties were missing, though she still had her flat canvas shoes on. The body was twisted, the legs splayed. The young woman's vagina was fully exposed. There is no dignity in death.

The girl's white embroidered panties were found 45 feet

1

from the body. They were twisted as if they had been rolled down when they had been taken off. Joggers had seen a tall young man in an Oxford shirt in the area. One thought he had seen a couple engaged in what he took to be sexual activity in the area at about 5.30 am.

Patricia Reilly ran to the Central Park boathouse to call the police, but the phones had been ripped out. She spotted a police truck. Its engine was running, but the doors were locked and there was no one inside.

She had to cycle as far as Madison and 50th before she found a pay phone that worked. She dialled 911 and reported the dead body she had found. The operator wanted to know exactly where the corpse was located. Reilly was told that each lamp post in Central Park carried a four digit number. The first two digits specified the number of the nearest cross street. But after discovering the body Patricia Reilly had somehow omitted to examine the nearest lamp post. All she knew was that the body was near the back of the Metropolitan Museum.

When the police arrived, they immediately concluded that the young woman had been the victim of a sex attack. A brown limousine with tinted windows had been seen in the area. The uniformed officers concluded that the woman was a prostitute. She had picked up a trick and been murdered elsewhere, then her body had been unceremoniously dumped in the park. But when the New York Police Department Detective Paul Chu turned up, he told them they were wrong. Apart from the outline of a high-cut bikini, the girl's body had a California tan. New York prostitutes traditionally stay out of the sun in an effort to effect a look of pallid innocence.

Around the neck of the victim Chu noticed multiple red wounds. The girl, it appeared, had been strangled. Against all the rules in the NYPD handbook, Chu pulled down the blouse and the skirt, destroying much of the evidence of how she was killed, but giving the innocent victim some privacy in death.

2

There was no money on the victim, apart from one torn dollar bill. Her jewellery was missing too. But a credit card found in the pocket of the girl's blood-splattered white Levi jacket gave Chu the victim's name – Jennifer Levin.

Jennifer was just eighteen. At ten o'clock on the previous night she had met two of her girlfriends at Juanita's Mexican restaurant on Third Avenue. They ordered margaritas. In New York State, it is illegal to serve minors under the age of twenty-one but no one asked for any ID. They had two cocktails a piece, then a man they did not know sent a bottle of champagne to their table. Soon after midnight, rather drunk, they took a cab uptown to Dorrian's Red Hand on 84th Street and Second Avenue, an old-fashioned restaurant and bar that was a hangout for 'preppies', and where alcohol was served all night to underage drinkers. Jennifer knew that handsome nineteen-year-old Robert Chambers would be there. She had talked about him to her girlfriends earlier that night. When they arrived, she made straight for him.

Chambers was a regular at Dorrian's, and was known as a cocaine user and trouble maker. Although Jennifer had a regular boyfriend she had also had sex with Chambers twice. That night, she went up to Chambers and told him straight out that he had given her the best sex she had had in her young life.

Chambers seemed offended by this. 'Jennifer, you shouldn't have said that,' he admonished as he walked away.

But Jennifer and her boyfriend were going off to college in Boston soon and she wanted to see Chambers again before she left. She inveigled a friend into asking him to meet her outside the bar in twenty minutes. Jennifer Levin was last seen alive leaving Dorrian's with Robert Chambers at around 2.30 am.

Early in the afternoon after the murder, Detective Frank Connelly and Al Genova from Manhattan North's crack homicide squad visited the penthouse apartment on New York's fashionable East 90th Street where Chambers lived

3

with his mother. They told Mrs Chambers that they were on a missing person's investigation and she let them in.

When Robert Chambers appeared, the detectives noticed that he had scratches on his face and cuts on the backs of his fingers. He agreed to accompany them to the precinct.

Although they read him his rights, he was still not considered a prime suspect at this point. He said that after he and Jennifer left Dorrian's, she had asked him for a cigarette. He did not have any. She went to a Korean deli to buy some, then headed off to see her regular boyfriend, Brock Pernice. He lived on the West Side, the other side of Central Park, Chambers said.

Chambers claimed that he had gone to a doughnut shop on East 86th Street, then walked home and watched *The Price is Right* on the TV. The scratches on his face and chest, he said, were inflicted by their pet cat that had jumped on him as he lay back watching TV. The cuts on his hands came from a neighbour's sanding machine, which had jumped when he was sanding the floor, he said.

The police accepted this tale at first and Chambers stuck to it for five hours of interrogation. Then veteran detective Mike Sheehan asked what sort of cat did Chambers have – a mountain lion?

Chambers started fidgeting – and changed his story. He and Jennifer had walked two blocks west from Dorrian's. At Lexington Avenue, they quarrelled and Jennifer had scratched his face. Then a friend of hers, a blond man in his twenties whose name Chambers did not know, came along and Jennifer went off with him.

While he was sticking to his original story, the detectives had given Chambers the benefit of the doubt. They liked him and did not think that he was a murderer. But once he changed his story, they were on him in a feeding frenzy. Within minutes, he admitted that he had killed Jennifer – but protested that it was not murder.

4

She had been a little drunk, he said. In Dorrian's, she had pursued him. He had tried to give her the slip, but when he left, she had followed. She asked him to go to Central Park to talk. Once there, she had begun to get mad and had cursed and scratched him. She took off her panties to go to the bathroom, then said that he would look cute if he was tied up.

He let her tie his hands behind him with her panties, then she pushed him down and sat on his face. She scratched his chest, then grabbed his penis and began jerking him off very roughly. He begged her to stop it. She licked his penis, then slapped it and hit him with a stick. She squeezed his balls, hard. Chambers claimed that the pain was excruciating. Jennifer was laughing. It had made him mad.

Chambers said that he had managed to wriggle one of his hands free, then he grabbed her neck and had pulled her over. Before he knew it she was dead.

Chambers went on to claim that Jennifer was into kinky sex. She had taken nude photographs of him after they had had intercourse on the roof of a friend's house. His attorney tried to subpoena her diary, which he alleged contained details of her kinky and aggressive sexual goings-on with other men. After studying the diary himself for more than three-and-a-half hours, the judge handed the diary back to the Levin family. It contained no details that might be pertinent to the defence.

Chambers claimed that he had been raped by Jennifer Levin – although no semen was found on the corpse. Throughout his three-month trial, he maintained that Jennifer had been the victim of rough sex that had gone too far.

The prosecution, Jennifer Levin's parents and friends were outraged by this defence. They claimed that Chambers was blaming the victim for her own death. It was he that was on trial, not her. Outside the court-room, women protesters demanded 'Justice for Jennifer'.

Inside the court-room there was more sympathy for the

defendant though. Despite the charges against him, his notorious trial seemed to make the handsome Robert Chambers more attractive to women. Throughout the trial, the public gallery was packed with his groupies, eager to get a glimpse of the object of their desire. He even had an attractive new girlfriend, Shawn Kovell, who attended the trial every day.

In the end, the jury was not even allowed to decide whether the 'rough sex' defence was a good enough excuse – even if it was true. While they were out considering their verdict, the prosecution and defence cooked up a plea bargain. Chambers pleaded guilty to manslaughter in the first degree and was sentenced to five-to-fifteen years in the state penitentiary.

After he was sent down, a videotape shot by Shawn Kovell surfaced. It showed Chambers, Kovell and three of her posh Upper East Side girlfriends cavorting in their underwear. It was shot while Chambers was out on bail. In one scene, he was pictured playing with a doll. He twisted its head off, turned to the camera and said: 'Oops, I think I killed it.'

The video was aired on Fox Television for two days, with record ratings. Public opinion, which had been behind Chambers and his 'rough sex' defence, dwindled rapidly.

England's most notorious 'rough sex' case had happened forty years before in London. Then, just a year after the end of World War II, the pubs and clubs of Britain's capital were crowded with servicemen determined to live it up after six years of war. And women, deprived of their menfolk for six years and consigned to monotonous war work, were out to have a good time.

Ex-serviceman Neville Heath was certainly a man who went to great lengths to enjoy himself and 31-year-old would-be film actress Margery Gardner was a certified good-time girl. Margery had left her husband and baby daughter in Sheffield to seek fame and fortune in London. She led a precarious existence in a succession of bedsits, occasionally sleeping with men in return for a meal and bed for the night Her companions were pimps, thieves, black marketeers and ex-officers on the make. In September 1945, she had been a passenger in a stolen car that had been chased by police through Hyde Park and she was on the files of the 'Ghost Squad' set up to investigate the post-war crime boom in London's West End.

No one can be sure quite when she and Heath met, but on 23 February 1946, the manager of the Strand Palace Hotel burst into a bedroom to find Heath beating a woman with a cane. Heath had been registered as Captain James Cadogan Armstrong of the South African Air Force. An electrician heard the woman's screams and had called the manager. Heath showed no embarrassment and demanded to know what the manager meant by his intrusion. The woman, later identified as Margery Gardner, refused to press charges and the two of them left arm in arm. According to her medical files, Gardner enjoyed being beaten and would offer her naked body for flagellation.

They met again on the evening of 20 June 1946. Heath had spent the day drinking with journalists in Fleet Street bars. His afternoon was spent at a private drinking club. Then, in the early evening, he picked up Margery in the Trevor Arms in Knightsbridge. They had dinner together in the Normandie Hotel and went dancing at the Panama Club.

Around midnight, they took a cab to the Pembridge Court Hotel in Notting Hill, where he was registered as Lieutenant-Colonel N.G.C. Heath. After tipping the taxi driver, he put his arm around the waist of his attractive young companion and let them into the hotel with his own key.

At 2 pm the following afternoon, the chambermaid knocked on the door of Heath's room. There was no reply. She let herself in. The curtains were still drawn. Only one of the twin beds in the room had been slept in. It was still occupied – and the occupant was not moving.

7

The chambermaid rushed downstairs to fetch the assistant hotel manager, Mrs Alice Wyatt. Back in the room, she pulled open the curtains. The empty bed showed traces of blood. Gingerly, Mrs Wyatt pulled back the covers from the motionless figure in the other bed. It was a young woman, naked. She was dead.

When the police arrived, they examined the severely mutilated body. There were the marks of seventeen lashes of a whip across the flesh – nine on her back, six on her breasts and belly and two across her forehead. Both her nipples and some of the soft tissue of the breast had been bitten away, and there was a seven-inch tear up through her vagina and beyond.

The woman had plainly consented to some sort of sexual activity. Her clothes were neatly folded on a chair. Her rings were still on her fingers and her handbag had not been touched. Inside, detectives found her wartime identity card giving her name as Margery Aimee Brownell Gardner.

In the fireplace, there was a short poker that Home Office pathologist Professor Keith Simpson said was responsible for her internal injuries. Severe though these were, they were not responsible for her death. She had died from asphyxiation either from a gag or from having her face pushed into the pillow.

The whip that had inflicted the welts on her body was nowhere to be seen. The marks showed the distinctive diamond pattern of a woven leather riding crop.

'Find that whip and you've found your man,' Professor Simpson told the police.

After a solid day's drinking – it is estimated that he had drunk between 30 and 50 pints of beer – Heath may not have been in control of himself when he brutally murdered and mutilated Margery. But after the frenzy had subsided, he was ruthless and controlled. He washed the riding crop and packed it in his suitcase, along with the cloth he had used to bind Margery's wrists and the scarf he had gagged her with Then he bought a first-class return to Worthing.

He phoned his girlfriend to say that he was in Worthing. They had met two weeks before at a dance in Chelsea. The following evening he had proposed to her in his room at the Pembridge Court and they were 'unofficially engaged'. He asked her to give him an alibi. Heath said that he had lent his key to a friend called Jack, who had a woman with him. The police said that there had been a horrific murder, and he had been asked to prove that he had not been in his room that night. Unfortunately, he told her, his true alibi was one that Scotland Yard would never accept.

This was not the story he told the police though. Two days after the murder, while a nationwide manhunt was underway, Heath wrote to Scotland Yard explaining that, after an evening with Mrs Gardner, she asked him if she could use his room until 2 am. After that, she intimated, she would spend the rest of the night with him. He agreed, but when he returned she was dead.

However, the police already knew that Heath had a long career as a conman. At eighteen, he had applied for a commission in the Royal Air Force. Within a year, he had been promoted to Flying Officer and was posted to No. 9 Fighter Squadron at RAF Duxford. There he began embezzling the mess funds and bouncing cheques. After winning his wings, he deserted. When the service police arrested him, he gave his word as a gentleman not to escape – then stole the sergeant's car and drove off. He was caught, court-martialled and dismissed from the service.

By this time, he was set on a life of petty crime. In 1938, he appeared in the Old Bailey and was sent to Borstal. When he was released, he joined the Royal Army Service Corps and served as a captain in the Middle East. In the brothels of Cairo, he would pay to whip naked girls who were tied over a waist-high wooden bar. In 1941, he was cashiered for

9

having two pay books and for bouncing cheques. On his way back to England, he jumped ship in Durban. There, he met and married Elizabeth Pitt-Rivers, daughter of one of the wealthiest families in South Africa. They had a son.

In May 1944, Heath was back in England, serving with Bomber Command. He forged his flying log to impress Wrens and wrote more worthless cheques. After being grounded, he returned to South Africa where he faced charges of fraud. By this time, the Pitt-Rivers family were sick of him and paid him £2,400 to divorce Elizabeth. Soon afterwards he was deported, returning to England early in 1946.

Throughout his career of petty crime, Heath also displayed an unhealthy interest in causing pain to women. Even at school there were incidents. When a young girl dropped her pencil and reached down to get it, Heath stamped on her hand. On another occasion, he was found spanking a girl with a ruler.

When he was stationed at Duxford, one woman had refused to spend the night with him.

'I'll never forget his face,' she recalled, 'that horrible, sadistic look which twisted and contorted it grotesquely. Then I got it – two vicious smacks across the face.'

She had broken free and run to safety in a nearby hotel.

Heath's new girlfriend called Scotland Yard, telling them that Heath was in Worthing. The postmark on the letter he had sent also indicated that he was in Worthing. But by the time the police had tracked him to the Ocean Hotel, the bird had flown.

As Group Captain Rupert Brooke, Heath had booked into the Tollard Hotel in Bournemouth. He insisted on a room with a gas fire and seemed to have decided to kill himself. But first he would have one final fling.

In the bar he ran up a huge drinks bill, regaling his fellow drinker with tales of his life in South Africa. On the promenade he met a pretty nineteen-year-old, Doreen Marshall. A former Wren, she was staying at the Norfolk Hotel, recuperating from a bout of measles and the flu. They went for a walk and Heath invited her to dinner at his hotel.

The evening went well. Doreen seemed impressed by his tales of flying dangerous missions over enemy-occupied Europe. But towards the end of the meal, Heath must have said something out of place. Doreen blanched.

In the lounge, she managed to catch the attention of one of the other guests and asked him to call her a taxi. But Heath cancelled the cab. He told the night porter that he would walk Doreen back to the Norfolk, saying that he would be back in half an hour.

By 4 am, the night porter was still waiting up to let him in. He went to Heath's room to check if he was there. He found Heath in bed. Heath explained that he had played a practical joke. Knowing the porter would wait up, he had placed a ladder against his window and climbed up.

The next day, one of the other guests remarked on the scratches on Heath's neck. Then the manager of the Norfolk Hotel phoned, expressing concern about the disappearance of one of his guests – a young lady from Pinner. Heath was asked about it. He said the young lady he had entertained for dinner was definitely not from Pinner. Nevertheless, the manager suggested that he get in touch with the police.

With the supreme confidence of the professional conman, Heath phoned the local police station and spoke to Detective Constable George Souter. He agreed to come down to the station and take a look at a picture of the missing girl. But when he entered the station he almost bumped into Doreen's sister. The two women bore a striking resemblance. Heath broke into a cold sweat before he was able to compose himself. But it was enough to trigger Detective Constable Souter's suspicions. He came right to the point.

'Isn't your name Heath?' he asked.

Heath said it wasn't. Then he said that many people had

commented on the likeness. However, the police had not released any pictures of Heath to the press, in case it undermined identification evidence at the trial. The only people who knew what Heath looked like were the police and Heath himself.

In Heath's pocket, there was a cloakroom ticket from the railway station. When the police handed it in, they were given a suitcase. It contained the riding whip and a blood-stained scarf. Heath meekly wrote a statement.

Before Heath was charged, a dog sniffing in some undergrowth disturbed a swarm of flies. Under a pile of clothes, there was the naked body of a woman. Her throat had been cut. But before she died, her right nipple had been bitten off and jagged cuts had been made along the length of her torso. It was the body of the once pretty Doreen Marshall.

Heath wanted to plead guilty to both murders, but his barrister persuaded him to enter an insanity plea. The defence tried to build a picture of a normal man who was occasionally overwhelmed by irresistible impulses. But Heath's whole career as a petty criminal showed that he had little concept of right and wrong.

Heath was found guilty and was sentenced to death by hanging. He refused to enter an appeal, saying that, since he had lost his wife and child, he had had nothing to live for.

He faced death calmly. He accepted the traditional offer of a glass of whisky to steady his nerves, saying: 'While you're at it, make it a double.'

When the hangman Albert Pierrepoint arrived, Heath said: 'Come on, boys, let's get on with it.'

Chapter 2

Rape

By the age of nineteen, Colin Pitchfork had been arrested twice for indecent exposure. It was a compulsion he could not control – and it led, eventually, to rape and murder.

Pitchfork had his good side too. He did voluntary work at Dr Barnardo's Children's Home. It was there that he met eighteen-year-old Carole, who was an 'Auntie' to the children. They fell in love and started living together.

But the compulsion to expose himself to women had not left him. They had been together for two years when he was arrested again for flashing. He told a counsellor: 'You get that need. You go out sometimes and cover 50 or 60 miles looking for an opportunity. It's the high I needed.'

In 1981, the couple married. Pitchfork got a good job in a bakery and his skill at decorative icing attracted the attention of the local paper. But once again he was caught flashing and sent to have psychiatric help.

In 1983, his wife was pregnant and he no longer found her attractive. He started an affair with a student he had met at evening classes. Pitchfork even made love to her in his wife's

13

bed – the idea that his wife might catch them there added to the excitement.

When his wife found out, she threw him out of the house, but took him back again when the baby was born. But she never felt happy in the house again. They decided to move to Naborough where she would be closer to her family. Friends decided to hold a leaving party for them. That evening, Pitchfork felt the overwhelming urge to expose himself again. But this time a harmless flash turned into something much more deadly.

A pretty fifteen-year-old schoolgirl (known only as Jane X in court) was walking home from a friend's house, not far from Pitchfork's new home. Pitchfork was out in the car with the baby when he started cruising around. He spotted Jane walking along the street and decided that she would make the perfect victim.

He knew the area well. His psychotherapy sessions were held at the Carlton Hayes Hospital nearby. He got out of the car and exposed himself to Jane, intending to make his escape down a footpath that ran down behind the hospital. But Jane, terrified, ran down the pathway, cutting off his escape route. He chased after her and grabbed her. His desire was now even more overwhelming. She was too terrified to scream or even resist. If she had screamed, he said later, he thought he would have been scared off. At it was, he knocked her unconscious with a single punch and brutally raped her. Then he realised that he had to kill her.

'She knew I was married,' he told the police later. 'She saw the ring. I also realised I'd got a bloody earring on. And I'd been losing my hair. She could describe those things. Almost certainly she would see me in the village. There was no way out I was trapped. So I strangled her.'

Throughout the rape and murder, Pitchfork's baby lay innocently gurgling in the carry-cot in the back of his car. When he had finished, he drove home to the leaving party as if nothing had happened.

For the police, there was little to go on. The only clue was the rapist's semen that was found in Jane's pubic hair – indicating that the killer was so excited by the rape that he had ejaculated prematurely, even before he had forcibly penetrated her.

Jane's own stepfather was the police's first suspect. But the analysis of the semen indicated that the killer had a different blood group and he was eliminated from the inquiry. The sperm count in the semen also indicated that it came from a younger man. Every man between the ages of seventeen and thirty-four in the surrounding three villages was interviewed. They also checked on anyone in the region who had been charged with a sex offence in the past five years. But Pitchfork still lived outside the catchment area. By the time Jane was buried, the police enquiries had hit a dead end.

Pitchfork found it difficult to settle in his new home. He was restless, discontented. He told his wife that sex with her was 'boring' and he took a new lover. In January 1987, his mistress gave birth to a stillborn child. Pitchfork returned from the hospital in tears and confessed the affair to his wife – expecting her sympathy.

Even his new lover did not quell the urge to expose himself. He claimed to have flashed at over a thousand girls. Flashing, he thought, was a game that had to be played by strict rules. He cruised an area looking for a likely victim, usually an attractive young girl – someone who would be shocked and frightened. Then he would pick an appropriate spot.

'No matter where I expose myself, they always have room to walk by me,' he later told the police. 'It's the easiest way. You shock them. They walk by you and then you get your exit route clear.'

Fifteen-year-old Jane had not walked by him. She ran away, blocking his escape. So Pitchfork considered what happened to her as her own fault. Another fifteen-year-old

15

girl (who we shall call Susan Y) did not follow the rules of Pitchfork's flashing game either – and paid for it with her life.

Pitchfork was out on his motorbike on 31 July 1981 in the same area where Jane had been murdered. When he spotted Susan, he decided to stop and flash at her. But instead of walking by him, she ran into a field.

Pitchfork claimed that he killed her because he knew she could have recognised him from his motorcycle jacket. He felt trapped again and he had killed once before, so what did another one matter.

He seemed to have taken more time with his second victim. Again she had been knocked out. But this time, she was naked from the waist down with her bra pushed up to expose her breasts. There was blood around her vagina. She had been strangled and there was semen in her pubic hair. Once again there was little for the police to go on. All they knew was that they had to catch this brutal rapist-murderer before he struck again.

A seventeen-year-old kitchen porter named Richard Buckland was caught hanging around on his motorbike in the area, seemingly fascinated by the police activity. He had a history of sexual violence. He referred to women as 'slags, dogs, whores and bitches'. A former girlfriend told the police that he liked rough sex. He used to slap and bite her viciously and keep up a torrent of insulting names during intercourse. He also preferred anal sex.

Within 24 hours, Buckland had confessed to the murder of Susan. Many of the details about the murder were surprisingly accurate, but there were nagging inconsistencies. And Buckland knew nothing about the earlier murder of Jane X.

One of the detectives on the case had heard about the 'genetic fingerprinting' which had just been developed at Leicester University. He sent the semen samples from the two girls' bodies and a sample of Buckland's blood over to the labs at Leicester. They quickly concluded that the two semen samples had come from the same man – but not from the man who had given the blood sample. Buckland was released.

Now there was only one way forward. The police took blood samples from every man between 17 and 34 in the three surrounding villages – and from all current and former patients and inmates at Carlton Hayes Hospital. This would include Colin Pitchfork. The police tested samples of blood from over 5,000 men – at £120 a time – and still came up with no match to the DNA in the semen. The detectives were in despair. They had spent over £250,000 and still seemed no closer to catching the killer. Then, purely by chance, there was a breakthrough.

One evening at the Clarendon Pub in Leicester, a number of bakery workers were out having a drink. The conversation turned to the murder hunt and the blood samples that were being taken in the area of Naborough. One of the workers, Ian Kelly, claimed that he had supplied Colin Pitchfork's blood test for him.

The bakery's manageress was worried by this. She intended to report it to a policeman she knew, who was, in fact, the son of the owner of the Clarendon. But he was away on leave. When he returned six weeks later, she told him what Ian Kelly had said.

Pitchfork had moved into the area after the first murder, but before the second. So he had been interviewed about the murder of Susan. The police quickly compared the signature on his statement with the signature attached to the blood sample. They were different.

The police discovered that Pitchfork had offered several people money to take the blood test for him, saying that he had a record for indecent exposure and the police were trying to frame him. Ian Kelly wanted no cash. He took the blood test for Pitchfork purely as a favour.

Pitchfork coached him to answer questions that established his identity – the birth dates of his children, his

17

mother's maiden name – and gave him his passport as proof of identity. Pitchfork had already removed his own picture and pasted Kelly's picture in, resealing it carefully.

Pitchfork was arrested and confessed. He also admitted two other indecent assaults and one kidnapping. While the manhunt for Swan's killer was on, he had given a lift to a girl who had just had a row with her boyfriend. He drove her off into open countryside with the intention of indecently assaulting her. When she realised what was happening, she grabbed for the steering wheel, causing the car to skid to a halt. Pitchfork turned around and headed homewards, but then stopped in a layby to molest her. The girl leapt out and ran home.

Pitchfork was sentenced to two life sentences for the murders, two ten-year sentences for the rapes and another three years for attempting to pervert the course of justice.

Genetic fingerprinting soon caught on in America. Tommy Lee Andrews, a 24-year-old warehouseman, was the first American convicted by the weight of DNA evidence. He had been caught prowling at night in an area of Orlando, Florida, where there had been a series of brutal rapes. Two of the victims claimed to recognise him, but they had only glimpsed their assailant briefly. His blood type matched that of the semen recovered from the victims – but so did the blood of 30 per cent of Americans.

The prosecution case was not looking strong until the Assistant State Attorney Tim Berry read about the Pitchfork case in England. He discovered that Leicester University had licensed their genetic profiling procedure to ICI and that the techniques were now available through the Lifecodes Corporation in New York. Berry rushed samples of the semen and of Andrews' blood there. There was a perfect match.

But genetic fingerprinting made its major breakthrough in a murder case in the States with the prosecution of the Southside Slayer. In late 1987, there were a series of horrific rape-murders in Richmond, Virginia. All four women had been attacked in their own homes. Debbie Davis was found naked and dead in her apartment on 17 September 1987. The 35-year-old woman had been tied up, raped and strangled. Dr Susan Hellams, 32, a neurosurgeon, was murdered two weeks later. Her husband, a law student, came home to find her corpse bound and gagged, and stuffed into a wardrobe. On 22 November, fifteen-year-old Diane Cho was found naked and dead in her bedroom. And in December, 42-year-old Susan Tucker was raped and murdered in her home. Her body was discovered a week later.

The killer had left a telltale clue. He was extraordinarily neat. This reminded one detective of a case he had worked on years before that of Timothy Spencer, a cat burglar who got a thrill breaking into people's homes while they were there, asleep.

Spencer had a record of a series of arrests for burglary, but none for sex offences. When he was interviewed, he was asked for a blood sample. 'Does the blood thing have anything to do with rape?' he asked.

The DNA in the blood sample matched that in the semen. It was enough to convict Spencer. On 22 September 1988, a Richmond County jury sent him to Death Row.

Rapists often turn out to be the most surprising of people. Mild-mannered Gerald Thompson lived with his grandmother in Peoria, Illinois, and held down a good job at the Caterpillar Tractor Company. He was respectable and hardworking, and had never been in trouble in his life. But he boasted to a friend that, in the previous year, he had raped over fifty young women.

He would pick them up and drive them to some desolate spot. The passenger door handle was wired to the battery. If the woman tried to escape, she got an electric shock. Then he would cut away her clothing with a pair of scissors and rape her. Afterwards he would make his victim perform other sex acts with him in the headlights of the car while he photographed the action with an automatic camera. He noted down the names and addresses of his victims and intimidated them into silence by the obscene pictures he had taken.

This well-thought-out plan worked well until Mildred Hallmark, the daughter of another Caterpillar worker, fought back. She drew blood with her fingernails and managed to stab Thompson repeatedly with a pen. He went berserk and overpowered her. During the vicious beating he administered, his victim died. Thompson dumped her lifeless body into a narrow gorge and went home for a good night's sleep.

Acting on a tip-off, probably from the friend he had boasted to, the police picked up Thompson. They found his bloodstained clothes and car cushion, along with his rape diary and collection of pornographic photographs. Thompson eventually confessed and was sent to the electric chair in 1935.

Itinerant American engineer Robert J. Thompson also began as a rapist and turned into a killer. In August 1958, a Philadelphia woman was on vacation in Mexico when she agreed to visit an out-of-the-way village with him. In the car, he gave her a bottle and she took a swig from it. The next thing she remembered was waking up naked, having been raped, robbed and beaten.

A few weeks later, a New York woman had a lucky escape when a group of men interrupted her attacker. But a retired Chicago school teacher was found dead at the roadside nearby the next day. Her stomach contained a powerful sedative. And a 52-year-old interior decorator died of her wounds, after being robbed, raped and beaten. But she had taken a couple of photographs of the man who had picked her up. Interpol caught Thompson and he was sentenced to life imprisonment.

Even a failed rape can have fatal consequences. Craig Crimmins, a dim-witted stagehand at New York's Metropolitan

20

Opera House, killed after failing in his attempt to rape 30-year-old Helen Mintiks in the 1980 'Phantom of the Opera Case'. Crimmins had been a hulking, withdrawn child, given to somnambulation. His parents once found him outside, sleep-walking in a blizzard. He had no recollection of the incident.

After high school, his father got him the job at the Met, where he found himself attracted to a pretty young violinist who worked in the orchestra pit. On the evening of 23 July 1980, when the performance was over, Crimmins followed her into the backstage lift. The gauche Crimmins had no idea of how to woo a woman and simply asked Mintiks for sex. She turned bright red and slapped him.

In a panic, she hit the wrong button in the lift. At the next floor, she got out. Crimmins followed her. She realised that she was alone with Crimmins on a deserted level near the roof. Anger and embarrassment turned to fear. She tried to strike up a friendly conversation with Crimmins. He picked up a hammer and told her to undress.

Mintiks obeyed. When she was naked, Crimmins tried to rape her, but failed. In frustration, he bound her with rags and tied her to a pipe. He later claimed that he had no intention of hurting her and that he was going to call someone to let them know where she was. But while he was leaving he saw her break free from the pipe. He went back and pushed the bound and naked woman through an opening in the air-conditioning shaft. Her body was found there the next day.

When the police were called in, they began photographing and fingerprinting all the staff of the Met. When it came to Crimmins' turn, detectives noticed that he was extremely nervous. His palm print matched one they found on the pipe where Mintiks had been tethered. Later that day Crimmins confessed.

He was sentenced to twenty-years-to-life. He was denied parole in 2000 and 2004 at the age of forty-five

Sometimes rapists-turned-murderers kill more than just their rape victims. On 27 October 1975, one young Ottawan virgin craved sex so much that he lured a girl into his bedroom, raped and killed her – then went on to kill three more people and wound six.

Robert Poulin was born in 1957. He was described as a 'strange quiet boy'. When he was twelve, his third sister Jody was born, and Poulin moved into the basement to make room for the new baby. He lived there alone.

He had an innocent passion for childish war games. He played out heroic battles on the basement floor, where he manoeuvred his huge armies of troops and artillery. But he had another, darker obsession – sex. The walls of his basement were plastered with pictures of nude women and his room was piled high with soft-core pornographic magazines.

Poulin's diary showed that he was a desperately lonely boy. Since puberty, he yearned for contact with the opposite sex and he was deeply tormented by his shyness and his inability to deal with girls.

One entry read: 'Today is September 5, 1972, a Tuesday . . . There are some girls at school that I would love to be good friends with but I know that I am still too shy to go up and talk to any of them. I wish I could overcome this fear of women.'

Among Poulin's possessions were found women's bras, panties and negligees. He even had a condom-type vibrator device that a man could put his penis into. But at some point, Poulin's interests seemed to change from straightforward sex to bondage, forced sex and rape. Four pairs of handcuffs were found in his room, along with a collection of pornographic books. Some showed women tied up, gagged and handcuffed to bedposts.

One of Poulin's notebooks contained the names, addresses and telephone numbers of eighteen local women. None knew Poulin intimately, but several had received phone calls from an anonymous heavy breather.

In a neatly typed diary entry, on 7 April 1975, when he had just flunked a biology test, Poulin wrote: 'For the last couple of weeks, I have been fairly depressed . . . [and] thought of committing suicide, but I don't want to die before I have had the pleasure of fucking some girl. So I decided to order a model gun from an ad in a *Gallery* magazine (April 1975). With this I was going to threaten a girl in one of the dark streets around here and rape her. I planned to carry my father's scout knife strapped to the inside of my right leg. If the girl caused me any trouble I would kill her, for I was planning to kill myself anyhow, and I have nothing to lose. After that, I would wait for a reason for killing myself. The day I would kill myself would be a Sunday, for if I was going to die, the people that make up my family were going to suffer.'

Poulin was brought back from the brink by an advert for 'Everything' Dolls he found in *Playboy* magazine. It was $29.95 and he sent off for it. In his diary, he recorded his pathetic hopes that it would be 'lifelike'. 'Now I no longer think that I will have to rape a girl,' he wrote, 'and I am unsure whether or not I will still commit suicide.'

Then on 5 May 1975, he found that the plastic blow-up woman with a gaping mouth and vagina was not everything he hoped for. He noted: '"Everything" Doll arrived – a big disappointment.'

Around that time there were a number of sexual assaults and attempted rapes in the area. The perpetrator wore a balaclava. It may have been Poulin. According to his diary, he planned to rape and use a balaclava to disguise his identity. The attacker answered the same general description as Poulin.

In early October, he ran a small ad in the *Ottawa Journal* for a week. It read: 'Male, 18, looking for companionship. PO Box 4021.'

He received three replies – all from homosexuals. Poulin

wrote a reply to one, but had left the letter unposted. It read: 'I have never had a homosexual experience, though the thought has crossed my mind before. However, I'm not only interested in sex but in sharing other pastimes and hobbies. My favourite hobbies are, in order: wargaming, reading (science fiction) and collecting (a variety of things, including stamps and models). I hope you have the same sort of hobbies especially wargaming.'

This letter, more than anything, reveals Poulin's utter desperation and loneliness. Despite his strongly heterosexual feelings, he was even prepared to dabble with homosexuality in order to find a friend.

Soon after he had written that unposted letter, Poulin went to a local store and bought a Winchester pump-action shotgun. Then, in his lonely basement, he sawed off the barrel.

The following day at about 1 pm, the Ottawa fire department received a call to a routine domestic fire. Poulin's mother reported that smoke was pouring from a second-storey window of her home. When firemen arrived ten minutes later, they discovered that the fire was in the basement. Two fire-fighters donned oxygen masks and made their way down into the cellar. The smoke was thick and they had to feel their way. But even through the breathing gear, the firemen noticed an unpleasant smell. It was burning flesh.

The firemen entered the basement bedroom and found the charred body of a girl spread-eagled on what remained of the bed. It was naked except for a bloodstained blouse.

She had not died from the effects of the fire, but as the result of asphyxiation. There was a plastic bag over her head.

The intense heat soon forced the two firemen to retreat. Visibly shaken, they asked another officer to call the police and report a murder.

When the fire was out, the basement was left flooded with several inches of water. The police waded back into the bedroom and found the dead girl had been handcuffed to the bedpost by her left wrist. Handcuffs hung from the other bedpost. This suggested that her right wrist had also been fastened at one time. There were ski bindings around the posts at the foot of the bed, which indicated that her feet had also been tied.

The girl, it was discovered, had been tied down and raped. The bloodstains on the remains of her plaid blouse showed that she had then been stabbed to death.

A trail of half-charred sex magazines ran up the stairs. They had been doused with camping fuel and set alight. Robert Poulin had plainly intended to burn down the whole house. But he had forgotten to open the tiny bedroom window. Starved of oxygen, the fire had effectively snuffed itself out.

Robert Poulin did not have a girlfriend, so investigators were baffled as to the identity of the victim. Poulin's sister had a suggestion to make. Robert, she said, had been interested in a seventeen-year-old Sri Lankan girl named Kim Rabot, who lived a few doors away. He had once invited her over to the house. It was soon found that Kim Rabot was, indeed, missing.

The last person to have seen her was her thirteen-year-old brother. He had been with her at the bus stop on their way to school at 8.30 am that morning when Robert Poulin had approached them. Paulin had told Kim that he had something to show her. A gentle girl sensitive to other people's feelings, Kim had agreed to go with him.

Poulin had taken Kim to his basement bedroom where he showed her his shotgun. At gun point, he forced her to undress and handcuffed her to the bed. Then he raped her. At one point, he untied her feet and unhandcuffed one wrist to turn her over and have her again from behind. The postmortem showed that she had been sodomised as well as raped. Then, when he was sexually satisfied for the first time

25

in his life, he stabbed her fourteen times with a hunting knife.

Mrs Poulin had interrupted her son's activity at some point. She went downstairs to the basement at around 10 o'clock. The curtains that closed off his bedroom were drawn. She called out: 'Knock, knock, can I talk to you for a minute?'

'Yeah,' Poulin said. 'But don't come in.'

Poulin came upstairs an hour later for his peanut butter sandwiches. Then he had returned to the basement, spread the magazines up the stairs and set the room alight. He strapped his hunting knife across his chest, put his 12-bore shotgun in a blue duffel bag and cycled across town on his ten-speed racing bike to his two o'clock theology class.

He was a little late for class. The students were already listening to the teacher, Father Robert Bedard, talk about Christ and the problems of modern society. At 2.30 pm, the door of the classroom creaked slowly open. The students at the back glanced around and saw Robert Poulin, who seemed to be in a kind of a trance. He was carrying a shotgun. He raised it and started to fire.

Suddenly the air was filled with screams. Father Bedard flung himself to the floor. He shouted at his students to do the same. For some, it was too late. The firing continued for about two minutes, then stopped.

The deathly silence that followed was broken by the sound of just one more shot. It came from outside the classroom.

Panic erupted. Students were smashing the windows with chairs and hurling themselves out. The wounded moaned but Father Bedard remained calm. He picked himself up and walked to the classroom door.

Outside the door Robert Poulin lay sprawled on the floor. A sawn-off Winchester shotgun lay beside him. Half the teenager's face was blown away. Despite this, Father Bedard recognised him as one of his students.

Chapter 3

Unwanted Lovers

It seems almost unfair that the mild-mannered Dr Crippen should have gone down in history as one of the world's most notorious murderers. Plenty of vicious killers have committed far more heinous crimes but have remained in relative obscurity. But it was the method of his capture and the world-wide media attention that it created that captured the public's imagination for the best part of a century.

Born in 1862, in Coldwater, Michigan, Dr Hawley Harvey Crippen served his internship in New York, where he met and married Irish student nurse Charlotte Jane Bell. But the sexual side of their marriage was far from satisfactory. Mrs Crippen was a strict convent girl and rushed to the priest to confess each time they made love. She died in childbirth in 1892.

The second Mrs Crippen was the daughter of a Polish grocer who had ambitions to go on the stage. Her name was Kunigunde Mackamotzki but she was known by her stage name Belle Turner. Crippen met her when he treated her after a miscarriage.

He was immediately attracted to her and won her away from her lover, a wealthy Brooklyn businessman. But when they married Crippen found he was unable to satisfy the sexual demands of his inexhaustible wife. He was modest, she voracious. She taunted him with the nickname 'Pyjama Top' because of his shyness when it came to nudity.

Crippen's practice could not sustain his wife's financial demands either. To keep up with her growing expenditure, Crippen began selling patent remedies which were usually nothing more than coloured sugar water with alcohol or opiates added. Meanwhile, his wife began a series of brief affairs.

In 1897, Crippen joined the growing empire of patent-medicine king Professor Munyon and was sent to London to open a British branch. His salary was enormous and he hired the Old Marylebone Music Hall where Belle – this time as Cora Motzki – performed in operetta. The audience was unenthusiastic, though, and the show was taken off after a week.

Belle blamed Crippen for her failure and began flaunting her new lovers in front of her cuckolded husband. Meanwhile, he lost his job and was reduced to selling his own quack medicines again.

They had moved into a large house at 39 Hildrop Crescent, Camden, and Crippen struggled to make ends meet. Belle took up with an American actor named Bruce Miller while Crippen took a lover of his own, his pretty young assistant Ethel LeNeve.

Belle began to suspect that he had a lover and grew jealous. Crippen told Ethel that he was going to divorce his second wife and marry her. But Belle would not hear of it.

Bruce Miller went back to America, where he had a wife and children, and Belle announced that she was taking all the money from Crippen's savings account to follow him. This would ruin him. So Crippen hatched a plot. He bought five grains of the deadly poison hydrobromide of hyoscine.

Belle was last seen alive at a dinner party on 31 January 1910, where she regaled friends with tales of her, now non-existent, music-hall career. Crippen went to bed early and Belle saw her guests to the door at around 1.30 am.

Sometime that night, Crippen poisoned his wife and dragged her heavy body down into the cellar. There, he cut off her head and limbs, removed the genitals and stripped the flesh from her body. He dug a hole in the cellar floor and buried the soft tissue there, wrapped, ironically, in his pyjama top and covered in quicklime. Over the next few days, he burnt the bones in the basement stove.

Belle had been an active member of the Music Hall Ladies' Guild. Two days after the murder, Crippen wrote a note to the Guild. In it, he formally resigned her position, explaining that Belle had rushed back to the States and had no time to write herself. Later Crippen placed an announcement in a theatrical magazine, saying that Belle had recently died of pneumonia in California.

Crippen could easily have got away with it. Belle's friends knew of her temperament, the problems in her marriage and her love for the recently departed Bruce Miller. But Crippen was in love. He moved Ethel LeNeve into 39 Hildrop Crescent as his 'housekeeper'. The neighbours were outraged. Ethel was also seen wearing Belle's clothes and she turned up to the grand ball of the Music Hall Ladies' Guild on Crippen's arm and wearing Belle's jewellery. Belle's acquaintances found this scandalous and promptly informed Scotland Yard.

Inspector Walter Dew came to visit Crippen at his surgery and was easily taken in by the mild-mannered doctor. Crippen freely admitted that it was quite untrue that his wife had died in America. She had, Crippen said, left him for another man and he had placed the announcement of her death to cover his humiliation and embarrassment. He invited Inspector Dew up to the house for lunch and showed him around. They even visited the cellar.

Inspector Dew was satisfied with Crippen's explanation. But Crippen lost his nerve. He was convinced that Dew had seen through him and that he was about to be arrested at any minute.

Even then he could have made a clean escape, if it had not been for his love of Ethel LeNeve. Crippen fled to Holland, taking Ethel LeNeve with him. Trying to tie up all the loose ends for his report exonerating Crippen, Inspector Dew wanted to know the exact date that Belle had left for America. He visited the house to find Crippen and LeNeve gone.

Scotland Yard tore the house apart, even pulling back the wallpaper and digging up the garden. Only after several days' exhaustive search did they come across the human remains hidden under the cellar floor. A scar on the flesh of the abdomen allowed the police to identify the body as Belle's from her medical records.

Crippen read in a Continental edition of the *Daily Mail* that he was wanted. He and Ethel made for Antwerp. There, with Ethel dressed as a boy, they boarded the *S.S. Montrose*, bound for Canada. They travelled as Mr Harvey Robinson and his son.

The captain of the Montrose, Captain Kendall, fancied himself as something of an amateur detective. He spotted that Crippen and his companion held hands on deck and realised that they were rather more intimate than a father and son should be. Master Robinson had a very feminine face and his ill-fitting clothes revealed a more voluptuous body than you would expect of a teenage boy. Even though Crippen had shaved off his bushy moustache and was growing a beard, Captain Kendall soon identified his passengers as the London cellar murderer and his mistress.

The *Montrose* had just been fitted with Marconi's new wireless telegraphy equipment. Kendall transmitted his discovery back to the shipping line, who contacted the police. Inspector Dew jumped the *Laurentic*, a faster ship out of

Liverpool, in an attempt to reach Quebec before the fugitives.

News of the chase set the world on fire. It was the first time a criminal had been hunted down by radio. Newspapers around the world splashed the story across their front pages. Music hall songs about the fleeing lovers were written and performed. Meanwhile, on board the *Montrose*, Dr Crippen and Ethel LeNeve were totally unaware of the world-wide media storm that was breaking around them.

The *Laurentic* passed the *Montrose* in the middle of the Atlantic. At one point they were even in sight of each other. When the *Montrose* arrived in Quebec harbour, Inspector Dew boarded from a small tugboat. He made his way to the bridge and Captain Kendall pointed out Crippen on the deck.

Before the Montrose had finished tying up, Inspector Dew approached his transatlantic quarry.

'Good morning, Dr Crippen,' he said. 'I am Chief Inspector Dew of Scotland Yard. I believe you know me.'

Crippen was handed the arrest warrant which charged him with murder and mutilation.

'Oh God,' said Crippen as he was led away.

Extradited back to the UK, Crippen stood trial in the Old Bailey and was found guilty. The death sentence for murder was mandatory. He accepted his fate. Throughout, he maintained Ethel LeNeve's innocence. He was greatly relieved when she was acquitted of being an accessory after the fact.

Home Secretary Winston Churchill turned down his final appeal. On that same day, Inspector Dew resigned from Scotland Yard.

In his last letter, Crippen wrote that 'the love of Ethel LeNeve has been the only good thing in my life'. He was buried with a picture of her beside him in the coffin after he was hanged on 23 November 1910.

After her acquittal, Ethel LeNeve left for New York where she worked as a typist. She returned to Britain in 1916, under an assumed name. She married a man who resembled Crippen. He died in 1943 without ever discovering her real identity. In 1954, Ethel co-operated in the writing of the novel *The Girl Who Loved Crippen* with author Ursula Bloom. She died in 1967 and was buried with a locket which contained a fading photograph of Crippen.

Captain Kendall received £250 from Scotland Yard for his detective work. And the house at 39 Hildrop Crescent remained empty until World War II, when it was hit and demolished by a German bomb.

Since his hanging, doubts have been raised over Dr Crippen's guilt. The great defence barrister Sir Edward Marshall Hall, who had been engaged to lead Crippen's defence but gave up the brief, said that Crippen had been treating his wife with hyoscine, accidentally gave her an overdose and panicked when she died. The novelist Raymond Chandler marvelled that Crippen could successfully dispose of his wife's head and limbs, but not her torso which he buried ineptly under the cellar floor.

Then in October 2007, a team from Michigan State University compared mitochondrial DNA from the remains found under the cellar floor to those collected from Belle's relative and showed that the corpse was not Mrs Crippen at all. Leading the investigation, Dr John Trestrail, head of the regional poison centre in Grand Rapids, Michigan, pointed out that poisoners rarely cut up the corpses of their victims as they hope to pass the murder off as a death from natural causes. He believed that Crippen had been carrying out illegal abortions, botched one, killed the patient, then had to dispose of the body. But further tests showed that the remains were those of a man. However, the remains are nearly a century old and could have been contaminated or mislabelled. It has also been alleged that Belle's great-nieces the DNA samples were taken from were not blood relatives of Mrs Crippen at all – it is known that she had a step-family in Brooklyn.

The jury at the trial were convinced that the remains belonged to Mrs Crippen because of a distinctive scar on the abdomen. The research team argued the identification was mistaken as the tissue in question had hair follicles, whereas scars do not.

A letter to the jailed Crippen, purporting to be from his wife, was dismissed by the police who claimed it was not in Belle's handwriting. But it was not shown to Crippen or to his defence counsel. Evidence that Mrs Crippen had instructed a carter to remove boxes and packages from the house in the days before her disappearance was also withheld from the defence. So what happened to Mrs Crippen? The 1920 US census lists a female 'singer' living relative in Brooklyn, under one of Mrs Crippen's stage names. However, this new evidence has yet to be evaluated by a court, so it is too early to proclaim Crippen's innocence. After all, someone's body was buried under the cellar floor.

Lydia Thompson was certainly an unwanted lover, but it was never established if she was murdered by her husband together with his secretary and lover Helen Budnik, who married just four months after Lydia's headless corpse was found in a swamp.

Lydia and her husband Victor Louis Thompson were British and had emigrated to Detroit where they started a successful business. But a lovely home and a lavish social life were not enough and the couple began to drift apart. Early in 1945, Lydia discovered that her husband was seeing other women. When confronted, Louis Thompson confessed and begged his wife's forgiveness. But in May, she heard that he was having an affair with his secretary, Helen Budnik, who was accompanying him on a trip to Miami. She flew to Florida and caught them together in a motel. This time there would be no forgiveness. Louis Thompson moved out.

Lydia began to fear for her life. She had already paid out a great deal of money on detectives and some say that she was planning to hire a contract killer to rub out her husband's lover.

She was last seen alive outside her suburban home on 11 October 1945, talking with a man and a woman. When her body was recovered, two days later, it showed signs of torture and mutilation.

Louis and his new wife, Helen, were arrested for murder and conspiracy to murder eighteen months later. But less than two months after that, they were released for lack of evidence.

The beautiful Vicki Morgan found herself an unwanted lover after her long-time lover, Alfred Bloomingdale, owner of the famous New York department store, died. She was unwanted by the Bloomingdale family, who had fended off her $10-million palimony suit, and she was unwanted by the Reagan administration, who were afraid of the allegations which she said she would make in her forthcoming kiss-and-tell biography.

Vicki was a Valley Girl who had always dreamed of moving to Beverly Hills. Daughter of a GI bride, she was sent to school in England with Bloomingdale's daughter. At 15, she enrolled in a modelling course which soon transformed her from a lanky adolescent into a transcendent beauty. She turned men's heads and, almost immediately, fell pregnant.

Vicki was yanked from school and consigned to a run-down maternity home in a seedy corner of Los Angeles. She kept her son Todd. He lived with Vicki's mother, whom he referred to as 'Mom' so as to distinguish her from 'Mommy'. Meanwhile, Vicki had had a taste of the rough side of life and vowed never to be poor again.

Modelling jobs were not thick on the ground in Los Angeles. But older men were. At sixteen, Vicki married 47-year-old clothing wholesaler Earle Lamm. He was the type who favoured open-necked shirts and gold chains. They married in a Las Vegas chapel. Soon after, Vicki discovered he wore a toupee.

With a reputation as a middle-aged 'swinger', Earle was both intensely jealous and a closet voyeur. He introduced his young bride to threesomes. Later, he preferred to watch her in action alone with another man or another woman.

He was generous, but not overly so. When he bought her a Cadillac, she pestered him to trade it in for a Mercedes 280-SL.

Alfred Bloomingdale was lunching at the Olde World restaurant on Sunset Boulevard when he spotted Vicki Morgan striding by. He loved leggy blondes and leapt from his table, deserting his lunch guests. Out on the street, he stopped her and persuaded her to come back into the restaurant with him. As they sat down at his table, he discreetly tucked a cheque for $8,000 into her hand. It was nothing he said. He was always seized by generous impulses in the presence of beauty.

Bloomingdale bombarded Vicki with phone calls. On their third date, she was told to go to Schwab's Drugstore, where legend has it Marilyn Monroe and Lana Turner were discovered. There, she was told to drive to a huge house on Sunset Plaza Drive. A servant let her in and she was served iced tea. Then she was taken upstairs to a bedroom where Bloomingdale was whipping two naked prostitutes bound hand and foot. Thus aroused, he made love to Vicki.

Their affair lasted for twelve years. During that time Vicki lived in the lap of luxury. Alfred Bloomingdale was the confidant of President Reagan and had considerable influence in Washington. But in his sleazy private life he and Vicki experimented with almost every sexual permutation.

Then Alfred died. At his wife's instigation, Vicki's $18,000 a-month allowance was cut off and she was kicked out of her home on Los Angeles' Tower Grove Drive, where

35

she and Alfred used to make love next to the swimming pool overlooking the city.

She sold her Mercedes convertible and her jewellery and moved into a small apartment in Studio City, North Hollywood. She also checked into a drying-out clinic after years of drug and alcohol abuse.

Vicki engaged Marvin Michelson, the legal wizard who had first floated the idea of 'palimony' for the discarded live-in lovers of Hollywood stars. However, Michelson soon discovered he had a problem. Alfred Bloomingdale was a careful man and he and Vicki had never even so much as checked into the same hotel room together. Nevertheless Michelson reckoned that the Bloomingdale family would still make a huge settlement to hush up details of his bizarre sex life out of court. He was wrong. The court relished every detail of Vicki's role as ring master in sado-masochistic orgies featuring legions of prostitutes, but the judge concluded that she was no more than a well paid mistress.

Vicki had not saved a penny from her days with Bloomingdale. Her future lay in a tell-all book she was writing with young scriptwriter Gordon Basichis. There were a great many people in Washington who had reason to fear such a book and it was reported that ex-President Gerald Ford had personally stepped in to stop the prestigious William Morris Agency from handling it. But with Vicki still strung out on booze and drugs, the book was progressing agonisingly slowly. Her ghost-writer Basichis had also become her lover.

Thirty-three-year-old homosexual Marvin Pancoast also lived in the apartment. Vicki had met him at the clinic. She kept him around to borrow money for her. But she would dismiss him with a peck on the cheek every time she and Basichis wanted to be alone. Despite Pancoast's financial contributions, they were about to be evicted.

At 3.40 am on the morning of 7 July 1983, Pancoast

stumbled into the North Hollywood police precinct and told the desk sergeant: 'I've just killed Vicki Morgan.'

At the apartment, the police found Vicki sprawled across her monogrammed bedsheets. Her body was still warm. There was blood up the walls. Her head had been stoved in with a baseball bat. Pancoast said that he had killed her because he could not stand her whining.

'I was tired of being a slave boy,' he said later. He could not stand her habit of stubbing out cigarettes on a wad of chewing gum any more.

Vicki's funeral was at Forest Lawns. But there was no body. The coroner refused to release it. Mourners made do with a glossy photograph of Vicki on the altar and Simon and Garfunkel on the chapel's stereo system.

A friend of Vicki's, lawyer Robert Steinberg, chose that same day to announce that he had compromising video tapes showing top government officials engaged in sexual activity with Vicki and other women. Apparently a mysterious blonde woman had dropped them by at his office in a Gucci carrier bag. After 24 hours in the national spotlight, Steinberg claimed that the tapes had been stolen from his office. Larry Flynt, publisher of Hustler magazine, offered a million dollars for the tapes, but no one ever came forward with them.

Meanwhile Marvin Pancoast recanted on his confession. He claimed that on the night of Vicki's death he had been chloroformed. When he awoke, he found himself lying on the bed next to her dead body. He staggered downstairs to find the front door unlocked and their dog Katy outside. After stopping off for a hamburger, he went to the precinct and confessed, simply assuming that he must have been the murderer.

This recantation came as a shock to the Los Angeles Police Department. Without his confession, they had not a single shred of evidence to link Pancoast to the crime. Many people thought that it was just too convenient that Vicki Morgan had been murdered as the result of a domestic squabble by a masochist with a guilt complex – exactly the sort of person who would confess to something he did not do.

The rumour circulated that the video tapes did exist. They were supposed to show Vicki dressed as a dominatrix sticking pink carnations onto the genitals of members of the Reagan cabinet at a stag party.

Pancoast assured his defence attorney that there had been such tapes. Once, when he had suggested hiring some porno-graphic movies, Vicki had said that she had some of her own, and pulled three video cassettes from a black lacquer cabinet. Pancoast maintained that they showed Bloomingdale with Vicki and other women. But one of them also showed Vicki with a key member of the Reagan administration.

The defence lawyers took this with a pinch of salt – until they managed to make some of the other anecdotes Pancoast told about Vicki stand up. She had told him that she had had an affair with ageing Hollywood star Cary Grant, had bedded the King of Morocco and had had a lesbian relationship with a Saudi princess. These stones all checked out. They also discovered that Bloomingdale had been blackmailed once before, after being filmed with a prostitute.

In the 1960s, Bloomingdale had had links to prostitution and organised crime. The FBI file on his criminal activities had been handed over to the LAPD who had, mysteriously, lost it. It also came to light that after Pancoast had turned himself in, the apartment was left unguarded and unsealed, and had been ransacked – perhaps by someone looking for the tapes.

The trial was a farce. The jury was shocked at the police incompetence. They had not even taken fingerprints from the murder weapon.

The defence promised to produce witnesses who had viewed the missing video tapes and to subpoena the big-named government officials shown on them. The recently appointed attorney general Ed Meese was named, but he insisted that he had never even met Vicki Morgan. The judge ruled that any further mention of the missing video tapes was inadmissible.

Pancoast's attorney tried to blame Gordon Basichis, Vicki's ghostwriter and lover. Pancoast and Vicki's mother claimed he was responsible for some old bruises found on her body. He denied beating her up, though he admitted that they had had a row, but they made up the night before Vicki's murder.

Pancoast himself was never called to the stand. He was kept heavily sedated throughout the trial. His own lawyers insisted that he be kept that way. It was said that sometimes he would repeat his confession – and insist that he had killed soul singer Marvin Gaye as well. Throughout the trial, he paid little attention and read Stephen King's *The Shining*.

The jury took just four-and-a-half hours to find Pancoast guilty of first-degree murder. Despite a long history of mental illness, they also rejected his plea of not guilty by reason of insanity and he was given 27-years-to-life.

Pancoast claimed that he was the victim of a conspiracy involving Bloomingdale's widow and President Reagan. In jail, he retreated into paranoid self-delusion. But he had enjoyed his brief moment of fame. He kept all his press cuttings, which he shows to anyone who visits him in San Quentin.

The only person unwanted in the passionate relationship between Denise Labbe and Jacques Algarron was her two-year-old daughter Cathy. To prove that she loved him, Algarron demanded that she kill her own child.

Cathy's father was a young doctor. But she had been born while he was away fighting in Indo-China. When he returned, Denise wanted nothing further to do with him and struggled to bring Cathy up on her own.

In 1954, she met Jacques Algarron, a cadet at the top French military academy of Saint-Cyr. He was cold and arrogant. After just two dances, Algarron wrote to her, saying that he wanted to make her his mistress.

Their affair was sado-masochistic. She wrote to him, 'The scratchmarks on my back are beginning to heal, I notice with despair this morning.'

Although she was passionately in love with him, he demanded that she be unfaithful, so that she would have to beg his forgiveness. She complied with his wishes, ladening herself with self-loathing and disgust.

True lovers, Algarron claimed, would go to any lengths – even murder – to show their love for one another. At first, he suggested the random murder of a taxi driver to make them an 'extraordinary' couple.

Then Denise found herself pregnant. Algarron already had two illegitimate children. He did not want any more and demanded that she have an abortion. And, to prove her love for him, he insisted that she should murder two-year-old Cathy.

Denise thought he was joking, but he was in deadly earnest. He threatened to abandon her if she did not make this sacrifice. Witnesses testified that she truly loved the child, but her lover's threats and sexual blackmail wore her down. She dangled the baby over the balcony, but could not go through with it.

A few days later, she dropped the baby off a bridge into a canal. But her nerve went again. Her cries alerted a lock-keeper who rescued the baby. Algarron mercilessly rebuked her. Plainly she did not love him enough.

Denise went through with the abortion. It was bungled and she was haemorrhaging when she tried – and failed – to kill baby Cathy yet again. While Denise was having an operation on her womb, Algarron left for Paris. He later visited her in hospital, but simply repeated his demand that she kill the child.

A few weeks later, when she was up and about again, she took baby Cathy out into the yard and drowned her in a pail of water. She sent a postcard to Algarron. It read: 'Catherine dead. See you soon.'

Algarron's reply was: 'I find it all very disappointing. It means nothing to me now.'

Their trial became a cause célèbre. Denise was sentenced to life imprisonment. Algarron got twenty years' hard labour.

Chapter 4

Lady Killers

Murdering women can be a lucrative profession for a man, if he has enough sex appeal to get them to the altar first. Although poorly educated and far from good looking, East End petty criminal George Joseph Smith found that he had what it takes to become a lady-killer. He would marry his victims and despatch them when they were naked and at their most vulnerable, in what became known as the famous 'Brides in the Bath' case.

By the age of twenty-five, Smith had spent most of his short life in jail for petty thieving. But this time, he vowed to go straight. He opened a baker's shop at 25 Russell Square, Leicester, under the name of George Oliver Love. From behind the counter, his beady eye fell on 18-year-old Caroline Thornhill, the friend of one of his shop-girls. Within weeks he had wooed and wed her.

His pledge to stay out of trouble was short lived. When his shop failed, he set off on a new life of crime with his young wife as an accomplice. She would find employment as a housemaid with a rich family and steal their valuables. He would dispose of them and they would move on.

Caroline was a clever thief and the two of them got away with it for nearly two years. But then when she tried to pawn some silverware she had just stolen from her employers, the pawnbroker grew suspicious. She was arrested and her husband bolted. After a night in the cells, she was tried and sentenced to a year's imprisonment. This taught her a lesson and she resolved to free herself of her callous and cowardly husband.

While she was in custody, Smith had made his way to London, where he took rooms. Unable to afford to pay for the room, he took the simple expedient of bigamously marrying his landlady and he began to develop his taste for married life.

Released from jail, Caroline went to London where, entirely by chance, she bumped into her erstwhile husband in Oxford Street. She immediately called a policeman and had him arrested. He was sentenced to two years' hard labour.

When he got out, he discovered that his first wife had emigrated to Canada. He moved back in with his second 'wife' but things did not work out. She later complained: 'He came home and thrashed me till I was nearly dead.'

George Smith then set out on a career as a swindler and a bigamist. In 1908, with £90 he had taken from an unsuspecting spinster, he opened a second-hand store in Bristol. He hired a housekeeper, 28-year-old Edith Pegler, whom he married within a month – bigamously, of course.

His business gave him the perfect excuse to travel the country in search of new victims. When he was away for an even longer period than normal, he claimed to have been abroad where he said he sold a Chinese idol for £1,000. Edith did not question him.

Smith occasionally took Edith on business trips with him. They were in Southampton together when he spotted a likely target. Edith was packed off home while Smith wooed Sarah

Freeman. She resisted stoutly and it took him nearly four months to get her up the aisle. She had £50 in cash.

As soon as they were married, by special licence, they set off for London. Taking lodgings in Clapham, Smith spotted his new wife's bank book. He lost no time in suggesting that she take all her money out of the bank and hand it over to him. Soon he was £300 the richer.

Then, for a treat, he took her to the National Gallery. Once inside, he sat her down on a bench and said he was going to the lavatory. He did not come back. After about an hour, Sarah asked an attendant to go into the loo to look for him. He was not there. When she returned to their lodgings, she found that he had stolen her jewellery, clothes and other belongings. She was left with just a handful of coppers which he had generously left for her.

This ploy was typical. Florence Wilson, a widow from Worthing, also accepted Smith's hand in 1908. Her dowry, which she cheerfully handed over after the nuptials, was twenty gold sovereigns and two large white fivers. Smith explained that he would take care of them for her. After all, she had no pockets. He then suggested that they visit the Anglo-French exhibition at White City. Seating her on a bench, he said he was going to buy a newspaper. He did not come back.

Bessie Mundy, a handsome woman in her mid-thirties, fell for a similar trick. She had married Smith, believing him to be a George Williams. After a few weeks, she returned home to find her husband, and her life savings, gone. He had thoughtfully left behind a note accusing her of giving him a venereal disease.

Eighteen months later, much to her surprise, she spotted him on the promenade at Weston-Super-Mare. She approached him.

'Henry?' she asked timidly.

'My dearest Bessie,' he exclaimed. 'I have been searching

the country for you. It was all a terrible mistake. I can explain.'

He took her by the arm, sat her on a promenade bench and begged her forgiveness. He thought, mistakenly, he had contracted venereal disease and decided to do the honourable thing – leave home rather than risk passing it on to her. The £150 he had 'borrowed' from her, he had used to pay back a loan. By the time he had realised that he did not have VD after all, he had lost track of her. Since then he had been combing the country in search of her. He was only in Weston-Super-Mare, he said, because one of her relatives – he did not say which – had told her she was there.

Bessie listened wide-eyed. She swallowed every word of it. Soon they were locked in a tearful embrace. Back at her lodgings, Bessie announced to the incredulous residents that she was reconciled with her husband. Her landlady was not impressed and telegraphed Bessie's aunt to come at once. But by the time she arrived, the couple were gone.

To seal their new-found happiness, the reconciled couple went to a solicitor and had wills draw up each naming the other as sole beneficiary. This seemed fair enough, but Bessie had £2,500, while her husband was penniless.

They moved to Herne Bay in Kent, where he set up as an art and antiques dealer. The house they rented was nice enough, but it did not have a bath. This was soon to be remedied. On a hot July day, a £2 bath was ordered from the local ironmonger. Bessie was sent round to bargain 2/6d off the price, because it did not have taps or fittings. The next day, when the bath was delivered, Smith neglected to pay.

The day afterwards Smith took Bessie to see the local doctor. He explained that his wife had blacked out during a fit. Bessie seemed perfectly fit. The doctor was puzzled, but he gave her bromide of potassium, a sedative.

In the early hours, two days later, Smith woke the young doctor by beating on his door. Bessie had had a second fit.

The doctor came to examine her. She was in her night-dress. Although her body was hot and clammy – it was a humid night – she exhibited no other signs of having had a fit. Nevertheless, he prescribed another bottle of bromide.

Next day, Bessie seemed in radiant health, but the following morning the doctor received another note from her husband asking him to come right away. His wife, the note said, was dead.

When the doctor arrived, he found Bessie's naked body lying face up in the bath. Her mouth and nose were under the water. In her right hand she clutched a bar of soap. Her husband said that he had gone out to buy herrings for breakfast. When he returned, she was dead.

He sobbed at the inquest, which returned a verdict of accidental death, then bundled his wife's remains into a pauper's grave. The bath was returned to the ironmongers. He still had not paid for it. The will was settled and he sold up and moved away.

The following year, Smith turned up in Southsea under his real name. Within weeks, he had married a 25-year-old nurse called Alice Burnham, the buxom daughter of a rich fruit farmer. Money was soon transferred out of her account into his. With it, he insured her life for £500. Alice also made a will in his favour.

The happy couple set off for a belated honeymoon in Blackpool. The first boarding house they tried was delightful. It had a piano, but no bath. They were directed to a second boarding house where they took a room, with bath, for ten shillings.

Within days of arriving in Blackpool, Alice became ill. She sent a postcard to her mother, complaining of headaches. A local GP prescribed some tablets. On the evening of Friday 12 December, the landlady was having dinner with her family when one of them noticed a damp patch on the ceiling. It grew bigger. Then Smith came in with some eggs, which he said he had bought for their breakfast in the morning.

He went upstairs. Moments later he cried for them to call a doctor. The doctor found Smith in the bathroom. He was supporting his wife's head. She was in the bath, naked, and quite dead.

The hastily arranged inquest again returned a verdict of accidental death. Alice was given the cheapest possible funeral and Smith made off with her estate of £600.

Next, Smith picked up Alice Reavil while listening to a band in Bournemouth, a few weeks after the outbreak of World War I. In less than a week, they were married – he as Charles Oliver James, a gentleman with a private income from land in Canada.

He announced that he intended to open an antiques shop and persuaded her to take £76 out of her post-office savings account. She also sold a few items of furniture and handed over the £14 she made. That evening the rest of her belongings were loaded onto a barrow and taken away. Alice's husband informed her that they would be moving to new accommodation.

The following morning he took his new bride for a walk in a nearby park, sat her on a bench and went to find a lavatory. He did not return. All she had left were a few shillings and the clothes she stood up in. But at least she was alive.

In December 1914, Smith married again. He introduced himself as John Lloyd, an estate agent. His intended was Margaret Lofty, a clergyman's daughter, but he called her Peggy. They married in Bath. Immediately after the service, they travelled to London and found rooms in Bismarck Road, Highgate. The next evening the landlady boiled up a copper for Mrs Lloyd's bath. She heard splashing, then a sigh. The front door slammed. A few minutes later, Lloyd returned with a bag containing tomatoes. They were for his wife's supper, he said, mentioning that he would go up and ask whether she was ready for them. There was no answer. Peggy was already dead.

Smith haggled with the undertaker. Margaret Lofty was buried, for a pound off the standard price, in a common grave. Smith then returned to Bristol to spend Christmas with Edith. Her present? Margaret Lofty's dresses, straight from her trousseau. But, this time, Smith had made a mistake.

Usually, his murders had taken place in seaside resorts, where details of the inquest only made the local papers. But he had drowned his latest bride in a bath in London. The mass circulation *News of the World* picked up the story, which they printed under the headline: 'Bride's tragic fate on the day of her wedding.' Alice Burnham's father read it over breakfast that Sunday morning. So did the neighbour of the Blackpool boarding house where Alice died. Scotland Yard were soon alerted to the similarities between the two cases.

The inquest in Highgate, yet again, returned a verdict of accidental death. But detectives began to keep a watch on 'Mr Lloyd'. A month later, they arrested him at the offices of a lawyer in Shepherd's Bush where he was trying to hurry probate. He was charged with making a false entry on his marriage certificate. He soon admitted that his name was, in fact, George Joseph Smith.

While Smith was held in Bow Street, the bodies of his dead wives were exhumed. The famous Home Office pathologist Dr Bernard Spilsbury was soon able to establish that the victims had died by neither accident nor suicide. He believed that Smith had entered the bathroom while his latest wife was luxuriating in the bath. He had knelt down by the bath, put one arm under her knees and pulled them up. With his other hand placed on the top of her head, he had pushed her under the water. The whole thing would have happened so fast, Spilsbury thought, that the woman would have died of shock rather than drowning.

Scotland Yard's investigations took them to forty seaside resorts. More than 150 witnesses were interviewed and the police discovered thirteen similarities between the untimely deaths of Margaret Lofty, Alice Burnham and Bessie Mundy. On 23 March 1915, George Joseph Smith was formally charged with the murder of these three women.

Despite the fact that Britain was in the middle of the Great War, there was intense interest in the Brides in the Bath case, especially among women. Even Smith's real wife – Caroline Thornhill – made the two-week trip from Saskatchewan to attend the committal hearings. When she burst into tears, so did more than half a dozen other women in the court-room. Smith, himself, remained unmoved. His only reaction was to abuse the prosecutor and the witnesses against him. He was committed for trial at the Old Bailey. Although he had been charged with three murders, he was only tried for the murder of Bessie Mundy. Details of the other two cases were simply used as corroborating evidence.

Throughout his trial, Edith Pegler stood by him. So did a flock of his female fans. The criminologist H.B. Irving recalled sitting alongside two fashionably dressed women who vied with each other in the fulsome praises of the prisoner's attractions. And the dock was often mobbed by crowds of eager young women.

Throughout the trial, Smith abused the prosecution witnesses and protested his innocence. In a private room, a nurse in a bathing dress was used to demonstrate Spilsbury's theory. The jury watched as she lay back in the bath. Inspector Neil of Scotland Yard grasped her feet and pulled them up, forcing her head under the water. She started to struggle and was immediately lifted from the water. Although she had been submerged for a matter of seconds, she had to be revived by artificial respiration.

A lifelong atheist, Smith became a Christian after being found guilty of murder and sentenced to death, and was confirmed in the condemned cell. In Pentonville, he wrote to Edith Pegler as his only 'true love'. The day his appeal was rejected, 29 July 1915, there was a violent thunder storm. Later he was moved to Maidstone Jail where he was hanged. The last words on his lips as the trap door opened were: 'I am innocent.'

The lodging houses where Smith murdered his brides in the bath are still standing today, though Bismarck Road in Highgate was renamed Waterloo Road after an outbreak of anti-German feeling during World War I. Smith's only legal wife, Caroline Thornhill, married a Canadian soldier the day after her first husband was executed. The bath from Bismarck Road where Margaret Lofty died was bought by Madame Tussaud's for display in their chamber of horrors. One of the other baths Smith used is kept by Scotland Yard's Black Museum.

Samuel Herbert Dougal was another professional woman-hunter. He spent twenty-one years in the army, largely in Nova Scotia. He married a Miss Griffiths there. She bore him four children then died suddenly after sixteen years of marriage. Five weeks later, Dougal married Marie Boyd who died two months later. Both deaths were attributed to oyster poisoning.

After leaving the army, he became an unsuccessful salesman. His house burned town and Dougal collected the insurance, but was later charged with arson. In court though, the jury was impressed by his military record and he was acquitted.

He moved to Ireland where he married again. His third wife, Sarah White, bore him two children, but two years later he was back in London where he was supported by another woman, Miss Emily Booty. She leased a house outside Oxford, but Dougal moved his wife and family in. Miss Booty took umbrage at this and there was a row. She went to the police, accusing Dougal of stealing from her. Again he was found not guilty.

The following year, he was not so lucky. In the Old Bailey,

he was convicted of forging a signature on a cheque and sentenced to 12 months' hard labour. In Pentonville Prison, he tried to hang himself and he was transferred to Cane Hill Lunatic Asylum in Surrey. He was diagnosed as suffering from acute melancholia, but was discharged later that year after being declared sane.

By now Dougal was fifty. His conviction had lost him his army pension. His wife left him and went back to Ireland. But then he met Miss Camille Cecile Holland.

Sexually, she was not to his taste. Throughout his life, he had preferred buxom, hot-blooded, young women. Miss Holland was a petite 55-year-old spinster. But she had been left a sizeable fortune by an aunt.

Dougal's powerful animal magnetism quickly overcame any inhibitions she may have had. They spent a romantic weekend together in Southend. Over Christmas and the New Year, they rented a house together. However, Miss Holland confided to her dressmaker that she thought Dougal was only after her for her money. Nevertheless, she bought Moat House Farm in Essex and they moved in together as Mr and Mrs Dougal.

Within a month, the serving girl they had hired moved out to escape the unwanted attentions from Dougal. Her replacement, Florrie, complained to Miss Holland that Dougal had crept up on her and kissed her. Two days later, he tried to break into Florrie's bedroom at night and she began sleeping with Miss Holland for protection.

After a week of this arrangement, Dougal and Miss Holland went shopping in nearby Saffron Walden. But only Dougal returned. He explained to Florrie that her mistress had gone to London.

That night Florrie slept in her clothes by an open window, so that she could jump out if Dougal attacked her. Next day, Dougal said that he had received a letter saying that 'Mrs Dougal' was taking a short holiday with some lady friends.

51

Later, Florrie's mother arrived to rescue her daughter from Dougal, giving him a good tongue-lashing into the bargain.

Forging Miss Holland's signature, Dougal transferred Moat House Farm into his name and started milking Miss Holland's bank accounts. He moved his wife in, introducing her to the neighbours as his widowed daughter, though many suspected the truth. Dougal also managed to carry on with other local women. It was rumoured that he carried on affairs with three sisters and their mother simultaneously. Kate Cranwell, a servant at a nearby farm, bore Dougal a child and successfully sued for maintenance. Her sister Georgina also fell pregnant by Dougal. It was even said that Dougal gave bicycle-riding lessons to nude girls in a field adjoining the farmhouse.

Neighbours began to suspect that Dougal had done away with his wife – Miss Holland, that is. The police began to investigate the forged signatures on Miss Holland's cheques and a warrant was issued for Dougal's arrest. When he was arrested in the bank, he made a break for it, but ran into a cul-de-sac.

The police still had a problem though. To make the charges stick, they had to locate Miss Holland. Suspecting that she had been murdered, they began searching the 100 acres that surrounded Moat House Farm. They emptied the moat that surrounded the farmhouse and raked through the smelly sludge at the bottom. It was so thick that a heavy stone would not sink in it. The police soon concluded that if a stone would not sink, neither would a body.

It was then that they spotted that a drainage ditch connecting the moat to a nearby pond had been filled in. Excavating it was even more unpleasant than searching the moat. It ran with liquid sewage. But after five weeks of digging, the police unearthed the fully clothed body of a woman. It was identified as Miss Holland. She had been shot in the head.

After a two-day trial, Dougal was found guilty of murder and sentenced to death. On the gallows, the chaplain asked Dougal one last time whether he was guilty or not guilty of murdering Miss Holland. After a long pause, he said: 'Guilty.' According to one newspaper report, before the word was out of his mouth, the trap door opened and Dougal jolted to his death.

The most notorious lady-killer was Henri Desire Landru who, the French police estimated, killed nearly 300 women. Despite his small stature, bald head and pointed beard, he had a power of attraction that allowed him to seduce almost any woman he pleased. Even while Landru was a conscript, he got his attractive young cousin Mademoiselle Remy pregnant and was forced to marry her.

When he left the service he was swindled by a conman and decided to become a conman himself. He was not very successful, and was arrested four times between 1900 and 1908.

In 1914, using a number of aliases, he put a number of ads in the lonely-hearts columns of a newspaper. The ads said that he was a wealthy bachelor seeking respectable female companionship. Landru had already fathered three illegitimate children outside his marriage and he maintained a separate address for his assignations. But that was for pleasure. He would now use his seductive skills to make a living. When women answered his ad, he would meet them, woo them, propose marriage, take the dowry and murder them.

His first known victim, Madame Izoré, vanished, along with 15,000 francs. Then a 39-year-old widow, Madame Cuchet, answered one of his ads. When she declared her intention to marry Landru, her family went to visit him. Landru was out, but they entered the villa he was renting and found a huge cache of love letters. They warned Madame Cuchet against Landru, but she did not believe them. She and her 16-year-old son disappeared soon after.

In 1915, a widow from Buenos Aires, named Madame Laborde-Line, moved out of her apartment in Pans, saying that she was going to live with a wonderful man in Vernouillet. She was seen in a villa there, then disappeared. He sold her securities and her furniture, piece by piece, from a garage in Neuilly. Landru then moved in another widow, Madame Guillin, who had 22,000 francs. She and the money disappeared – her furniture ended up on sale in Neuilly.

Landru forged Madame Guillin's signature to withdraw 12,000 francs from her bank account. When questioned at the bank, Landru explained that he was Madame Guillin's brother-in-law. She had suffered a stroke, he said, and was no longer able to handle her own affairs.

Having killed at least three women in Vernouillet, Landru moved to another villa in the village of Gambais. He enticed another widow there with the promise of marriage. She too disappeared and the inhabitants of Gambais began to remark on the black smoke that belched from the chimney of Landru's villa at odd hours.

Landru put another ad in the lonely hearts columns saying that he was a 'widower with two children, aged forty-three, with comfortable income'. He was, he said, 'affectionate, serious and moving in good company' and he desired to meet a 'widow, with a view to matrimony'.

The ad was answered by a 45-year-old Madame Collomb, who had been living with a man who would not marry her. She worked as a typist and had saved 10,000 francs. Landru proposed. His fiancée insisted that he should meet her family. He did, reluctantly. They disliked him and advised against marriage. But the lovesick Madame Collomb joined her intended at his villa in Gambais and was never seen again.

On 11 March 1917, nineteen-year-old Andrée Babelay told her mother of her wonderful news. She was going to be rescued from her life of poverty by a wonderful rich man she met on the Metro. He had proposed and they were on their way to his villa in Gambais. Andrée's mother never saw her daughter again. She was the only one of Landru's victims that yielded him no money at all, but she did satisfy his almost incessant need for sex.

His next conquest was 47-year-old Madame Buisson, a widow worth around 10,000 francs. They had been corresponding for some time. She told relatives that she was going to get married, then disappeared. Landru appeared at her apartment with a forged note, ostensibly from Madame Buisson, authorising him to remove her furniture. He took her possessions straight to his garage in Neuilly.

Madame Jaume had separated from her husband and a matrimonial agency introduced her to Landru. She was last seen leaving her apartment with him on 25 November 1917. A few days later Landru reappeared in Paris and withdrew 1,400 francs from her account.

Landru had been seeing 36-year-old Madame Pascal on and off for a year. She had very little money but he kept her for a while in an apartment in Paris. Then, when he tired of her sexual charms, he took her on a trip to Gambais.

Madame Marchadier did not have much money either, but she had a large house on the rue St. Jacques. She took her two dogs with her to Gambais. Landru was seen later selling Madame Marchadier's house and her belongings.

Landru had always avoided the relatives of his victims. But he had met Madame Buisson's sister Madame Lacoste. Nearly two years after the disappearance of her sister, Madame Lacoste saw Landru walking down the Rue de Rivoli in Paris with an attractive young woman on his arm. She followed them into a china shop where, under the name of Lucien Guillet, he ordered a delivery of crockery.

Madame Lacoste went to the police, who got Landru's address in the Rue de Rochechouart. The police visited his apartment, where they found Landru and 27-year-old clerk Fernande Segret naked in bed. The lovers were planning a trip to Gambais.

In Landru's pocket the police found a loose-leafed notebook which he used to keep track of his victims. They searched the villa at Gambais and dug up the garden. But all they found were the corpses of three dogs, the personal effects of his victims and of a large number of unknown women – but no bodies.

The prosecution maintained that Landru had drugged his victims and strangled them. Then he had chopped their bodies up into tiny pieces and burnt them. They produced the stove from the villa in Gambais as evidence. It contained ashes and tiny fragments of bone.

Landru's response throughout the trial was: 'Produce your bodies.'

Voluminous correspondence was also found in the villa. It was sorted into seven groups: 'No reply'; 'Without money'; 'Without furniture'; 'To be answered poste restante'; 'To be answered to initials poste restante'; 'Possible fortune'; and 'In reserve for further investigation'. The police maintained that Landru had written to 83 women. Almost none of them could be located.

The defence countered weakly that Landru was no mass murderer. He had simply sold the women into white slavery – they had been abducted and shipped to the brothels of South America. This suggestion was ridiculed by the prosecution. Most of the women were in their fifties and Landru had kept their false teeth, false hair and false bosoms.

Landru was brazen throughout. When the presiding judge asked Landru if he was a liar, Landru replied: 'I am not a lawyer.'

During his time in court, the women of Paris flocked to see him. Landru knew the effect he had on them. When the jury found him guilty and he left the court for the last time, he turned to them and said: 'I wonder if there is any lady present who would care to take my seat?'

On the day of his execution, a priest asked Landru if he wished to make a last confession. He pointed to the guards who were to escort him to the guillotine and said he was sorry, but he did not want to keep those gentlemen waiting.

Chapter 5

The Eternal Triangle

In 1992, seventeen-year-old Amy Fisher aimed to join the long tradition of jealous lovers who turned to murder. On 19 May, Amy walked up to the front door of a white, split-level house in Massapequa, Long Island. The door was answered by Mary Jo Buttafuacco, a slender blonde housewife. After a short conversation, Amy pulled a gun, pointed it at Mary Jo's right temple and pulled the trigger.

Amy stood motionless for a moment, then ran to the maroon Thunderbird driven by 21-year-old Peter Guagenti that was waiting for her. He roared off.

Although the bullet had entered Mary Jo's head above her right ear, shattered her jaw, ripped through her eardrum and come to rest in the base of her brain, she did not die. Recovering in hospital she learnt that her assailant, Amy Fisher, claimed to be having an affair with her husband, forty-year-old Joey. Joey denied it.

But the truth was even more complex. A pornographic movie showing Amy cavorting with another man surfaced. Since she had been sixteen, Amy had been working for an escort agency after school hours. She was much in demand and had to carry a pager. It was alleged that Joey Buttafuacco was not just an innocent panel beater in an autoshop, as his wife was led to believe. He also moonlighted as a driver for the escort agency and often tried it on with the girls. It was said that it was Joey who first brought Amy to the agency.

Amy fell in love with Joey, but continued her professional career. She also planned a confrontation with Mary Jo. She got a young male friend, Peter Guagenti, to stake out the house and check on her movements. He was rewarded with oral sex.

Amy Fisher pleaded guilty to reckless assault and was jailed for five to fifteen years. Charges of statutory rape brought against Joey Buttafuocco were dropped. Mary Jo Buttafuocco recovered, though she lost her hearing and the right half of her face is partially paralysed. She stood by her husband, despite Amy's allegation. The American people lapped it all up. *Amy Fisher: The Musical* played to packed houses off Broadway.

Amy Fisher's case is unusual only in that Mary Jo Buttafuacco survived. When a love affair becomes an obsession, people are often driven by jealousy to murder their lover's partner. In the summer of 1921, Percy and Edith Thompson met a sailor named Frederick Bywaters. The three of them got on and they went on holiday to the Isle of Wight together. During the vacation, there was some disharmony between the Thompson couple and Edith turned to Bywaters for consolation. The affair flourished during Bywaters' shore leaves.

The menage lasted until October of the following year, when Percy Thompson was stabbed to death as he and his wife were returning to their London home. Edith claimed that she did not know the assailant and had done everything she could to save her husband's life. The police believed her – until her affair with Bywaters came to light.

Bywaters' flat was searched and the police found letters from Edith in which she proclaimed her love and spelt out plans to poison her husband.

Thompson and Bywaters were arrested. At their trial at the Old Bailey, Bywaters confessed to stabbing Percy Thompson, but said he had done so in self-defence. Edith, he said, knew nothing of the crime. But under gruelling interrogation, Edith admitted to the affair and to discussing the murder of her husband with Bywaters. Both were hanged at 9 am on 9 January 1923 – she at Holloway, he a few miles away at Pentonville.

It is, of course, possible to become insanely jealous of a lover's former lovers – especially if you are insane to start with. And millionaire Harry K. Thaw was more than a little unstable.

Son of a Pittsburgh mining magnate, Thaw was sent down from Harvard for running a high-stake poker school off-campus. He moved to New York – where he moved into an apartment in one of Manhattan's finest whore houses and joined a prominent Ivy-League club – only to be blackballed for riding a horse through its hallowed portals.

He would pick up would-be Broadway show girls, take them back to his swanky flat, where he would rape and beat them. The madam of the brothel threw him out when she heard screams from his rooms and burst in to find a naked girl, tied to the bed and being thrashed with a whip.

Thaw was later thrown out of a Fifth Avenue fashion salon for the type of women he brought there. He took his revenge by driving a car through the shop front.

Fleeing from justice, Thaw went to Paris where he rented an entire floor of the Hotel Georges V. He spent $50,000 on a party for Paris's leading prostitutes which went on for several days. Thaw was finally asked to leave when he was caught whipping naked women down the corridors.

Back in New York, Thaw met 19-year-old beauty Evelyn

Nesbit and married her. She had formerly been the mistress of society architect Stanley White. Super-rich White was famous for designing Madison Square Garden and the arch in Washington Square. He was also well known as a womaniser. In his apartment, which occupied one of the towers of Madison Square Garden, he had a red velvet swing. He would get girls to sit on it, and swing them so high that he could see under their billowing skirts.

White's affair with Nesbit had been more than a passing fancy. She was a sixteen-year-old chorus girl when she caught the eye of Stanley White. He lavished jewels and clothes on her, hired a chauffeured limousine for her, installed her in a lavish apartment and paid for her education. White built up a huge collection of photographs of her in erotic poses, but after three years he tired of her. It was then that she met Thaw.

Thaw became obsessed with his wife's affair with White. He would tie Evelyn to the bed naked and beat her until she told him vile stories about White. Often she would end up covered in red welts. One of the stories she told Thaw was that White had tricked her into accompanying him back to his apartment. There he had stripped her and raped her, then forced her into obscene poses on the swing while he took photographs of her. Thaw vowed revenge.

At the opening of the musical *Mamzelle Champagne* at Madison Square Garden, Thaw spotted White in the rooftop restaurant. He went over to the ageing architect, drew a revolver and shot him. Pandemonium broke out. The manager screamed for the band to continue playing. A doctor pronounced Stanley White dead. And Thaw explained meekly that he had killed him 'because he ruined my wife'.

Thaw's doting mother paid $100,000 to Delphin Delmas, an attorney who claimed never to have lost a case, to keep her son out of the electric chair. He spent another $2 million of her money on a press campaign to blacken White's name,

61

which included linking him to under-age sex. A 15-year-old model claimed to have been lured back to White's flat, plied with drinks, seduced and abandoned. Delmas even arranged for a medium to come forward and say that Thaw was not guilty. She claimed to have talked to a spirit that had taken over Thaw's body and had guided his hand.

This campaign backfired to some extent. The details of Thaw's sordid private life also began to leak out. A complaint lodged three years before by Ethel Thomas made headlines. She had been swept off her feet by Thaw. But one day on her way back to his flat with her, he had stopped and bought a dog whip. She asked what it was for. He replied with a laugh: 'It's for you, dear.' She thought he was joking, but once inside the apartment he whipped her until her clothes were in tatters.

For fifteen months, while the battle raged in the press, Thaw languished in New York's famous downtown detention centre, the Tombs, dining on meals from the best hotels and being offered every comfort money could buy.

When the case came to trial, Delmas claimed that Thaw was suffering from 'dementia Americana'- the murderous rage that seized any red-blooded American male when the sacred virtue of his wife has been violated. Thaw was eventually found not guilty by reason of insanity. He escaped the electric chair but was sent to the New York Asylum for the Criminally Insane in Matteawan, upstate New York, for life.

Thaw's mother then arranged for his escape, by limousine, to Canada, where he holed up in a luxury apartment. But the US State Department put pressure on the Canadian Government to return him. The Canadian authorities turned Thaw over to the authorities in New Hampshire, where he returned to a luxurious life in prison while his attorneys fought his extradition back to New York State.

Eventually, they forced a new trial. This time Thaw was found not guilty – and sane. He was released. But, a year later, he was arrested for kidnapping, beating and sexually abusing a 19-year-old boy. At his first trial he was declared insane again. But at his second, he was declared sane and the charges were dropped – following a half-million-dollar donation to the boy's family by Thaw's mother.

Thaw continued his depraved ways throughout his life – and continued to stay out of prison due to his money. He died from a heart attack at the age of 76.

Evelyn Nesbit cashed in on the notoriety Thaw's trial had given her, appearing in vaudeville as 'the girl on the red velvet swing'. Her divorce settlement brought more money and she had another bite of the cherry eight years later, claiming that her newborn son had been fathered by Thaw. She had bribed Thaw's guards to let her into the asylum for a night of connubial bliss.

Playboy 'Playmate of the Year' Dorothy Stratten was killed by love, sex and overwhelming jealousy. Born plain Dorothy Ruth Hoogstratten, she was 'discovered' by small-time Hollywood hustler Paul Snider, working in a snack bar in East Vancouver. She was just eighteen.

Snider had worked as a promoter and pimp in Beverly Hills. He had decided to 'go straight' when he returned to his native Canada in 1978. But when he walked into the snack bar where Dorothy worked part time, he realised that the shy schoolgirl behind the counter was his meal ticket for life.

He wheedled her phone number out of her, invited her out and wined and dined her. He told her she was the most beautiful woman in the world and bought her a topaz ring set in diamonds and a white gown for her high-school graduation dance.

Dorothy aimed to become a secretary after high school, but Snider had other plans. He flattered her natural vanity by hiring a photographer. First he took her portrait. The photographer noted that she was eager to please. Then Snider persuaded her to be photographed naked.

The set of nude photographs were sent to Playboy

magazine and Dorothy, who was by then working for the phone company, was summoned to Los Angeles for more test shots. Flying there was her first time on a plane. The results of her second nude session were sensational. They seemed to show a subtle mixture of innocence and eroticism. She was 'so beautiful she seemed luminescent, as if lit from within,' *People* magazine raved after she was dead.

While waiting for her nude pictures to appear in the magazine, Dorothy worked as a cocktail bunny in the Playboy Club in Los Angeles. She and Snider began living together, first in an apartment, later in a small Spanish-style house off Santa Monica Boulevard. It was near Bel Air, where the big movie directors and producers live.

In June 1979, they married. In August, she was Playmate of the Month. Playboy publisher Hugh Hefner was particularly taken with her and invited her up to the Playboy mansion, where there were three girls for every man and regular skinny-dipping sessions in Hefner's private Jacuzzi. The property was guarded by fifty security men. Snider was excluded.

At a Playboy party, Dorothy met the movie director Peter Bogdanovich. There was an instant attraction. The party was televised and Bogdanovich's stunning companion was an instant star. A flurry of TV offers followed. She appeared in Fantasy Island, Buck Rogers in the 25th Century and Galaxina, where she played a delectable robot.

Snider had to content himself with running wet T-shirt contests and male strip shows. But he kept Dorothy away from his other sleazy businesses. She was special. He spoke of their 'lifetime bargain' and tried to protect her. He stopped her smoking and drinking, and taught her how to parry the plays men made for her when she was working for Playboy.

In 1980, Dorothy was picked as Playmate of the Year. She won $20,000, a Jaguar XJS and a $65,000 sable coat. She was given the lead in a low-budget Canadian movie and Peter

Bogdanovich cast her alongside Audrey Hepburn and Ben Gazzara in his movie *They All Laughed*.

Suddenly Dorothy was out of Snider's league. Although she told *Maclean's* magazine that 'many men in the world have my picture to look at, he has my heart', the strain was already showing.

Snider plastered their house with pictures of his wife and bought himself a brand new Mercedes with the licence plates STAR-80. 'We're on a rocketship to the moon,' he told Dorothy. But by now she had a business manager and an agent. She was even incorporated as Dorothy Stratten Enterprises and there was little room in her growing operation for a cheap hustler like Paul Snider.

Dorothy flew to New York in March 1980 to begin filming with Bogdanovich. He nurtured the newcomer and discreetly moved her into the Plaza Hotel, where he was staying.

Dorothy saw Snider briefly in Vancouver two months later, but in June he received official notification of their separation. She closed down their joint bank accounts and Bogdanovich's lawyers hired a private detective to keep an eye on Snider.

Dorothy and Bogdanovich took a fortnight's holiday in London, before returning to his luxurious Bel Air home where a welter of movie offers awaited her.

On Friday, 8 August, Dorothy phoned Snider and agreed to meet him at the house for lunch. He was elated. 'The queen is coming back,' he told friends. In fact, she had only come back to pick up some of her clothes. 'Give the rest to Patty' – the 17-year-old Stratten lookalike Snider was now promoting – she told him.

At a barbecue that Sunday, Snider told other guests that he was looking for a gun for 'protection'. He found a 12-gauge Mossberg pump-action shotgun in the small ads.

Dorothy agreed to meet Snider again, to clear up some financial matters. She arrived shortly after noon the following

Thursday. Calls to the house that afternoon were not answered. At 5 pm, Snider's new protégé Patty arrived. Snider's bedroom door was closed and she decide not to disturb him.

By this time, Bogdanovich's private detective was getting seriously worried. He called the police. When they arrived, they noticed a trail of tiny black ants leading to the bedroom. Inside they found Dorothy and Snider naked. Both were dead.

Dorothy's magnificent body lay sprawled across a low bed. Her face had been pulped by a shotgun blast. Near her head was a makeshift bondage machine, set up for rear entry. There were loops of tape on the floor. Dorothy Stratten had been sodomised after death. Beside her lay Snider with the shotgun alongside him. He had blown his brains out, point-blank.

Bogdanovich was racked with grief. He blamed Hefner and 'the Playboy sex factory' for Dorothy's death. Hefner later responded by accusing Bogdanovich of seducing Dorothy's sister Louise when she was underage. Louise filed suit against Hefner, but later dropped the action. She had met Bogdanovich when she was fourteen. He had helped pay for her schooling and later married her when she was twenty.

Clarence J. R. Rodgers made a big mistake for a pimp. He fell in love with one of his whores. When she was murdered, Rodgers – a leading figure of Boston's red light district, the Combat Zone – was the first suspect. But the culprit was, in fact, a mild-mannered professor of anatomy – one of her 'tricks' who had become insanely jealous of her.

Robin Benedict came from a stable middle-class background, but she craved the excitement that only the black pimp JR could give her. He introduced her to cocaine and put her on the game.

When she disappeared in early March 1983, he was beside himself with worry. Unable to go to the police for help; he hired private detective Jack DaRosa, to track her down. JR had last seen Robin two days before when she had gone to visit Dr William Douglas, an international authority on cell culture at Tufts University.

At Tufts, Douglas was known as a fussy workaholic. But at night he would visit the sleazy strip joints and pornographic bookshops of the Combat Zone. In April 1982, he had stumbled into a dimly lit dive named Good Time Charlie's, where he met Robin Benedict who was working under her alias Nadine. She ignored the overweight professor at first, but then took him out for a quick $50's worth. He came back again and again, and soon became obsessed with her.

They spent time together – shopping, cooking, eating – but always at her regular rate of $100 an hour. She introduced him to cocaine, which he paid for, and to her friends from Good Time Charlie's, including Savi Bastram, known as Indian Debbie, and her boy Taj, JR's son.

On the night she disappeared, Dr Douglas was supposed to have been helping her to fill in her tax forms. DaRosa visited Dr Douglas who confirmed that Robin had visited him. He claimed to be a friend of the family who had helped her out when she had been charged with soliciting.

JR called Robin's parents and told them that she was missing. As Robin was over twenty-one, she could not officially be listed as missing for another few days, but John Benedict, Robin's father, distributed photographs of his missing daughter to the media. The press took one look at the pictures and immediately splashed the story across their front pages as 'The Missing Beauty Case'.

Seeing the stories, State Trooper Paul Landry came forward with information. He had found a man's blue shirt and a woman's beige corduroy jacket, both bloodstained, along with a sledgehammer in a plastic garbage bag on Route 95, about five miles from Douglas's home. Lodged between the shaft and head of the sledgehammer was a long brown hair which Landry thought could be Robin's.

JR recognised the jacket. He had bought it for Robin himself. He also recognised her perfume on it.

The police now had good reason to believe that Robin had been murdered. JR was the prime suspect. They wanted to know where he had put the body. But during long hours of interrogation, JR only had one thing to confess – he loved Robin. They had never had a fight and planned to get married.

Dr Douglas was also interviewed. He said that Robin was a very nice girl who he had tried to help by commissioning her to do artwork to illustrate his scientific work. This conflicted with JR's story that Robin was a full-time prostitute for about two years. Douglas had been seeing her for about a year, almost every other night. He sent love letters to her almost daily and was incredibly jealous. He spied on her, and when she took other clients, he called the vice squad. Then he turned up as a character witness.

Early in 1983, Robin had called Douglas's wife and told her to make her husband stop pestering her. The night she had gone missing, JR said she had visited Douglas's home to tell him that she did not want to see him any more.

There were a couple of calls on Robin's answering service. They indicated that Robin was going to an all-night party being held by someone called Joe. Later, JR's service had got a message that Robin would 'be at John's'. JR said that Robin knew neither a Joe nor a John.

A Boston estate agent called the police, saying that he had recently rented an apartment to a girl answering Robin's description. Inside the police found a bed, condoms, paper tissues and a business card inscribed 'Nadine'. The tenant had given her occupation as 'research assistant' to Dr Douglas at Tufts University. She was indeed on the pay-roll there as an 'image analyst' and was cited as an assistant on one of Dr Douglas's papers in the British Journal of Cell Science. Indian Debbie was also on the staff.

The police obtained a search warrant and went around to the leafy cul-de-sac where Dr Douglas lived with his wife and three children. Mrs Douglas recognised the bloodstained blue man's shirt Landry had found, and pointed out the place where she had mended it under the armpit.

In a bedroom cupboard, the police found hard-core pornographic magazines and small ads offering erotic services. In an envelope addressed to the professor, there was a pair of pink panties and a piece of chewed gum.

They also found a coded address book and a handbag containing Robin Benedict's credit card. When asked how they got them, Dr Douglas said that JR must have planted them. More ominously, stuck to the inside of a blue windcheater hanging in the hallway, was a piece of grey tissue about the size of a penny. It came from deep inside a human brain.

Then John Benedict received a surprising telegram. It read: 'Happy Easter. I am working in Las Vegas and things are well. Please do not tell JR where I am. Love to everyone. Robin.'

Mr Benedict knew that it was a fake immediately. Robin was known in the family as 'Bin-Bin' and always signed herself that way.

Meanwhile, the police heard that the professor was picking up prostitutes more compulsively than ever. They also discovered that he had been suspended from the university over financial irregularities in his grant allocations. $67,000 was missing.

In one of his love letters to Robin, he had forlornly written: 'I need your help. I truly need a friend.' Her response was to calculate how much he owed her and to begin charging interest. Once she had visited the house demanding payment. Douglas no longer had any money, or access to it. On her second visit, she disappeared. But still there was no body and precious little to link Dr Douglas to her disappearance.

69

Through dogged detective work, the police discovered that, although suspended from the university, Dr Douglas was still using a Tufts charge card to make phone calls. One was traced to a phone box near where the sledgehammer and bloodstained clothes were found. It was made at the time Dr Douglas claimed Robin was leaving his home. Other calls coincided with the mysterious calls to Robin and JR's answering services.

Robin's car, a Toyota, was found near New York's Penn Station. The driver's seat had been pushed well back, to accommodate a large person. The floor and the upholstery were caked with blood. A rail ticket from Penn Station to Boston had been purchased on the professor's credit card the day after Robin's disappearance. His signature was on the sales slip.

Douglas's brother-in-law admitted that the sledgehammer belonged to Mrs Douglas's father, who had lent it to the professor for work in his garage. Dr Douglas was arrested at a car-rental company where he had found work as a driver.

He spent six months on remand while his attorney Tom Troy, who had once represented the Boston Strangler, tried to counter the yearlong sentimentalisation of 'The Missing Beauty Case' in the press. Robin Benedict, Troy maintained, was 'a blackmailing whore with a black pimp.'

The prosecution built an impressive forensic case against Douglas. But no murder case without a body can be cast iron. On a plea bargain, Dr Douglas pleaded guilty to manslaughter.

Dr Douglas was sentenced to 18-20-years imprisonment – the maximum sentence for manslaughter. In court, he made a mumbled apology and said that he had dumped Robin's body in an unidentified skip behind a large shopping mall.

His grotesque story was interrupted by a torrent of abuse from the back of the court. It came from Clarence J.R. Rogers who sat surrounded by the sobbing Benedict family.

Ruth Ellis gunned down her lover David Blakely outside

the Magdala Tavern in Hampstead in 1955 because of jealousy. She longed for a stable family life for herself and her children and the social status that a good marriage would bring – but she was fatally attracted to the type of men who could never be faithful.

Ruth Ellis, nee Neilson, gave birth to her first child, Andre Clare, in 1944 when she was just 17. She had expected the father, a French-Canadian soldier on wartime duty in Europe, to propose when she fell pregnant. It was only then that she discovered he already had a wife and family in Quebec.

Her older sister Muriel looked after the baby while Ruth pursued her career as a model – often posing nude for camera clubs. At the age of nineteen, she met Morris Conley, dubbed 'Britain's biggest vice boss' by the press. She became a hostess in Conley's Court Club in Mayfair, earning £20 a week to perch on a bar stool and let men ply her with overpriced champagne. Any extra money she made after hours was hers to keep. She lived well.

One of the club's clientele, George Ellis, pestered her for a date. He had money and could give Ruth all the things she craved. They married in 1950 and moved to Southampton. But George was an alcoholic and soon after their daughter was born in 1951 they separated.

Ruth went back to London where Conley made her the manageress of the Little Club in Knightsbridge. She earned £15 a week plus tips and commission. She also had a £10 entertainment allowance and could live rent-free in the two-bedroom flat above the club.

The Little Club was a gold mine. Apart from selling overpriced drinks to a rich clientele, there were also private rooms where customers could have sex with the girls. Two of the regulars were racing driver David Blakely and wealthy bachelor Dennis Cussen.

Cussen fell for Ruth straight away. He was a director of a respectable family business and offered status, money, and a good home for Ruth's two children. But it was the feckless womaniser David Blakely that she fell for.

Within a week Blakely had moved in with her. Despite his well-paid job and an inheritance of £7,000, he lived rent-free with Ruth and ran a free drinks slate in the Little Club. He declared undying love for her, even though he was engaged to textile heiress Linda Dawson.

Despite Blakely's reputation as a playboy, he could not hold his drink. His behaviour in the club soon turned other customers away. To get rid of him, Conley sacked Ruth. But Cussen took pity on her. He put Ruth and her son up in his flat in Baker Street and lavished money on them. He even allowed Blakely to sleep with her there.

Ruth was overjoyed when Blakely broke off his engagement with Linda Dawson – thinking that it was for her. Then she discovered love bites all over his back and realised that there was someone else. She threw him out, but soon took him back.

Ruth took a one-bedroom flat in Kensington, paid for by Cussen. Styling himself as Mr Ellis, Blakely would visit her there. Her divorce from the real Mr Ellis was almost complete when she fell pregnant again. Instead of proposing marriage, as she had hoped, Blakely punched her in the stomach inducing a miscarriage. He sent a dozen red carnations and a card saying 'Sorry Darling' to the hospital. Soon they were the best of friends again.

They spent the night of Thursday, 6 April 1955, together in her flat. In the morning, he left saying that he would meet her for drinks later. He never showed up. He did not show up the next day either. Ruth was beside herself.

On Sunday 9 April she was drinking Pernod with Cussen and complaining about Blakely's treatment of her. According to the statement Ruth Ellis made the day before she was hanged, Cussen gave her a loaded gun and took her to Epping Forest for some shooting practice. Then he drove her up to Hampstead.

Blakely was in the Magdala Tavern telling friends how he wanted to leave Ruth, but she would not let him go. Around 9 pm Blakely and a friend, Clive Gunnell, emerged from the pub laughing. Ruth was waiting.

'David,' she called. He did not hear her.

'David,' she called again. His face fell as if he were expecting another slanging match.

Instead, Ruth Ellis pointed a gun at him and pulled the trigger. Blakely stumbled back. Another shot rang out. Blakely fell bleeding. He screamed for Clive Gunnell to help him.

'Get out of the way, Clive,' Ellis said.

Blakely tried to make his escape up the hill. Ruth fired three more times. The first shot brought him down, the second mortally wounded him and the third was pumped into him at point-blank range, finishing him off.

Ruth Ellis then raised the gun to her own temple and pulled the trigger. Nothing happened. As her arm fell wearily from her head, she pulled the trigger once more. This time the gun fired. The bullet ricocheted off the pavement, hitting a bystander in the thumb.

'Fetch the police,' she said dejectedly.

An off-duty constable who had been drinking in the Magdala Tavern took the gun from her hand.

'I am the police,' he said.

On 13 July 1955, Ruth Ellis became the last woman to be hanged in Britain. After her death, capital punishment became so unpopular in the United Kingdom that within five years it was abolished altogether.

Chapter 6

Thrill Killers

Vampires are the stuff of myth and legend. But they also exist in real life. For some people the sexual thrill of drinking human blood is so strong that they will do anything for it – even kill.

Ex-Catholic schoolgirl Tracy Wigginton was a committed lesbian with an obsession with the occult. She went out only at night and avoided both sunlight and mirrors. Six foot tall and 17 stone, she was never seen to eat. Her only sustenance came from drinking blood which she collected from butchers' shops.

In Brisbane in 1989, Wigginton gathered around her a group of girls called the Swampies. They wore black clothes and heavy boots, and surrounded themselves with Gothic imagery.

Wigginton's lover, former heroin user Lisa Ptaschinski, would use a tourniquet to pump up the veins in her arm, then nick her wrist so that Wigginton could suck her blood. But this was not enough. Wigginton craved more human blood and was willing to kill to get it.

Wigginton, Ptaschinski, Acid House Swampy Kim Jervis and her lover, unemployed secretary Tracey Waugh, planned to commit the perfect murder to satisfy Wigginton's bizarre lusts. Meeting in gay clubs, they discussed how they could stalk, trap and kill a human victim so that Wigginton could drink his blood.

One night in Jervis's flat, which was hung with pictures of cemeteries and had a stolen headstone as a centre-piece, they came up with what they thought was the perfect plan. Waugh and Ptaschinski would pose as prostitutes and lure the victim into one of the inner city parks. In a secluded spot, Wigginton and Jervis would kill him and drink his blood. The women would then take his body to a cemetery, dump it in a freshly dug grave and cover it over. When the funeral party arrived the following day, a coffin would be lowered on top of the body, the grave would be filled in and the victim would be buried without anyone realising it. There would be no witnesses, no clues and no corpse.

On the night of Friday, 20 October 1989, the four women met at the Club Lewmors, a lesbian dive, where they sipped champagne. Wigginton and Jervis were carrying knives – but Wigginton bragged that she would kill with her bare hands if she had to.

Around 11.30 pm, they left the club and began cruising the streets in Wigginton's green Holden sedan looking for a likely victim. On River Terrace, they spotted 47-year-old Edward Baldock, clinging drunkenly to a lamp post. He had been out for a few beers and a game of darts with his mates in the Caledonian club and was now slowly making his way home to his wife of 25 years.

The women stopped and asked him if he wanted a lift home. He accepted and climbed in the back with Wigginton. They held hands. Wigginton instructed Ptaschinski to drive down to Orleigh Park, which was near Baldock's home. Ptaschinski parked under a fig tree near the deserted South

Brisbane Sailing Club. Wigginton asked Baldock whether he wanted a good time. He was all for it. They got out of the car and walked down to the river bank, where they both undressed.

A few minutes later Wigginton returned to the car, complaining that Baldock was too strong. Ptaschinski said she would help and Jervis handed her the knife. The two lesbian lovers walked back down to the river where Baldock sat, naked except for his socks.

Wigginton urged Ptaschinski to creep up on him and stab him, but she did not have the nerve. She could not kill a poor old drunk. Instead, she collapsed in the sand in front of him and began to gabble. Wigginton had no such qualms. She stabbed Baldock repeatedly in the neck and throat until his head was nearly severed, then she drank his blood.

She returned to the car satisfied, and the women drove back to Jervis's flat elated, convinced that they had committed the perfect murder. It was only when they arrived at the macabre apartment that Wigginton realised that she had lost her bankers' card. She had dropped it at the beach while she was undressing.

Panicked, the women drove back to Orleigh Park and scoured the area, but they could not find the card. They decided that Wigginton must have lost it elsewhere. On the way back to Jervis's flat, they were stopped for a routine check by a patrol car and Ptaschinski was breathalysed. The breath test was negative, but she had come out without her driving licence. The police took down the details of the car.

Next morning, Baldock's naked body was discovered by two women out for an early morning walk. They called the police. Within minutes of their arrival, detectives found Wigginton's bankers' card in Baldock's shoe, where he had tucked it, perhaps thinking it was his own. They quickly discovered that the green Holden that had been stopped by a patrol car in the area was also registered to a Tracey

Wigginton and put two and two together. At this point, they assumed that Wigginton was Baldock's mistress and she had murdered him in an argument over money.

Realising that their perfect crime might not be so perfect after all, the four women had cooked up what they thought was a foolproof alibi. They were to say that they had been out fooling about in the area earlier the day before. That's when Wigginton must have lost the card. This story did not take into account that they had been stopped in that same area by a patrol car that night.

Under questioning, Wigginton began to change her story. She mentioned that they had seen a suspicious-looking couple in the park – then, later, that she had gone to the park in the evening and had fallen over a dead body in the dark, but had been too frightened to report it.

Ptaschinski's nerve had gone once the night before. With Wigginton in custody, it went again. She could not stand the waiting. She left the flat and began walking about in a confused state. As she wandered about aimlessly, the guilt gradually ate into her. She turned herself into a nearby police station. Jervis and Waugh were arrested the next day.

Under relentless questioning, Tracey Wigginton admitted that she was a 'vampire'. She was sent for detailed psychological examination. The doctors discovered that Tracey had been abandoned by her father and mother when she was a baby and was brought up by her grandparents George and Avril Wigginton. George was a profligate womaniser and Avril took out her hatred of her unfaithful husband on the children in her care. She had beaten Tracey mercilessly and poisoned her mind against men.

Tracey had turned to her genial grandfather for affection, but claimed that he had demanded sex with her when she was eight years old. At her Catholic school, she became a notorious lesbian and was known for her strange and evil behaviour.

When she left school in 1982, she began calling herself Bobby. She went round and beat her grandmother up. She had a sado-masochistic relationship with a woman called Jamie who beat her with a strap and demanded social submission. She later underwent a lesbian 'wedding' performed by a member of the Hare Krishna sect and became a bouncer at a gay night-club.

After her 'marriage' broke up, she asked the club's owner, a man named John O'Hara, to help her have a baby. They had sex in front of six close friends. Tracey fell pregnant, but later miscarried. She began a stormy relationship with a woman named Donna Staib. They lived together but both were enormously promiscuous with other women. Around that time, Tracey dyed her hair 'midnight blue' and had her body tattooed with mystical signs. She and Staib shared a taste for horror videos. The night before Baldock's murder they had watched a sequence of a man being shot in the forehead, his skull exploding, over and over again in slow motion.

The police feared that Wigginton's warped upbringing might be used in an insanity plea. But Wigginton, 24, took responsibility for her acts and was aware of their consequences. She pleaded guilty and was sentenced to life imprisonment.

The other three women pleaded not guilty. They claimed that they had thought that Wigginton was not serious and had been forced by her overbearing personality to go along with her. Under cross-examination though, Ptaschinski admitted that she had been fascinated by the 'thrilling and chilling' plan to murder a man and to drink his blood.

In court, the three women claimed that Wigginton had occult powers. They said that she claimed to be the Devil's wife and practised mind control. The cross around Kim Jervis's neck had been broken by her diabolical power, and she could disappear leaving only the eyes of a cat.

Ptaschinski, 24, was found guilty of murder and sentenced

to life. Jervis, 23, got eighteen years for manslaughter. Only Waugh, 23, walked free from the court. Although she was the brightest of the four women, the jury decided that she was completely under the evil swathe of Tracey Wigginton.

Women are not often the perpetrators of sex crimes. More often they are the victims. The life of the nude model is especially fraught with danger. Most models have their stories of 'suspicious' customers. Many men just get a natural thrill by being close to a naked woman. Others are voyeuristic weirdoes. There is always the danger of rape. And some men can only get their kicks from the ultimate violation – murder.

Los Angeles Times journalist Robert Dull had separated from his pretty young blonde wife, Judy, because he objected to her modelling nude for other men. But he remained on reasonably good terms with her. On 1 August 1957, she had invited him round to talk about the break-up of their marriage, but when he arrived she was not at home. Her flatmate, Lynn Lykles, said that she had left several hours before with a photographer called Johnny Glynn.

Over the next two hours two more photographers called saying that nineteen-year-old Judy had failed to turn up for a session. No one replied on the number Glynn had left. Dull called Judy's family and friends. None of them had seen her. So he called the police.

Lynn gave them a description of Glynn. He was short with jughandle ears and looked rather scruffy and dishevelled. He had come around two days before and another flatmate, Betty, showed him Judy's portfolio. He was captivated.

That morning he had phoned, saying that he had a rush assignment. Judy was reluctant, she had a busy schedule. Betty's description of him made her rather suspicious too. But when he said that his studio was tied up and they would have to shoot the assignment in her apartment, she agreed.

When he turned up at the apartment, he had no photographic gear with him. A friend had lent him his studio, he explained. He agreed to her fee and the two of them left. That was the last time anyone saw her alive.

Descriptions of Judy and this mysterious photographer were circulated, but there was little else to go on. However the disappearance made the newspapers, and Police Sergeant David Ostroff was kept busy following up leads for weeks. Ostroff also studied the file of beautiful young actress Jean Spangler who had disappeared eight years before.

Five months after Judy's disappearance, a rancher and his dog discovered a skull in the desert near Interstate 60, over 100 miles east of Los Angeles. When the police arrived, they discovered a half-buried skeleton. The underwear and the remains of a brown dress, like the one Judy was wearing when she was last seen, showed that the body was that of a woman. Tufts of hair showed that she was a blonde. The skeleton was 5ft 4in, the same height as Judy.

Eight months after Judy Dull had gone missing, another woman in the Los Angeles area disappeared. A divorcee and mother of two, 24-year-old Shirley Bridgeford had gone out on a blind date. Her escort was a short dishevelled man with jug ears called George Williams. Sergeant Ostroff believed that the mystery photographer Johnny Glynn and George Williams were the same man.

Three months later, 24-year-old stripper and nude model, Ruth Rita Mercado – who used the stage name Angela – also vanished. Ostroff added her file to his dossier, but he was still no nearer catching the culprit. Then the police got lucky.

On the evening of Monday, 27 October 1958, Officer Thomas F. Mulligan of the California Highway Patrol turned into a dark street in the dusty town of Tustin, 35 miles south of LA. The light from his motorcycle headlamp picked out a couple struggling. He stopped and shouted over to them. The woman was holding a gun and her clothes were in a state of considerable disarray.

Office Mulligan pulled his own pistol and ordered them to stop. They put their hands up. The woman, who identified herself as Lorraine Vigil, claimed that the man was a killer who had tried to rape her. The man did not deny her allegations.

Lorraine was a secretary who was determined to break into modelling. A friend, who ran a modelling agency, had called her that evening and asked her if she wanted an assignment. Although the friend knew the photographer, who was called Frank Johnson, she warned Lorraine to be a little wary. But Lorraine accepted anyway.

The photographer picked her up from her apartment on Wiltshire Boulevard and headed downtown. He drove straight past the modelling studio on Sunset Strip, the agency had mentioned. When Lorraine drew this to his attention, he said he was taking her to his studio in Anaheim. But he drove right through Anaheim as well.

On the dark road in Tustin, he stopped and pulled a gun. He ordered her to keep quiet and produced a length of rope. Lorraine said that she did not want to be tied up and would do anything he wanted instead. At that moment, a car came by and Lorraine made a lunge for the door handle. The gun went off, grazing her thigh.

In the split second confusion, she threw herself at her assailant. The car door flew open and they fell out onto the road. Lorraine bit her attacker as hard as she could. He dropped the gun. She grabbed it and was trying to shoot the fake photographer who had attacked her when Officer Mulligan arrived.

At Santa Ana police station, the photographer who had called himself Frank Johnson revealed that he was, in fact, Harvey Murky Glatman, aged thirty. Glatman lived no more than a few blocks from Ruth Mercado's San Pico Boulevard apartment. When they went around to his address, the police found a run-down white shingle bungalow. Inside, they found the walls covered with nude pin-ups. In some, the girls were bound and gagged. Among Glatman's meagre possessions were a number of lengths of rope.

Glatman agreed to take a lie detector test. When the name Angela – Ruth Mercado's professional name – was mentioned, the stylus leapt. Within minutes, Glatman confessed to killing Ruth Mercado. Then he added: 'I killed a couple of other girls too.' He had quite a story to relate.

Harvey Glatman was born in Denver, Colorado, in 1928. He was a mummy's boy who did not get on well with other children. When he was twelve, his parents noticed red welts around his neck. Under persistent questioning, he admitted that tightening a rope around his own neck gave him some perverse sexual satisfaction. The family doctor said he would grow out of it.

With his jug ears, Glatman soon found that he was unattractive to girls. He would gain their attention by grabbing their purses. But this, he discovered, was not a very effective method of courtship. At seventeen, he took more direct action. He pulled a toy gun on a girl and ordered her to undress. She screamed and run away. Glatman was arrested. When he was released on bail, he fled to New York.

There he turned his urges into a way of life. He began robbing women at gunpoint. Later he graduated to burglary and spent five years in Sing Sing. In prison, he seemed to respond to psychiatric help and became a model prisoner. On his release, he went back to Colorado and begun working as a TV repairman. It was a job that allowed him to enter other people's homes, quite legitimately. Sometimes he would sneak into their bedrooms. His mother lent him the money to set up a TV repair business in Los Angeles.

Glatman admitted everything. Judy Dull, he said, was the girl of his dreams. After he picked her up, he drove her back to his makeshift studio. There he asked her to take off her dress and put on a pleated skirt and cardigan. He produced a length of rope and tied her up. The shots he was taking, he explained, were for the cover of a true-life crime magazine. She had to be bound and gagged.

He took some pictures, but the sight of pretty young Judy helpless before him was too much. There was no way she could resist as he slowly undressed her. He put a gun to her head and told her that he would kill her if she cried for help. She nodded and he untied her gag.

Glatman made her pose on the settee for more explicit bondage photographs, then raped her twice. When he had finished, he told her that he would take her to some remote spot in the desert where he would release her.

He let Judy put her brown dress back on. Then he drove her out into the Nevada desert. In a lonely spot he spread a blanket out on the ground and made her pose again for erotic photographs. In some of them, she had a noose around her neck. When Glatman grew tired of taking pictures, he tied the loose end of the noose around her ankles and pulled it until she was dead.

Glatman apologised to the corpse before he buried it in a shallow grave. He kept her shoes as a keepsake. Although he had originally been out to get a thrill from photographing, and raping, a beautiful woman – naked, bound and gagged – Glatman found that the killing gave him the greatest satisfaction. He was determined to do it again.

Glatman registered with a dating agency in the name of George Williams. The agency fixed him up with a date with Shirley Ann Bridgeford. But he could see by her reaction when he went to pick her up that she found him a disappointment. She went with him anyway.

Glatman drove her south out of Los Angeles, towards San Diego. He stopped in the Anza desert and tried to put his arm around her. She did not really feel that was appropriate behaviour on a first date. He suggested that they went for a meal. She seemed relieved. But he drove with one hand on the steering wheel. With the other, he tried to fondle her. Still she tried to fend him off. Soon he grew angry. He stopped the car and pulled out his automatic. He ordered her to get in the back of the car and undress. She refused, so he tore off her clothes then raped her.

But that was not the end of Shirley's hideous blind date. He drove her out into the desert. Unpacking his photographic gear, he made her pose on the blanket that he had killed Judy Dull on. Then he made her lie on her front. He tied a rope around her neck and garrotted her. He took her red knickers as a memento and left her body. The ground was too hard to dig a grave in, so he left her body covered with brushwood.

Five months later, Glatman spotted an advert in the newspaper, offering the services of a nude model called 'Angela'. He called her up and went round to visit her on the evening of 23 July 1958. She took one look at him and refused to let him in. But he liked the look of her. He pulled his gun and forced his way into her apartment.

At gunpoint he ordered her to undress, tied her up and raped her. Then he announced that they were going for a little picnic. He drove them out to a deserted spot about 30 miles from where he had murdered Shirley Ann Bridgeford. Much as he had enjoyed killing Shirley and Judy Dull, it had all been over too quickly. This time, he decided he would take his time. The two of them spent the day together. They ate, slept and drank. Occasionally, Glatman would force Angela, or Ruth Mercado as she was known outside of work, to pose for him. He raped her repeatedly.

Ruth was very compliant. She plainly decided that her only chance was to try and please him. But after 24 hours of toying with his victim, Glatman garrotted her in the same manner in which he had despatched his other two victims.

After his detailed confession, Glatman helped the police find the remains of Ruth Mercado and Shirley Ann Bridgeford. His lawyers suggested that he plead guilty but insane, but Glatman pleaded guilty without caveat, opting for a quick execution rather than a life in a mental institution. He died in the gas chamber on 18 September 1959.

In 1972, Gerald Schaeffer was sentenced to two life sentences by a Florida court for the murder of two girls – although his name was linked with thirty-four other murder enquiries. He was a vicious sadist who liked to hang girls, watch them choking, then stab them before they were dead. In his diaries, he confided that, even with his girlfriend, the only way he could reach orgasm was to think of hanging women. Even in jail he had daydreams about sexual murder. He was killed by a fellow inmate on 3 December 1995.

But one of the most prolific sex-thrill killers of this century was a well-dressed, soft-spoken, respectable German who lived quietly with his wife. His name was Peter Kürten. In 1929, he terrorised the city of Düsseldorf.

Kürten was born in Koln-Mulheim. His father was a violent drunk who physically and sexually abused his wife and thirteen children. Eventually, he ended up in jail, but he had already done his damage.

At the age of nine, Peter Kürten drowned two of his playmates in the River Rhine. A dog catcher who shared the Kürten's house taught Peter how to torture animals. Peter was precocious sexually. He began indulging his enormous sexual appetite with farm animals and found that stabbing the animal during the act increased his satisfaction.

Later he took up with a prostitute, but was arrested for theft. In jail, his sexual longings became sublimated into gruesome fantasy. On his release, he strangled a young woman in a wood while they were having sex. Back in prison, Kürten deliberately flouted prison rules so that he would be put in solitary confinement. There he would work on his erotic fantasies.

Out again, he added arson to his repertoire of crime. Then he was called up. He deserted, putting him back in prison

85

once again. In 1913, he was breaking into a house when he found a 13-year-old girl asleep in bed. He raped and strangled her. It was then that he discovered murder as a pleasure in its own right. Soon after he attacked two strangers in the street with an axe, achieving orgasm at the sight of their blood.

Kürten spent World War I in jail for burglary. When he was released, he posed as a returning prisoner of war. It was then that he met his future wife. He wooed her with a mixture of sweet talk and threats of appalling violence. She was stoical. A former prostitute, she had spent four years in jail for shooting a man who had abandoned her after promising to marry her. She felt that she had to endure whatever came her way to atone and she put up with Kürten's strange ways. Physically he was gentle with her, but he later admitted that he could only have sex with her by fantasising about violence with someone else.

During the early years of their marriage, they lived in the small town of Altenburg. He worked hard and was a political activist. But from time to time, he would seek out women for brutal sexual encounters. On one occasion assault charges were avoided only by the intervention of his wife.

They moved back to Düsseldorf, where Kürten took up arson again.

'I got pleasure from the glow of the fire, the cries for help', he said later. 'It gave me so much pleasure that I got sexual satisfaction.'

He also attacked four or five women, strangling them to the point of unconsciousness.

On 3 February 1929, his assaults reached a renewed ferocity. He attacked a woman in the street, stabbing her twenty-four times with a pair of scissors. A week later he stabbed a workman to death. He raped and strangled an eight-year-old girl, then mutilated her body with a knife.

He half-strangled four women during attacks, and murdered two children. He killed 20-year-old Maria Hann and buried her. Later he returned to her grave and dug her up, intending to nail her body to a tree in a mock crucifixion to frighten people. But he found her body too heavy to lift, so dragged her body to a new grave site and buried it again.

He killed two women with a hammer, severely injuring two others. Then he murdered a five-year-old girl, buried her and sent a map of the grave site to the newspapers. Kürten joined the crowd that rushed to the scene. He found a new source of sexual pleasure in their fear and outrage.

There were no more murders, but Kürten continued his attacks. Ten more women were battered or half-strangled. They survived to give descriptions of their attacker to the police.

By this time the police had a list of hundreds and thousands of suspects. More than 9,000 people were interviewed; 2,000 clues were followed up. Even Kürten's name had been reported, but the woman who had accused him of attacking her was fined for wasting police time.

But when a woman whom Kürten had raped bumped into him on the stairs outside his flat, Kürten knew his time was up. He confessed everything to his wife, urging her to go to the police and collect the reward. She did not believe his story. It was only when he started relating every detail of his assaults, with evident relish, that she was convinced.

He planned one more act of mass murder, but his wife was too quick for him. She went straight to the police and arranged for him to give himself up to an armed policeman outside the Rochus Church. Kürten made a full confession, including many crimes the police had not heard about before. Often he did not even know his victim's name.

'I went out with my scissors,' ran one typical confession. 'At the station a girl spoke to me, I took her to have a glass of beer, and we then walked towards the Grafenberg woods. I seized her by the throat and I held on for a bit . . . I threw her down the river and went away.'

After being found guilty, Kürten was studied by Professor Karl Berg who described him as the 'king of the sexual perverts.'

'I have no remorse,' Kürten told Berg. 'As to whether recollection of my deeds makes me feel ashamed, I will tell you. Thinking back to the details is not at all unpleasant I rather enjoy it.'

Kürten also received a huge mail bag while he was held in prison. Around half the letters he received spelt out the cruel and unusual penalties the writer would like to inflict. The other half was fan mail, including a large number of love letters from women.

The death penalty was very unpopular in Germany at that time and there were huge protests when Kürten was sentenced to death. Kürten himself was unconcerned. When he heard that he would be able to experience the ultimate pleasure of hearing the blood gush from his neck for the split second his head was being severed, he relished the prospect. And on 2 July 1930, after a meal of wiener schnitzel, fried potatoes and white wine, Peter Kürten went eagerly to the guillotine.

Chapter 7

Partners in Crime

The Moors Murderers Ian Brady and Myra Hindley are the world's most famous sex-killer partners. Their bizarre and deviant sexual relationship drove them to torture and murder defenceless children for pleasure in a case that appalled the world.

When Myra Hindley met Ian Brady he was already deeply warped. He was a 21-year-old stock clerk at Millwards, a chemical company in Manchester, but his mind was full of sadistic fantasies. He had a collection of Nazi memorabilia and recordings of Nazi rallies. In his lunch hour, he read *Mein Kampf* and studied German grammar. He believed then, as he believes now, in the rightness of the Nazi cause and regretted only that he could not join in its sadistic excesses.

Myra Hindley had problems of her own. She was nineteen when they met. She was known as a loner and a daydreamer. At fifteen, her boyfriend had died. She could not sleep for days afterwards and eventually turned to the Catholic Church for consolation.

At school it was noted that she was tough, aggressive and

rather masculine, enjoying contact sports and judo. But that hardly made her suited to working life in 1950s Britain. After a series of menial jobs, she became a typist at Millwards, where she met Brady. He impressed her immediately. Most of the men she knew she considered immature. But Brady was dressed well and rode a motorbike. Everything about him fascinated her. 'Ian wore a black shirt today and looked smashing... I love him,' she confided to her diary.

For nearly a year Brady took no notice of her. 'The pig. He didn't even look at me today,' she wrote more than once.

Finally, in December 1961, he asked her out. 'Eureka!' her diary says. 'Today we have our first date. We are going to the cinema. The film – *Judgment at Nuremberg*.

Soon Hindley had surrendered her virginity to Brady. She was madly in love with him and was writing schoolgirlishly: 'I hope Ian and I love each other all our lives and get married and are happy ever after.'

But their relationship was far more sophisticated than that. Hindley was Brady's love slave. He talked to her of sexual perversions and lent her books on Nazi atrocities. They took pornographic photographs of each other and kept them in a scrapbook. Some showed the weals of a whip across her buttocks.

Hindley gave up baby-sitting and going to church. Within six months, Brady moved with Hindley into her grand-mother's house. Hindley's grandmother was a frail woman who spent most of her time in bed, giving them the run of the place. Brady persuaded Hindley to bleach her hair a Teutonic blonde and dressed her in leather skirts and high-heeled boots. He called her Myra Hess – or Hessie – after sadistic concentration camp guard Irma Grese.

Hindley became hard and cruel, doing anything Brady asked. She did not even balk at procuring children for him to abuse, torture and kill. The first victim was sixteen-year-old

Pauline Reade who disappeared on her way to a dance on 12 July 1963. Somehow they managed to persuade her to walk up to nearby Saddleworth Moor, where they killed and buried her in a shallow grave.

Four months later, Hindley hired a car and abducted twelve-year-old John Kilbride. When she returned the car, it was covered in peaty mud from the moors. Brady and Hindley laughed when they read about the massive police operation to find the missing boy.

In May 1964, Hindley bought a car of her own, a white Mini van. The following month, twelve-year-old Keith Bennett went missing. He too was buried on Saddleworth Moor. At Brady's behest, Hindley joined a local gun club and bought pistols for them both. They would go up to the moors for practice. While they were there they would visit the graves of their victims. They would photograph each other kneeling on them.

On 26 December 1964, they abducted ten-year-old Lesley Ann Downey. This time they were determined to get their money's worth out of their defenceless victim. They forced her to pose nude for pornographic photographs. Then they tortured her, recording her screams, before strangling her and burying her with the others on Saddleworth Moor.

Even this did not satisfy the depraved Brady. He wanted to extend his evil empire. He aimed to recruit Myra's 16-year-old brother-in-law, David Smith. Brady began to systematically corrupt Smith. He showed the youth his guns and talked to him about robbing a bank. He lent him books about de Sade and got him to copy out quotations. 'Murder is a hobby and a supreme pleasure' and 'People are like maggots, small, blind, worthless fish-bait' Smith wrote in an exercise book under the guidance of Brady.

Brady believed he could lure anyone into his world of brutality and murder. He bragged to Smith about the murders he had already committed, saying he had photographs to

91

prove it. They were drinking at the time and Smith thought Brady was joking.

Brady decided to prove what he was saying – and ensnare Smith into his vicious schemes by making him a party to murder. On 6 October 1965 Brady and Hindley picked up seventeen-year-old homosexual Edward Evans in a pub in Manchester. Smith had been invited around midnight. When he arrived, he heard a cry. 'Help him, Dave,' Hindley said. Smith rushed through into the sitting room to find a youth in a chair with Brady astride him. Brady had an axe in his hands and smashed it down on the boy's head. He hit him again and again – at least fourteen times.

'It's the messiest,' Brady said with some satisfaction. Usually it takes only one blow.'

He handed the axe to the dumbstruck Smith. This was a simple attempt to incriminate Smith by making him put his fingerprints on the murder weapon. Although Smith was terrified by what he had seen, he helped clean up the blood, while Brady and Hindley wrapped the body in a plastic sheet. The couple made jokes about the murder as they carried the corpse downstairs.

Hindley made a pot of tea and they all sat down.

'You should have seen the look on his face,' said Hindley, flushed with excitement, and she started reminiscing about the previous murders.

Smith could not believe all this was happening, but he realised that if he showed any sign of disgust or outrage he would be their next victim. After a decent interval, he made his excuses and left. When he got back to his flat, he was violently ill.

He told his wife and she urged him to go to the police. Armed with a knife and a screwdriver, they went out to a phone box at dawn and reported the murder. A police car picked them up and Smith told his lurid story to unbelieving policemen. But at 8.40 am, the police dropped round to

Hindley's house to check it out. To their horror, they found Edward Evans's body in the back bedroom.

Brady admitted killing Evans during an argument and tried to implicate Smith. Hindley only said: 'My story is the same as Ian's . . . Whatever he did, I did.' The only time she showed any emotion was when she was told that her dog had died. 'You fucking murderers,' she screamed at the police.

The police found a detailed plan that Brady had drawn up for the removal from the house of all clues to Evans's murder. One of the items mentioned was, curiously, Hindley's prayer book. When the police examined the prayer book, they found a left luggage ticket from Manchester station stuck down the spine. At the left luggage office, they found two suitcases which contained books on sexual perversion, coshes and pictures of Lesley Ann Downey naked and gagged. There was also the tape of her screams, which was later played to the stunned court-room at Chester Assizes. Other photographs showed Hindley posing beside graves on Saddleworth Moor. These helped the police locate the bodies of Lesley Ann Downey and John Kilbride.

At the trial the true, horrific, sexual nature of the crimes was revealed. The pathologist disclosed that Edward Evans's fly had been undone and he had found dog hairs around Evans's anus. John Kilbride's body was found with his trousers and underpants around his knees. Hindley, it seemed, got turned on by watching Brady perform homosexual acts on his victims. Later Brady let it slip that both he and Hindley had been naked during the nude photographic sessions with Lesley Ann Downey. But otherwise they refused to talk.

They were sentenced to life. Brady did not bother to appeal. Hindley did, but her appeal was rejected. They were also refused permission to see each other, though they were allowed to write.

Brady has shown no contrition in prison and has refused to be broken. He sees himself as a martyr in his own perverted cause. Gradually, he has gone insane. Hindley broke down and petitioned to be released. When that was refused, a warder, who was Hindley's lesbian lover, organised an escape attempt. It failed and Hindley was sentenced to an additional year in jail.

She took an open university degree and gave additional information on the whereabouts of the victims' graves in a bid for mercy. But Brady countered her every move by revealing more of her involvement in the crimes. He saw any attempt on her part to go free as disloyalty.

'The weight of our crimes justifies permanent imprisonment,' Brady told the Parole Board in 1982. 'I will not wish to be free in 1985 or even 2005.'

Myra Hindley died in prison in 2002, after hinting that there may have been one more victim, a young hitchhiker. Brady has never addressed the matter and it is very unlikely that he will ever be released. After all, he has never shown any remorse and the families of their victims are still suffering.

America's most prolific serial killer, Henry Lee Lucas also had a partner in crime. With his accomplice, Ottis Toole, he confessed to over 360 murders – 157 of these have been checked out by the authorities and proved to be true.

Lucas's mother was half-Chippawa. She was drunk most of the time on corn liquor which she bought with the proceeds of prostitution. She was known to be 'as mean as a rattlesnake' and packed the seven children from her first marriage off to a foster home. Lucas's father worked on the railways and lost both legs in an accident. He was brought up by another of his mother's bizarre lovers, Andrew Lucas.

Lucas's mother beat the children constantly. Henry was made to grow his hair long and wear a dress. After one beating he was unconscious for three days and suffered damage to his brain. Another accident left him with a glass eye.

At the age of ten, Henry Lucas was introduced to sex by Bernard Dowdy, yet another of his mother's lovers. Dowdy was mentally retarded. He would slit the throat of a calf and have sex with the carcass, and would encourage the boy to do the same. Lucas enjoyed this and, from childhood onwards, he associated sex and death.

Throughout his childhood he continued to have sex with animals, sometimes skinning them alive for sexual pleasure. At fourteen, he turned his perverted attention to women. He beat a seventeen-year-old girl unconscious at a bus stop and raped her. When she came to and started screaming, he choked the life out of her.

At fifteen, he was sent to reformatory for burglary. Two years of hard labour on a prison farm did nothing to reform him. When he was released, he returned to housebreaking. He was caught again and sent back to jail.

He escaped, then met and fell in love with a girl called Stella. They stayed together for four years and she agreed to marry him. Then his mother turned up demanding that her son take care of her. After a violent row, Lucas killed her. This time he got 40 years.

By 1970, the authorities considered Lucas a reformed character and released him. He killed a woman within hours of getting out. In 1971, he was arrested for attempting to rape two teenage girls at gunpoint. His only excuse was that he craved women all the time.

Released in 1975, he married a woman called Betty Crawford. The marriage broke up when Betty discovered that he was having sex with her nine-year-old daughter and trying to force himself on her seven year-old. Lucas then moved in with his sister, but was thrown out when he started having sex with her daughter too.

In 1978, he met another sex murder freak called Ottis Toole in a soup kitchen in Jacksonville, Florida. He was a sadist with homosexual tendencies. He often dressed as a woman and picked up men in bars. He even started a course of female hormones as part of his ambition to have a sex change. Toole was also a pyromaniac, getting an orgasm at the sight of a burning building.

Lucas and Toole became lovers and together they began a series of violent robberies which frequently involved murder – often for the sheer pleasure of it. In Toole's confession, he admitted that around that time they saw a teenage couple walking along a road after their car had run out of petrol. Toole shot the boy, while Lucas forced the girl into the back of the car. After he had finished with her, he shot her six times and they dumped her body on the roadside. This was one of the cases the police could confirm.

Another occurred outside Oklahoma City. There they had picked up a girl called Tina Williams when her car broke down. Lucas shot her twice and had sex with her dead body.

In 1978, Lucas and Toole were in Maryland, when a man asked them whether they would help him transport stolen cars. This was too tame a sport for such hardened criminals, they explained. So he asked them whether they were interested in becoming professional killers. They said that were. The one proviso was that they had to join a Satanist cult.

Lucas and Toole claimed to have been inducted into the Hand of Death sect in Florida by a man named Don Meteric. As part of the initiation Lucas had to kill a man. He lured the victim to a beach and gave him a bottle of whisky. When the man threw his head back to take a swig, Lucas cut his throat.

As part of the cult activity, Lucas and Toole kidnapped young prostitutes who were forced to perform in porno-graphic videos which often turned out to be 'snuff movies'. They also abducted children and took them across the border into Mexico where they were sold or used as sacrifices in satanic ceremonies. These children may have been delivered to Adolfo de Jesus Constanzo, the homosexual high priest, and his one-time lover, the beautiful, American-college-educated Sara Maria Aldrete, known as 'La Bruja' – The Witch. They murdered and mutilated children in Mexico during satanic rites. Their victim's genitals were cut out and their brains boiled. The flesh of 'gringos' was especially in demand.

Around that time, Toole introduced Lucas to his eleven-year-old niece, Becky Powell, who was slightly mentally retarded. She lived in Toole's mother's house in Florida where they were staying. Toole had been seduced by his older sister Druscilla, before he became a homosexual, and he enjoyed watching his pick-ups make love to Becky or her older sister Sarah.

When Druscilla committed suicide, Becky and her brother Frank were put in care. Lucas decided to rescue them. By January 1982, they were on the run together, living off the money they stole from small grocery stores. Becky called Lucas 'Daddy'. But one night, when he was tickling her innocently at bedtime, they began to kiss. Lucas undressed her, then stripped off himself. Becky was only twelve, he said, but she looked eighteen.

During his time with Becky, Lucas continued his murderous rampage with Toole. Lucas outlined a typical two weeks in Georgia. In that short space of time, they kidnapped and murdered a sixteen-year-old girl then raped the dead body, and abducted, raped and mutilated a blonde woman. Another woman was abducted from a parking lot and stabbed to death in front of her own children. In the course of one robbery, the store owner was shot. Another man died in a second robbery. In a third, the store owner was stabbed. And in a fourth, a woman was tied up before being stabbed to death. Toole also tried to force his sexual attentions on a young man. On being spurned, Toole shot him. Becky and her brother Frank were often in on the robberies and witnessed several of the murders.

Eventually, Lucas and Toole parted company. Toole took Frank back to Florida, while Lucas and Becky got a job with a couple named Smart who ran an antique shop in California. After five months, the Smarts sent Lucas and Becky to Texas to look after Mrs Smart's eighty-year-old mother, Kate Rich.

A few weeks later, Mrs Smart's sister visited her mother to find the place filthy. Lucas had been taking money to buy beer and cigarettes. She found him drunk in bed with Becky and the two of them were fired.

They were hitchhiking out of town when they were picked up by the Reverend Rueben Moore, who had started a religious community nearby called the House of Prayer. Lucas and his fifteen-year-old common law wife quickly became converts and lived in a converted chicken barn. While they were staying at the House of Prayer, Becky seems to have had a genuine change of heart. She was homesick and she wanted to go back to Florida. Reluctantly, Lucas agreed and they set off hitchhiking.

At nightfall, they settled down with their blankets in a field. It was a warm June night. A row broke out about Becky's decision to return home. She struck him in the face. He grabbed a knife and stabbed her through the heart. Then he had sex with her corpse, cut her body up and scattered its dismembered pieces in the woods.

After killing Becky, whom Lucas later described as the only woman he had ever loved, he returned to the House of Prayer. He too seems to have had some sort of change of heart. One Sunday, he dropped around to Mrs Rich's house to offer her a lift to church. She accepted. But during the journey, she began to question him about the whereabouts of Becky. Lucas pulled a knife and stabbed it into her side. She died immediately. He drove her to a piece of waste ground where he undressed and raped her corpse. He stuffed her naked body into a drainage pipe that ran under the road. Later he collected it in a garbage bag and burnt it in the stove at the House of Prayer.

Sheriff Bill F. 'Hound Dog' Conway of Montague County, Texas, had begun to have his suspicions about Lucas when he reappeared without Becky. Now he was linked to the disappearance of two women. Lucas was hauled in for questioning.

Lucas was a chain smoker and caffeine addict. Conway deprived him of both cigarettes and coffee, but still he refused to break. Lucas maintained that he knew nothing about the disappearance of Kate Rich, and that Becky had run off with a truck driver who promised to take her back to Florida. Finally, Sheriff Conway had to release him.

Soon after, Lucas told the Reverend Moore that he was going off to look for Becky. He headed for Missouri, where he saw a young woman standing beside her car in a petrol station. He held a knife to her ribs and forced her back into the car. They drove south towards Texas. When she dozed off, Lucas pulled off the road with the intention of raping her. She awoke suddenly to find a knife at her neck. He stabbed her in the throat, pushed her out onto the ground and cut her clothes off. After he had raped her dead body, he dragged it into a copse and took the money from her handbag. He abandoned her car in Fredericksburg, Texas, and returned to the House of Prayer.

While he had been away, the Reverend Moore had told Sheriff Conway that Lucas had given Becky a gun for safe-keeping. Lucas was a convicted felon and had, consequently, forfeited his right to bear arms. It was enough to put him back in the slammer. Sheriff Conway again deprived him of coffee and cigarettes. This time he began to crack. He was found hanging in his cell with his wrists slashed.

After being patched up in the prison hospital, Lucas was put in a special observation cell in the women's wing. The next night, he cracked completely. In the early hours of the morning, he started yelling. When the jailer arrived, Lucas claimed that there was a light in his cell and it was talking to him. The night man, Joe Dan Weaver, knew that Lucas had already smashed the bulb in his cell and told him to get some sleep. Later in the night, Lucas called the jailer again and confessed that he had done some pretty bad things. Joe Don advised him to get down on his knees and pray. Instead, Lucas asked Joe Don for a pencil and paper.

Lucas spent the next half hour writing a note to Sheriff Conway. It read: 'I have tried to get help for so long, and no one will believe me. I have killed for the past ten years and no one will believe me. I cannot go on doing this. I have killed the only girl I ever loved.'

When the confession was finished, Lucas pushed it out of the cell door's peep hole. Joe Dan read it and called Sheriff Conway. He knew the Sheriff would not mind being woken in the middle of the night.

When Sheriff Conway arrived, he plied Lucas with coffee and cigarettes – and asked about the murders. Lucas said that he had seen a light in his cell and it had told him to confess his sins. Then he told the sheriff that he had killed Kate Rich.

Later, Sheriff Conway and Texas Ranger Phil Ryan asked Lucas what had happened to Becky Powell. Tears flowed from his one good eye as Lucas told how he had stabbed, raped and dismembered her. The story left the two hardened law officers sick and wretched.

'Is that all?' asked Ryan wearily, half-hoping it was.

'Not by a long way,' said Lucas. 'I reckon I killed more than a hundred.'

The next day, Montague County police began to check out Lucas's story. Near the drainage pipe where Lucas had temporarily hidden Mrs Rich's body, they found some of her underclothes and her glasses, broken. At the House of Prayer, they found some burnt fragments of human flesh and some charred bones.

Lucas took them to the field where he had killed Becky. They found her suitcase, full of women's clothing and make-up. Her skull, pelvis and other parts of her body were found in the woodland nearby, in an advanced stage of decomposition.

He began to confess to other murders too – often in breath-taking detail. These too checked out.

A week after he had begun to confess, Lucas appeared in court, charged with the murder of Kate Rich and Becky Powell. When asked whether he understood the seriousness of the charge against him, Lucas said he did and confessed to about a hundred other murders.

The judge, shocked, could scarcely credit this and asked Lucas whether he had ever had psychiatric examination. Lucas said he had, but 'they didn't want to do anything about it . . . I know it ain't normal for a person to go out and kill girls just to have sex'.

Lucas's sensational testimony made huge headlines and the news wires carried the story to every paper in the country. Police departments in every state and country began checking their records and Lucas's confessions were run through the computer at the newly formed National Center for the Analysis of Violent Crime.

Toole, it was discovered, was already in prison. He had been sentenced to fifteen years for arson in Springfield. In jail he was regaling a cellmate with the tale of how he had raped, murdered, beheaded, barbecued and eaten a child named Adam Walsh. Suddenly, the police were taking his stories seriously.

Lucas and Toole began to confess freely. They admitted to a series of robberies of 'convenience' stores. At one, they had tied up a young girl. She had wriggled free, so Lucas had shot her in the head and Toole had had sex with her dead body.

Lucas went on a 1,000-mile tour of murder sites. In Duval Country, Florida, Lucas confessed to eight unsolved murders. The victims had been women ranging in age from seventeen to eighty. Some had been beaten, some strangled, some stabbed and some shot. Lucas said that the Hand of Death said he should vary the M.O.

Near Austin, Texas, Lucas pointed out a building and asked whether it had been a liquor store once. It had. Lucas confessed to murdering the former owners during a robbery in 1979. In the same county, Lucas led them to a field where he had murdered and mutilated a girl called Sandra Dubbs. He even pointed out where her car had been found.

Lucas and Toole had cruised Interstate 35, murdering tramps, hitchhikers, men who were robbed of their money and old women who were abducted from their homes. They had killed more than twenty people up and down that highway alone, over a period of five years. One was a young woman who was found naked except for a pair of orange socks near Austin. She had been hitchhiking on Interstate 35 when Lucas had picked her up. She refused to have sex with him, so Lucas strangled her and took what he wanted. She was never identified but Lucas was sentenced to death for her murder. Although he withdrew his confession to the Becky Powell murder and pleaded not guilty, he was found guilty anyway and sentenced to life. On top of that he received four more life sentences, two sentences of seventy-five years each and one of sixty-seven years, all for murder.

During his confessions, Lucas told the police that Toole had poured petrol over a 65-year-old man and set him alight. They had hidden so that they could watch the fire engines arrive. The police identified the man as George Sonenberg. He had died four days later. Until then, they had assumed that the fire was an accident. Toole freely admitted the murder and claimed to have started hundreds of other fires. But it was for this particularly horrific murder that Toole, as well, was sentenced to death.

Both Lucas and Toole enjoyed their brief celebrity and

102

took a certain relish in revealing the ghoulish details of their shocking crimes. But further information about the Hand of Death is not forthcoming.

Chapter 8

House of Horrors

Another couple who killed were Fred and Rosemary West, who lived in an ordinary three-storey house at 25 Cromwell Street in central Gloucester in the south-west of England. On 24 February 1994, the police turned up with a warrant to dig up the back garden. The door was answered by Stephen West, the 20-year-old son of Fred and Rosemary. The police told him that they were looking for the body of his sister Heather, who had disappeared in May 1987 at the age of 16. Stephen's parents had told him that she had left home to go and work in a holiday camp in Devon and he believed that she was now living in the Midlands.

'I wanted to know the reasons why they thought Heather was buried there but they wouldn't tell me,' said Stephen, disingenuously. Among the surviving West children there was a running joke that Heather was buried under the patio.

'I told one of the detectives that they were going to end up making fools of themselves,' said Stephen. 'He just replied "That's up to us".'

As the police went about their business, Stephen and his

mother Rosemary tried to contact his father Fred, who was working on a building site about 20 minutes' drive from Gloucester. Eventually they got through to him on the mobile phone in his van.

'You'd better get back home,' Rosemary told Fred. 'They're going to dig up the garden, looking for Heather.'

That was at 1.50 p.m. Fred did not turn up at home until 5.40 p.m. It has never been explained what he was doing during the intervening four hours. Fred said that he had been painting and that he had taken ill as a result of the fumes while he was driving home. He had had to pull over and passed out at the roadside. Others suspect that he was disposing of evidence.

When Rosemary was interviewed, she told the police that Heather had been both lazy and disagreeable, and they were well rid of her. Fred said that she was a lesbian who had got involved in drugs and, like his wife, seemed unconcerned with her disappearance.

'Lots of girls disappear, take a different name and go into prostitution,' he said, seemingly more concerned about the mess the police were making raising the paving stones of his patio.

That night Fred and Rosemary West stayed up all night, talking. Geoffrey Wansel, author of *Evil Love* based on 150 hours of taped interviews with Fred West, says that they cooked up a deal. Rosemary was to keep silent, while Fred said that 'he would "sort it out" with the police the following day, and that she had nothing to worry about as he would take all the blame'.

The next morning, Fred stepped into a police car outside and told Detective Constable Hazel Savage, who had instigated the search: 'I killed her.'

At Gloucester police station, Fred told detectives how he had murdered his daughter, cut her body into three pieces and buried them, adding: 'The thing I'd like to stress is that Rose knew nothing at all.'

When Rose was told of Fred's confession, she claimed that Fred had sent her out of the house the day Heather disappeared. She had no knowledge of Heather's death.

But 20 minutes, after he had confessed, Fred West retracted everything he had said.

'Heather's alive and well, right,' he insisted. 'She's possibly at the moment in Bahrain working for a drug cartel. She has a Mercedes, a chauffeur and a new birth certificate.'

West was adamant that the police could dig as much as they liked, but they would not find Heather. However, later that day, the excavation team unearthed human remains. When confronted with this, West again confessed to murdering his daughter. Heather, he said, was headstrong. During an argument he had slapped her for insolence, but she had laughed in his face. So he grabbed her by the throat to stop her. But he gripped too hard. She stopped breathing and turned blue. When he realised what he had done, he tried to resuscitate her, but he did not have any medical training. In desperation, he dragged her over to the bathtub and dowsed her with cold water.

It was then his story struck a disturbing note. To run cold water over her, he said, he found it necessary to take her clothes off. When the cold water treatment did not work he lifted her naked body out of the tub and dried her off. He tried to put the corpse in the large rubbish bin, but she would not fit. He realised that he would have to dismember her, but first he would have to make sure that she was dead, so he strangled her with her tights.

'I didn't want to touch her while she was alive,' said West. 'I mean, if I'd have started cutting her leg or her throat and she'd have suddenly come alive…'

According to his own account, West was squeamish. Before he began his gruesome task, he closed Heather's eyes.

'If somebody's sat there looking at you, you're not going to use a knife on that person are you?' he told the police.

First he cut off her head. This made a 'horrible noise . . . like scrunching'. It was very unpleasant. Then he began cutting her legs off. Twisting one of her feet, he heard 'one almighty crack and the leg come loose'.

With the head and legs removed, Heather's dismembered corpse fitted neatly into the rubbish bin. That night when the rest of the family was asleep, he said, he buried Heather in the garden, where she had lain undiscovered for seven years. Now the police had found her. But hers was the only body in the garden, he told them, so they could call off the excavation.

However, Professor Bernard Knight, the pathologist the police had called in, soon realised that among the remains the excavation team had unearthed, there were three leg bones. Clearly, there was more than one body buried in the garden at 25 Cromwell Street.

Again, Fred West was forced to make a confession, though again he tried to limit the damage. He agreed to accompany the police back to the garden and show them where he had buried the two other girls – 17-year-old Alison Chambers and 18-year-old Shirley Robinson, who had both disappeared in the late 1970s. However, he did not tell them about the six other bodies he had buried underneath the floor of the cellar and bathroom of the house. West did not want to be labelled a serial killer. He was also house-proud and did not want the police tearing apart his home.

Born in 1941 in the village of Much Marcle, some 14 miles north-west of Gloucester, Fred West was the last of a long line of Herefordshire farm labourers. His parents, Walter and Daisy West, had six children over a ten-year period who they brought up in rural poverty.

A beautiful baby with blond hair and piercing blue eyes, Fred was his mother's favourite. A doting son, he did everything she asked. He also enjoyed a good relationship with his father, who he took as a role model. However, as he grew, he lost his good looks. His blond hair turned dark brown and curly. He had inherited some of his mother's less attractive features – narrow eyes and a big mouth with a large gap between his front teeth. Some put this down to gypsy blood. Crueller commentators called him simian.

Scruffy and unkempt, West did not do well at school. He was a troublesome pupil and was thrashed regularly. His mother, now seriously overweight and always badly dressed, would turn up at his school to remonstrate with the teachers. This led to him being teased as a 'mummy's boy'. He left at 15, practically illiterate and went to work, like his father before him, as a farmhand.

By the time he was 16, West had begun to take an interest in girls. He tidied himself up a bit and aggressively pursued any woman that took his fancy. This included his next of kin: West claimed to have made his sister pregnant and that his father had committed incest with his daughters.

'I made you so I'm entitled to have you,' West claimed his father said. But then, West was a practised liar.

At 17, West was involved in a serious motorcycle accident. One leg was broken and was left permanently shorter than the other. He also suffered a fractured skull that left him in a coma for a week. A metal plate had to be put into his head. Dr Keith Ashcroft of the Centre for Forensic Psychophysiology in Manchester believes that damage to his frontal lobes left West with an insatiable need for sex. After the accident he was prone to sudden fits of rage and seems to have lost control over his emotions.

It was then that he met a pretty 16-year-old girl named Catherine Bernadette Costello, nicknamed Rena. She had been a petty thief since childhood and was constantly in trouble with the police. The two misfits quickly became lovers, but the relationship was halted when Rena returned home to Scotland a few months later.

Eager for more sex, Fred became offensively forward. One

night while standing on a fire escape outside a local youth club, he stuck his hand up a young woman's skirt. She reacted furiously, knocking him over the balustrade. In the fall, he banged his head again and lost consciousness. This may well have aggravated the frontal lobe damage caused by the motorcycle accident.

Fred West then embarked on a career in petty theft. In 1961, he and a friend stole cigarette cases and a watchstrap from a local jewellers. They were caught red-handed with the stolen goods on them and were fined. A few months later, he was accused of getting a 13-year-old girl, a friend of the family, pregnant. Fred was unrepentant. He did not see anything wrong in molesting underage girls.

"Doesn't everyone do it?" he said.

He was convicted but his general practitioner's claim that he suffered from epileptic fits saved him from serving a jail sentence. However, he showed no sign of changing his ways. His family threw him out and he went to work on building sites where, again, he was caught stealing. There were more allegations that he was having sex with underage girls.

West's parents eventually relented and let him return to the family home in Much Marcle. Then in the summer of 1962, Rena Costello returned from Scotland and took up with Fred again. By this time Rena had added burglary and prostitution to her rap sheet, which hardly recommended her to his parents.

Fred and Rena married secretly that November and they moved to Scotland. Rena was pregnant and Fred's parents believed that the baby she was carrying was his. In fact, the child's father was an Asian bus driver. When Rena's daughter Charmaine was born in March 1963, Fred got Rena to write to his mother, explaining that their baby had died and they had adopted a mixed-race child.

West's voracious sexual appetite was also causing problems, though his interest in straightforward vaginal sex was minimal; he preferred bondage, sodomy and oral sex. Although she had been a prostitute, Rena was not always willing to comply with Fred's urges. However, at the time, West was driving an ice-cream truck, which gave him easy access to other young women and he was unfaithful on a daily basis. Their marriage went through a rocky patch with frequent separations. But in 1964, Rena gave birth to West's child, Anne-Marie.

West was involved in an accident in the ice-cream truck that had resulted in the death of a young boy. The accident had not been his fault, but he was concerned that he might lose his job. Fred and Rena had also met a young Scottish woman named Ann McFall whose boyfriend had been killed in an accident. Together, the three of them, plus Rena's two children, moved to Gloucester, where West got a job in a slaughterhouse. It was while working there that West developed a morbid obsession with corpses, blood and dismemberment.

West's marriage became increasingly unstable. Rena fled back to Scotland but Fred refused to let her take the two children with her. Missing her daughters, Rena returned to Gloucester in July 1966 to find Fred and Ann McFall living together in a caravan. Around the time there had been eight sexual assaults in the area committed by a man who matched West's description. Increasingly worried about the safety of her children, Rena went to the police and told them that her husband was a sexual pervert and totally unfit to raise her daughters. This was when Constable Hazel Savage first became involved in the case.

By the beginning of 1967, McFall was pregnant with West's child. She put pressure on him to divorce Rena and marry her. In July, West responded by killing McFall and burying her in 'letterbox field' in Much Marcle, near the caravan site. She was eight months pregnant. West not only murdered his lover and their unborn child, he painstakingly dismembered the corpse, removing the foetus, which he buried alongside McFall's body parts – though some were missing. When the corpse was unearthed in 1994, the fingers and toes could not be found. This was to be his hallmark in future crimes.

After Anne McFall's disappearance, West was noticeably nervous. But when Rena moved into the caravan with him, West became his old self again. With West's encouragement, Rena went to work as a prostitute again. Meanwhile, he began to openly molest four-year-old Charmaine.

On 5 January 1968, pretty 15-year-old Mary Bastholm was abducted from a bus stop in Gloucester. She had been on the way to see her boyfriend and had been carrying a Monopoly game. The pieces were found strewn around the bus stop. West always denied abducting Mary Bastholm, but he knew her. He was a customer at the Pop-In Café, where Mary worked. Mary often served him tea when he had been employed to do some building work behind the café. Mary had also been seen with a woman answering the description of Anna McFall and one witness claimed to have seen Mary in West's car. Most people who have studied the case are convinced that Mary Bastholm was another of Fred West's victims.

A month after Mary Bastholm went missing, West's mother died after a routine gallbladder operation and West became seriously unstable. He changed jobs several times and launched into a series of petty thefts. Then his life changed. On 29 November 1968, while working as a delivery driver for a local baker, he met the 15-year-old girl who would become his second wife and partner in crime.

Rosemary Letts was born in November 1953 in Devon. Her background was disturbed. Her father, Bill Letts, was a schizophrenic. He demanded total obedience from his wife and children, and used violence to get his way.

'If he felt we were in bed too late,' said Rose's brother Andrew, 'he would throw a bucket of cold water over us. He

111

would order us to dig the garden, and that meant the whole garden. Then he would inspect it like an army officer, and if he was not satisfied, we would have to do it all over again.'

A martinet, he enjoyed disciplining his children and was always on the lookout for reasons to beat them.

'We were not allowed to speak and play like normal children,' said Andrew. 'If we were noisy, he would go for us with a belt or chunk of wood.'

His wife Daisy also suffered in the violent outbursts.

'He would beat you black and blue until Mum got in between us,' Andrew said. 'Then she would get a good hiding.'

His savage attitudes and his mental instability did little to recommend him to employers and he drifted through a series of low-paid, unskilled jobs. Short of housekeeping money and in the thrall of a violent husband, Daisy Letts suffered from severe depression. She had already given birth to three daughters and a son when she was hospitalised in 1953 and given electroshock therapy. At the time she was pregnant with Rosemary and it is thought that these shocks could have had an effect on the child as she developed in her mother's womb.

Rosemary was noticeably different from the other Letts' children. In her cot she developed the habit of rocking violently and sometimes she rocked so vigorously that she could move her pram across the room, even when the brake was on.

As she grew older, she rocked only her head – but for hours on end as if she was in a trance. The family soon realised that she was a bit slow. They called her 'Dozy Rosie'. However, with big brown eyes and a clear complexion, she was a pretty child. This appealed to her father and, by doing everything he asked without question, she became the apple of his eye and escaped the beatings he meted out to the other children although there were rumours that she had an incestuous relationship with her father and that he molested young girls.

Things did not go well for Rosemary when she went to school though. With no appreciable intellectual gifts, she did not do well academically. As she grew older, she developed a tendency towards chubbinesss and was teased relentlessly. In response, she lashed out.

As an adolescent, Rose became precocious sexually. After taking a bath, she would walk around the house naked, then climb into bed with her younger brother and fondle him. Her father forbade her to go out with boys her own age. Not that many were interested. Both her reputation as an ill-tempered, sullen, aggressive loner and her chubbiness put the local boys off. Instead she concentrated on the older men in the village.

After 15-year-old Mary Bastholm disappeared from a bus stop in Gloucester in January 1968, girls in the area were on their guard. But Rosemary's growing interest in sex meant that she would not stay home and, on one occasion, one of the older men she was seeing raped her.

At the beginning of 1969, Daisy Letts could stand life with her violent husband no longer. She left and moved in temporarily with her older daughter Glenys and her husband, Jim Tyler. Free from her father's strictures, the 15-year-old Rose spent all her time going out. Her brother-in-law said that Rose carried on with a numer of older men and that she had even tried to seduce him. After a few months, to everyone's surprise, Daisy moved back to Bill, bringing Rose with her. It was then that Rose met 28-year-old Fred West.

Whatever Bill Letts's shortcomings as a parent, he tried to keep his underage daughter away from West. When Bill discovered that Rose was having sex with West, he reported him to the Social Services. This proved ineffective, so Bill turned up at West's caravan and threatened him. The relationship was halted briefly when West went to prison for theft and failure to pay fines. But Rose was already pregnant with West's child. At 16, she left her father's house and moved into West's caravan to take care of Rena's two daughters.

In 1970, Rose gave birth to the ill-fated Heather. With Fred in jail, no money and three children to take care of, the teenage Rose found it hard to cope. Her temper flared constantly. She particularly resented having to take care of another woman's children and treated Charmaine and Anne-Marie abominably.

In the summer of 1971, eight-year-old Charmaine went missing. Rose told Anne-Marie that their mother Rena had come to get her. There is no doubt that Rose killed her. Colin Wilson, author of *The Corpse Garden*, believes that she was not responsible for her actions. He thinks that Rose 'simply lost her temper, and went further than usual in beating or throttling her. She was, as Anne-Marie said, a woman entirely without self-control; when she lost her temper, she became a kind of maniac.'

West could not have killed Charmaine as he was in jail at the time. However, he was complicit in concealing her body under the kitchen floor of 25 Midland Road, a house in Gloucester they had recently moved into. When the body was found, the fingers and toes were missing, just like Anna McFall's. Fred and Rose were now bound together by their crime. Later, when Rose's father came to take her away from West, West said: 'Come on, Rosie, you know what we've got between us.'

This upset Rose, Bill Letts noted. Afterwards Rose told her parents why she could not leave.

'You don't know him!' she said. 'You don't know him! There's nothing he wouldn't do – even murder!'

In the 1960s, a large number of West Indian immigrants had come to Gloucester. They were largely single men and Rose invited many of them over to the house for sex – both for fun and to earn a little extra money. Fred encouraged this. He was a voyeur and enjoyed watching her have sex through a peephole. Although over-sexed, Fred would only join in if the sex involved bondage, sadism, lesbianism or vibrators. He

114

also took suggestive pictures of Rose, using them in advertisements in magazines for 'swingers' and other publications where he advertised her services as a prostitute.

Eventually Rena came to look for her daughter Charmaine. Unable to get any sense out of Fred or Rose, Rena visited Fred's father, Walter, in August 1971, hoping he could shed some light on what happened to Charmaine. As a result, Fred decided to kill Rena. It seems that he got her back to the house in Midland Road, got her drunk and strangled her. He dismembered her body, put the bits in bags and buried her in 'fingerpost field' near Much Marcle in the same general area as he buried Anna McFall. Again the fingers and toes were missing.

Fred and Rose began employing their neighbour, Elizabeth Agius, as a babysitter. On more than one occasion, when the Wests returned home, Elizabeth asked them where they had been. They said they had been cruising around looking for young girls, preferably virgins. Fred explained that he had taken Rose along, so then they would not be afraid to get into the car with him. Elizabeth thought they were joking, but later Fred propositioned her. The Wests later drugged and raped her. They were deadly serious.

In January 1972, Fred and Rose married at Gloucester Registry Office. And in June, they had another daughter who they named Mae. They decided they needed a bigger house to raise their growing family and accommodate Rose's prostitution business and they moved into 25 Cromwell Street. It had a garage and a spacious cellar. Frank as ever, Fred told Elizabeth Agius that he planned to convert the cellar into a room where Rose could entertain her clients. Or he would soundproof it and turn it into his 'torture chamber'. This, in fact, was what he did.

Its first inmate was his own eight-year-old daughter, Anne-Marie. He told her that he and Rose were such caring parents that they were going to teach her how to satisfy her husband when she got married. They stripped her and gagged her. Her hands were tied behind her back and Rose held her down while Fred raped her. This hurt her so much that Anne-Marie could not go to school for several days. She was warned not to tell anyone, otherwise she would be beaten. The rapes continued. On one occasion she was strapped down so her father could rape her quickly during his lunch hour.

Fred and Rose continued cruising the vicinity, looking for young girls. At the end of 1972, they picked up 17-year-old Caroline Owens, who they hired as a live-in nanny, promising her family that they would take care of her. Caroline was very attractive, and Fred and Rose both tried to seduce her. She found them repellent, but when she said she was leaving, they stripped her and raped her. Fred threatened that if she told anyone about it: 'I'll keep you in the cellar and let my black friends have you. And when we're finished we'll kill you and bury you under the paving stones of Gloucester.'

Caroline believed him. Terrified, she kept silent. But she could not hide her bruises from her mother, who wrung the truth from her and called the police.

The matter came to court in January 1973, but West was able to convince the magistrate that Caroline had consented to sex. Despite West's long criminal record, the magistrate did not believe that the Wests were capable of violence and they got off with a small fine. By this time Fred was 31. Rose was 19 and pregnant for the third time.

The Wests still needed a nanny and seamstress. Lynda Gough moved into 25 Cromwell Street to take care of the children. Soon after, they murdered her. Then Fred buried her dismembered body under the floor of the garage. Again he removed her fingers and toes, although this time her kneecaps were missing too. When Lynda's family asked what had happened to her, they were told she had moved on. The police were not called and there were no repercussions. Soon after, in August 1973, the West's first son, Stephen, was born.

Having got away with so much, the Wests began killing just for the fun of it. In November 1973, they abducted 15-year-old schoolgirl Carol Ann Cooper and took her back to Cromwell Street where they amused themselves with her sexually. After about a week, they got tired of her and killed her, either suffocating or strangling her. Then her body was dismembered and buried under the house.

The following month, 21-year-old university student Lucy Partington went home to Gotherington near Cheltenham for the Christmas holidays. She was the cousin of novelist Martin Amis. On 27 December, she went to visit a disabled friend. She left to catch a bus shortly after 10 p.m. and was waiting at a bus stop on the outskirts of Cheltenham when the Wests offered her a lift. It is almost certain that she would not have got into the car if Rose had not been there. The Wests took her back to Cromwell Street where they raped and tortured her for about a week, then murdered her, dismembered her body and buried it under the house.

Fred cut himself while dismembering Lucy's corpse and went to the hospital to have the wound stitched on 3 January 1974. By then Lucy – like Carol Ann Cooper – had been reported missing, but there was nothing to connect either of the girls to the Wests. Their bodies were concealed in Fred's home improvement scheme. This involved enlarging the cellar and turning the garage into an extension to the main house. The only thing remotely suspicious about this was that Fred's home improvements were done at strange hours of the night. However, West did attract police attention. To pay for his home improvements – and the concrete he covered the corpses with – he committed a series of thefts and fenced stolen goods.

Three more young women – 15-year-old schoolgirl Shirley Hubbard, 19-year-old Juanita Mott from Newent in Gloucestershire and 21-year-old Swiss hitch-hiker Therese Siegenthaler – ended up under the cellar floor at 25

Gloucester Street. They had been tortured and dismembered. The Wests had subjected them to extreme bondage, using plastic covered washing lines and ropes to suspend them from one of the beams in the cellar, and gagging them with tights, nylon socks and a brassiere. In 1976, the Wests enticed a young woman from a home for wayward girls back to Cromwell Street where she was taken to a room where two naked girls were being held prisoner. She was forced to watch while the two girls were tortured. Then she was raped by Fred and sexually assaulted by Rose. Later during the court case, she gave evidence as 'Miss A'.

It is likely that one of the girls was Anne-Marie, Fred's daughter who was the regular target of the couple's sexual sadism. But Fred not only raped and tortured his own daughter, he brought home other men to have sex with her.

By 1977, Fred had extensively remodelled the house. Upstairs he had constructed extra bedrooms so they could take in lodgers. One of them was 18-year-old Shirley Robinson. A former prostitute with bisexual inclinations, she had sex with both Rose and Fred.

Rose fell pregnant by one of her West Indian clients and gave birth to Tara in December 1977. At the time Shirley was also pregnant, carrying Fred's child. Rose was unhappy about this. She feared that Shirley would displace her in Fred's affections. So she had to go. In July 1977, Shirley Robinson was murdered. By this time, the cellar was full, so Shirley and her unborn child were buried in the back garden at 25 Cromwell Street.

In November 1978, Rose gave birth to another daughter. She was Fred's child and they named her Louise. There were now six children in the household and, from an early age, they were aware of what was going on. They knew that Rose was a prostitute and that Anne-Marie was being sexually abused by her father. Anne-Marie eventually fell pregnant by Fred, but it was an ectopic pregnancy which took place in the fallopian tube rather than the womb itself and the foetus had to be aborted. She then moved out to live with her boyfriend, so Fred turned his sexual attentions on Heather and Mae. Heather tried to resist and was beaten.

Not even the loss of Rose's father, who died of a lung ailment in May 1979, put the Wests out of their stride. Several months later, they abducted a troubled 17-year-old from Swansea named Alison Chambers, raped and tortured her, then murdered her and buried her in the back garden.

In June 1980, Rose gave birth to Fred's second son, Barry. In April 1982, Rose had Rosemary Junior, who was not Fred's child. Then in July 1983, Rose had yet another daughter, Lucyanna. Like Tara and Rosemary Junior, she was mixed race. It is thought that the Wests kept on carrying out sexual abductions throughout this period. But as they did not bury any of the victims at 25 Cromwell Street and refused to confess to any murders during the early 1980s, we cannot be sure.

However, having eight children in the household took its toll on Rose's temper. She became increasingly irrational and beat them without provocation. This began to loosen the children's bond of loyalty. Their continued silence was the Wests' only protection. In May 1987, 16-year-old Heather told a girlfriend about her father's sexual abuse and the beatings, and her mother's profession. The girl told her parents, who were friends of the Wests. When Fred and Rose heard of this, they murdered Heather and told the other children that she left home. However, Fred asked his 13-year-old son Stephen to help him dig a hole in the back garden where he later buried Heather's dismembered body.

Fred and Rose set out to expand the prostitution business by advertising in specialist magazines. They were on the lookout for young women to pimp, who might also be willing to join in their sadistic perversions. A prostitute named Katherine

119

Halliday joined the household. But when she was introduced to the Wests' collection of whips and chains, the black bondage suits and masks, she took fright and left.

The Wests' campaign of rape and murder had been going on for 25 years, but only now did they begin to run out of luck. One of the very young girls that they had abducted and raped told her girlfriend what happened. The girl went to the police and the case was assigned to Hazel Savage, now a detective constable. She knew of Fred from 1966 when Rena had told her about his sexual perversions.

On 6 August 1992, the police arrived at 25 Cromwell Street with a search warrant. They were looking for evidence of child abuse, found a mountain of distasteful pornography and arrested both Fred and Rose. Fred was charged with the rape and sodomy of a minor and Rose was charged with assisting him.

DC Savage set about interviewing the Wests' friends and family members. Anne-Marie talked openly about the abuse she had suffered at Fred's hands. She also expressed her suspicions about the fate of Charmaine, who Savage had known from her investigations in 1966. Rena, it seemed, had also gone missing. Savage checked tax and national insurance records which showed that Heather had not been employed, drawn benefits or visited a doctor in five years. Either she had moved abroad or she was dead.

The younger children were taken into care. Unable to cope without Fred, Rose tried to kill herself by taking an overdose of pills. But her son Stephen found her in time and saved her life. In jail Fred became self-pitying and depressed. But still his luck held. The case against him collapsed when two key witnesses decided not to testify against them and he was released.

However, DC Savage now launched an inquiry into the whereabouts of Heather. The West children joked that she was under the patio. They said Fred had threatened them that if they did not keep their mouths shut about the goings-on in 25 Cromwell Street they would end up under the patio like Heather.

Digging up a 900-square-foot garden was a huge undertaking and was bound to attract media attention, especially since the extension to the house had been built over part of the garden. But Detective Superintendent John Bennett eventually got a warrant.

Fred West knew that it was only a matter of time before the evidence of his long murder spree would be unearthed. He told his son that he had done something really bad and would be going away for a while.

'He looked at me so evil and so cold,' said Stephen. 'That look went right through me.'

After the discovery of the bones in the garden, Fred was charged with the murder of Heather, Shirley Robinson and Alison Chambers. To protect Rose, Fred took full responsibility for the murders.

The police now broadened the investigation to look into the disappearance of Rena and Charmaine. Fred was assigned an 'appropriate adult' named Janet Leach. She was usually assigned to befriend and assist juveniles or the mentally subnormal when they were taken into custody, Fred West was thought to fall into this second category. Leach asked Fred whether there were any more bodies. West admitted that there were and sketched a map of the cellar and bathroom, showing where six more bodies lay. He admitted to murdering the girls he had buried there, but not to raping them. The girls, he insisted, wanted to have sex with him. However, he did not even know the names of some of his victims. One he called simply 'Scar Hand' because of a burn on her hand. Therese Siegenthaler he referred to as 'Tulip' under the mistaken impression that she was Dutch, though she was, in fact, Swiss. This made it difficult for the police to identify the bodies. With large numbers of people being reported missing

121

each year, it was a mammoth task to match a set of remains to a missing person's report.

Of course, Fred West did know the names of some of his victims. He admitted to murdering his first wife Rena and his lover Ann McFall and burying their bodies in the fields near Much Marcle. He also admitted to the murder of Charmaine, Rena's eldest daughter. With his help the bodies of Rena, Ann McFall and Charmaine were found. However, he refused to co-operate with the Mary Bastholm case and her body has never been located.

From the start the police were convinced that Rose West was involved in the murders, even though she feigned shock at her husband's confessions and denied everything. She played the naive and innocent victim of a murderous and manipulative man. Along with Stephen and her eldest daughter Mae, she was moved to a police safe house in Cheltenham. The house was bugged by police but she never said anything which implicated herself. However, on 18 April 1994 she was charged with a sex offence and taken into custody. The murder charges would come later.

By this time the world's media had turned up in Gloucester. There were TV crews from America and Japanese film interviews in the street. Journalists quickly dubbed 25 Cromwell Street the 'House of Horrors'.

The fact that a serial killer had been operating in Gloucester for over 25 years came as a shock to its citizens. They had got away with it because, with the exception of Lucy Partington, the Wests had deliberately targeted people who drifted in and out of society and whose disappearance would not be noticed. Nevertheless the international attention the Wests had brought the city came as a terrible blow to Gloucester's civic pride.

On 13 December 1994, Fred West was charged with 12 murders. He and Rose appeared together in court. In the dock, Fred tried to comfort Rose, but she pulled back from him, telling the police that he made her sick. Fred found the rejection devastating. He wrote to her, saying: 'We will always be in love . . . You will always be Mrs West, all over the world. That is important to me and to you.' She did not respond.

Just before noon on New Year's Day at Winson Green Prison in Birmingham, 54-year-old Fred West hanged himself with strips of bedsheet. He had picked his moment well. The guards were at lunch and he had clearly planned his suicide so that he would not be discovered and resuscitated.

This left Rose alone to face ten counts of murder. Clearly she could not have been involved in the murder of Rena and Ann McFall as they had been killed before she knew Fred. Her trial opened on 3 October 1995. However, there was little direct evidence to link her to the murders. Instead the prosecution, led by Brian Leveson QC, aimed to construct a tight web of circumstantial evidence to prove Rose's guilt.

A number of key witnesses – including Caroline Owens, Miss A and Anne-Marie – testified to Rose's sadistic assaults on young women. The most damning evidence came from Anne-Marie, who fixed her stepmother with a withering stare as she described how she and Fred had embarked on a campaign of sexual abuse when she was eight.

Another witness, Caroline Raine, a former beauty queen, told the court of the night in 1972 when Fred and Rose abducted her when she was hitchhiking across Gloucestershire and sexually assaulted her. The prosecution suggested that this was a blueprint for how the Wests picked up their victims. In this case, Caroline Raine escaped with her life and the Wests were prosecuted and fined over the incident at the time. From then on, it was clear that Fred and Rose had made up their minds that future victims would not be allowed to live to tell the tale.

Fred's confidante Janet Leach also gave crucial evidence. She testified that Fred had told her privately that Rose was involved in the murders – and that Rose had murdered

Charmaine and Shirley Robinson by herself. However, he said that he made a deal with Rose to take all the blame himself. At the time, this confession, given in confidence, had put her under so much stress that she suffered a stroke. It was only after Fred's suicide that she felt the bond of confidentiality had been lifted and she told the police what he had said to her. Giving testimony put her under enormous stress. She collapsed and had to be taken to the hospital, and the trial was adjourned for several days.

The defence, led by Richard Ferguson QC, maintained that evidence of sexual assault was not the same thing as evidence of murder. He made the case that Rose did not know that Fred was murdering the girls they had abused and burying them around the house.

Ferguson made the mistake of putting Rose on the witness stand. She did not impress the jury. The prosecution rattled her by making her angry. She appeared obstructive and defiant. The prosecution also managed to force her to confess how badly she had treated the children and she gave the general impression of being unscrupulous and dishonest.

The defence played taped interviews with Fred West, where he said that he had murdered his victims when Rose was out of the house. But it was not difficult for the prosecution to show that Fred was an inveterate liar, so everything he said was open to doubt.

In his closing speech, Leveson maintained Rose was the dominant force in the Wests' murderous partnership. She was, he told the jury, the 'strategist'.

'The evidence that Rosemary West knew nothing is not worthy of belief,' he said.

Ferguson, closing for the defence, maintained that the evidence for murder only pointed to Fred. There was no proof that Rose had known anything, let alone participated. The jury did not believe him. It quickly came to the unanimous verdict that Rosemary West was guilty of the murders of

Charmaine West, Heather West, Shirley Robinson and the other girls buried at the house. The judge sentenced her to life imprisonment on each of the ten counts of murder. In 1996, her request to appeal was turned down. David Blunkett, the Home Secretary during this period, later told Rosemary West that she would never be allowed out.

In October 1996, Gloucester City Council demolished 25 Cromwell Street. There were calls to create a memorial garden on the site, but there were fears that it would be turned into a ghoulish shrine, so it was left as a landscaped footpath leading to the city centre.

Four years after Rose West was sentenced her son Stephen revealed to the police that he was convinced that his father had killed 15-year-old Mary Bastholm. He said that, while visiting his father in prison shortly before he died, West had boasted that Bastholm's body would never be found. He also talked of a number of other victims and crowed: 'They are not going to find them all, you know, never.'

When Stephen asked specifically asked him about Mary Bastholm, West replied: 'I will never tell anyone where she is.'

However, to the police, West had continued strenuously denying that he had killed Bastholm, although she had been seen in his car. Mary Bastholm's brother Peter said he was relieved by the news, though his parents had both died without learning the fate of their only daughter.

Later in 1998, Fred West's cousin William Hill was jailed for four years after being convicted of one count of rape and three charges of indecent assaults. Like West, Hill preyed on young women and one of his convictions was for a series of indecent assault on a 15-year-old girl over an extended period in the early 1980s. He tried to kill himself in jail but failed. Fred West's brother John succeeded in hanging himself in jail while awaiting the verdict after being tried for raping Anne-Marie.

Anne-Marie tried to kill herself by throwing herself from a bridge near Gloucester, but was rescued. She had previously tried to kill herself during the trial by taking an overdose, but was rushed to hospital and had her stomach pumped. Stephen West tried to hang himself at his home in Bussage, near Stroud, after his girlfriend left him. He survived when the rope snapped.

In December 1998, Gordon Burn, the author of *Happy Like Murderers*, another book about the Wests, claimed that the bones removed from the victims' bodies – usually fingers, toes, but in some cases kneecaps and entire shoulder blades – had been buried near Pittville Park in Cheltenham, close to the bus stop where Fred first met Rose in 1970. Burn said that the location held an 'almost spiritual' significance for the Wests.

He was interviewed by Chief Constable of Gloucestershire, Tony Butler, and Detective Chief Inspector Terry Moore who had taken over the case after Detective Superintendent John Bennett had retired.

'Out of all the books it's probably the best written and the most interesting,' said Moore. 'He has got some things right and some things wrong."

As to the bones, Moore said: 'There are various theories but nothing has come to light. The secret has gone to the grave with Fred and Rose is not saying anything.'

In 2000, Rosemary West secured legal aid to launch a new appeal. Her lawyer, Leo Goatley, said that West may 'unearth new photographic evidence, which would prove that her husband, Fred West, was the sole killer'. The hope was that she would 'be cleared by anatomical photographs of women which were taken by Fred West and seized by police during an earlier investigation in 1992'. The photographs, he asserted, were time stamped and would help his client prove she was not present at the time. The originals, he said, had been destroyed, but Goatley was confident that 'copies would have been made or details of the photographs chronicled by police'. He also said that excessive publicity and chequebook journalism prevented her getting a fair trial, and an application was made to the Criminal Cases Review Commission on 20 October 2000.

But the application was doomed to failure when a TV documentary aired an interview with Janet Leach who revealed that Fred West had confessed to killing many more than the 12 victims he had been charged with murdering.

'Fred said that there were two other bodies in shallow graves in the woods but there was no way they would ever be found,' she told the interviewer. 'He said there were twenty other bodies, not in one place but spread around and he would give police one a year. He told me the truth about the girls in the cellar and what happened to them so I don't see why he would lie about other bodies.'

She also said that West had confessed to the murder of Mary Bastholm. She was one of two young woman 'in shallow graves in the woods, but there was no way they would ever be found'.

'No one has even scratched the surface of this case,' said the documentary's producer. 'Social services had three hundred missing files and one hundred missing girls. There were two girls from Jordansbrook children's home who were making a living as prostitutes from twenty-five Cromwell Street.'

The programme also described how West had told his solicitor that he believed 'the spirits of his victims were coming up through the floor from the cellar where they were entombed'.

'When they come up into you it's beautiful,' West is alleged to have said. 'It's when they go away you are trying to hold them, you feel them flying away from you and you try to stop them. You can't send them back to where they were.'

Soon after this Rosemary West abandoned her appeal and told the press that she had resigned herself to spending the rest of her life in Durham's high-security prison. She also apologised to her step-daughter Anne-Marie for 'the abuse she suffered' and expressed a desire to be reconciled to her.

Then, on 22 January 2003, the BBC reported that 'the wedding between jailed serial killer Rose West and session musician Dave Glover has been called off – just days after it was announced. The pair have been writing to each other for a year, but Mr Glover is reported to have pulled out because of the publicity.' Bass player Glover, 36, had been working regularly with the band Slade for 18 months, but his contract was then terminated.

A spokesman for the band said: 'It has all come as an incredible shock. At no point had Dave Glover discussed this. It's like marrying Hitler.' West and Glover had announced their intention to marry on 19 January. Rose West explained that she wanted to give 'this young man his life back'.

Chapter 9

Sex Slaves

Josefina Rivera had been on the streets most of her twenty-five years. Of mixed African American and Puerto Rican stock, she had been educated in a Catholic school. But she had dropped out as a teenager and turned to prostitution. The children she bore had been taken by the welfare authorities and put up for adoption. Life on the streets of Philadelphia – the city of brotherly love – had made her tough, tough enough to survive the ordeal that killed at least two others.

Josefina used the professional name 'Nicole' when she approached johns in the street. She was working the corner of Girard and Third on Philly's run-down north side on a cold November evening in 1986 when a brand new white and grey Cadillac pulled up. The trick was a stranger, but she was glad to see him. She was freezing her butt off on the street that night.

It was the evening before Thanksgiving and she was dreaming of turkey, yams and pumpkin pie. She even let the john beat her down on the price. She took $20 for a 'short time'. Then she would quit for the night.

The john's name was Gary Heidnik. He took her to a nearby McDonalds where he had a coffee. He bought her nothing, but while he drank his coffee, she examined him closely. He wore a Rolex watch and expensive jewellery. These clashed oddly with the fringed cowboy jacket he wore. He was none too clean either and his blue eyes were as cold as marble. They sent a shiver down her spine, she said later.

Heidnik suggested that they go to North Marshall Street, which was known, at that time, as OK Corral because of a recent shootout between drug dealers. He had a house there.

When Heidnik parked his new Cadillac in the garage, Josefina was surprised to see that Heidnik had several other cars, including a 1971 Rolls Royce. He also had an unusual door-locking system which, he explained, he had devised himself. Only he could work it, he said.

Inside the house, Heidnik asked if she wanted to watch a pornographic video to put her in the mood. She was a professional – she did not need to be in the mood. She looked at her watch and said she had to be getting home. Anger flashed across his face. To calm him, she said that she had three children at home and had to relieve the baby-sitter.

They went upstairs. The stairway, she noted, was papered with $1 and $5 bills. In the bedroom, there was a waterbed. Heidnik flung a grubby $20 at her, stripped off and jumped onto the bed. She stripped off too and the sex act was over, thankfully, in a few minutes. Relieved, Josefina reached for her blue jeans, to get dressed and go home.

Suddenly, Heidnik grabbed her by the throat. Josefina had been a prostitute for too long to risk antagonising a violent client. Half-strangled, she gasped her surrender. Heidnik handcuffed her and dragged her naked from the room. On the way, he grabbed back his $20.

He pulled Josefina down the stairs to the cellar and chained her to a pipe. The room was cold and damp. The walls and floor were filthy, the light dim and there were tiny windows high above the floor.

In the middle of the floor, a pit had been dug. Josefina feared that it would be her grave. She began to scream. Heidnik slapped her and threw her down on a filthy mattress. He lay down, rested his head on her naked lap and slept like a baby.

The next day, she found that her chain was long enough to allow her to reach one of the basement's boarded up windows. It was at about head height, but she managed to prise the boards off and squeezed her way out. Out in the garden she began to yell. But the neighbours were used to screaming, loud music and even the sound of gunshots coming from Heidnik's house, day and night. They took no notice. Heidnik heard her too and came running. He dragged her back into the basement by her chains. He slung her in the pit covered it with boards and heavy sacks, and turned the radio up full blast.

Gary Heidnik wanted to have babies and he would do anything to get them. He was born in 1943. His parents separated when he was 17 months old. His father accused his mother, a Creole, of being a drinker and wild woman. She accused him of gross neglect of his marital duties.

Gary and his older brother Terry stayed with their mother until school age, then they moved in with his father, who had remarried. Gary's father was a strict disciplinarian. If he messed the bed, he would show the soiled sheets to his neighbours. Sometimes he would even dangle the boy feet first from an upstairs window as punishment.

Gary Heidnik's reaction was to embrace the American dream. He joined the boy scouts and told friends that he was going to become a millionaire. But, in his early teens, he fell on his head out of a tree and suffered permanent brain damage. Later he tried to kill his brother.

After a number of suicide attempts, Terry was committed

131

to a mental hospital. When he was discharged, he went to a military academy but he was still suffering from psychiatric problems. He made at least three suicide attempts. He flunked out of the academy, but life was so intolerable back with his father that he enlisted in the army. In his army papers, he described himself as 'coloured' like his mother. She had gone on to marry twice more and had become an alcoholic by the time she died of cancer in 1971. He never spoke to his father again.

Heidnik had an IQ of around 140 – near genius. In the army he learnt he could make money without working for it. He became a loan shark, making more than his army pay in extortionate interest rates. When he was suddenly posted to Germany before he could call in his debts, he learnt that he needed to be his own boss. Still in the army, Heidnik began to exhibit strange psychiatric symptoms. He was discharged with a 100-percent disability pension – $2,000 a month. After he left the army, he never had a permanent job again.

From childhood, Heidnik had followed the stock market reports. For him, it was a splendid mathematical puzzle. He quickly turned his army pension into huge amounts of money. But, apart from fine cars, he did not flaunt his wealth. He bought pornographic magazines and books – featuring black women – and prefered to live around black people, where he felt at home. It also gave him access to black prostitutes. He was addicted to them. He liked to buy them fancy wigs and flamboyant clothes. Best of all, he liked retarded girls who had no defence against his intellect. He wanted to have children by them.

One of his girlfriends, an illiterate black girl called Aljeanette Davidson, had an IQ of just 49. When he got her pregnant, he refused to let her see a doctor, saying that he would take care of her himself. But he beat and starved her. Rescued by her sister, she was rushed to hospital. She was so emaciated that she had to give birth by Caesarean section.

She was unable to look after the child, which was put into care.

Heidnik also tried to shoot a man who rented a room in his house. The bullet grazed his cheek, but the charges were inexplicably dropped. When he moved house, the owners of his old place found stacks of pornographic magazines and a pit dug in the basement. They had no idea what it was for.

Heidnik started a church – the United Church of the Ministers of God. It performed a double function. American churches have taxfree status, so it allowed him to keep more of the money he made on the stock market. Its funds grew from $1,500 to $45,000 in just twelve years. And under the guise of doing good works, it gave him innocent access to mentally retarded black girls.

His own church also gave him, Heidnik, a direct line to God. And God told Gary Heidnik that he must make babies.

The run-down neighbourhood Heidnik lived in was a good cover for his activities. It was full of drug dealers and prostitutes and the police were so stretched they took no notice of his strange antics. One neighbour filed a complaint about his activities, but they gave an incorrect spelling of his name and the police did not follow it up.

Heidnik already had a criminal record. In 1978, he had been charged with kidnapping, rape, false imprisonment and involuntary deviant sexual intercourse. He had taken his girlfriend Aljeanette to visit her sister Alberta, who had an IQ of just 30 and had been an inmate of the state mental hospital for twenty years. Heidnik suggested that 35-year-old Alberta went on an outing with them. She was found, days later, locked in a garbage bin in Heidnik's basement. Alberta was deemed unfit to testify, but Heidnik was sentenced to three-to-seven years for the lesser charges of abduction and assault.

Heidnik spent most of his sentence in state mental institutions. Periods of hospitalisation continued after he was released, but no one kept an eye on him when he was on the street. Even when Aljeanette Davidson disappeared, no one suspected Heidnik though he was later thought to be responsible for her murder.

In 1985, he married Betty Disto, a Filipina who he contacted through a pen-pal agency. But when she arrived in the US, she found a black woman sleeping in Heidnik's bed. She was a lodger, he explained. And a week after their wedding she found him making love to three black women in exotic positions in their bedroom. This was an American custom, her new husband said.

Other women were brought to the house and his bride was forced to watch him make love to them. He also beat her and refused her food. She left after just three months, charging him with indecent assault, rape and other felonies. When she did not turn up in court, the charges were dropped. She was pregnant and only dared tell Heidnik by postcard. The family courts looked into his ability to pay maintenance. But still he did not have the children he craved.

Three days after Josefina was first chained up in Heidnik's basement, he dropped her down the pit again and covered it over. Then he went out looking for 25-year-old Sandra Lindsay, a former lover he had known for four years. He had a grudge against her. He had made her pregnant and he had offered $1,000 to keep it. But she had had an abortion.

Heidnik found Sandy and brought her back to the house. She, too, was stripped and chained up in the basement. Josefina was hauled from the pit and introduced to her. Heidnik then spelt out his plans for a baby farm. Soon there would be more naked black women chained up in the basement and Heidnik would move between them like a butterfly pollinating beautiful flowers. He then forced the two women to perform various sexual acts with him. The rest of the night, he spent digging out the punishment pit, making it deeper and wider.

The next morning there was hammering at Heidnik's door.

It was Sandra's sister Teresa and two cousins. Heidnik did not answer the door and, eventually, they went away. Sandra's mother complained to the police. They scarcely bothered to look into it. Sandra was just another black whore who had gone missing. And she was classified as mentally retarded. Heidnik forced Sandra to write a postcard to her mother, telling her not to worry, she would call, and posted it.

As good as his word, Heidnik captured other sex slaves. Over the Christmas and New Year of 1986, he imprisoned 23-year-old prostitute Deborah Dudley, eighteen-year-old prostitute Jacquelyn Askins, nineteen-year-old Lisa Thomas, who denied being a prostitute but admitted accepting $50 'for clothes', and Agnes Adams who had worked in a strip club with Josefina.

All the girls were shackled and chained, and Heidnik forced them to have sex with him every day. But being half-starved, they did not get pregnant. This made Heidnik angry and he beat the girls.

He found Sandra Lindsay most troublesome. He tied her wrists to an overhead beam and left her dangling there for a week, force-feeding her. Eventually, weakened, she choked on a piece of bread and died. He cut her down and kicked her dead body, then left it lying on the floor while he fed the other girls ice-cream.

When they had finished, he put Sandra's body over his shoulder and carried her upstairs. Later they smelt cooking flesh. The odour was so strong that neighbours complained. A young policeman knocked on the door and peered through the kitchen window. There was a pot on the stove, but the cop could not see what was in it. The crowd in the street told him to break in, but Heidnik opened the door a few inches and explained that he had just burnt his dinner.

Deborah Dudley also fought back against Heidnik. She would not easily submit to his sexual demands. As a punishment, he unchained her and took her upstairs. When she returned to the basement, she was dazed and silent. Josefina asked what had happened. Deborah said that she had seen Sandra's head boiling in a pot. Her ribs were in a roasting pan and her other body parts were being prepared for the freezer. Heidnik told Deborah that if she did not submit to his will, she would end up that way too.

After Sandra was dead, the girls' diet improved. Along with the bread and water, they got dog food mixed with minced body parts.

Occasionally, one of the girls would be taken from the basement and washed in the tub. Then they would have to perform a sexual act with Heidnik before he returned them to their shackles.

In the meantime, Heidnik went about his regular business. He stayed in touch with his broker and kept up with his stock transactions all the time he had the girls in his basement. He visited car showrooms and went to court over his maintenance payments. He even went out on dates with his latest girlfriend, a black nurse.

When he was out, he would put the girls in the pit and cover it over with planks, weighed down with heavy sacks. They found it hard to breathe in there and would scream. This gave him another excuse to beat them. To hide their screams from neighbours, he would play religious music loudly day and night.

Despite what she had seen, Deborah Dudley continued to be defiant and Heidnik devised a new punishment for her. He pushed Deborah, Jacquelyn Askins and Lisa Thomas into the pit and got Josefina to pour water over them. Then he touched their bodies or their chains with live electric wires. In the process, Deborah was electrocuted.

Heidnik decided not to dismember Deborah. He unchained Josefina and together they drove out into the wilds of New Jersey where they dumped Deborah's body. Josefina had seen Heidnik kill two other girls by now. There was only one way out of the basement alive, she realised. She would have to get him to trust her completely. She manoeuvred herself into the position of confidante. She signed a confession, saying that she had willingly helped him kill Deborah. Heidnik believe this would prevent her leaving him.

She began to flirt with him. This put the other girls' backs up. They thought she was conniving with their sadistic jailer. But Josefina was smarter than they were – and she, a common prostitute, was smarter than Heidnik with his IQ of 140.

Heidnik began to take her out to McDonalds and to buy her wigs. But he never let her out of his sight. He warned her that if the police ever caught up with him, he would plead insanity and she would get life for murdering Deborah because of the confession she had signed. He also said that if she tried to escape, he would kill the other three girls.

Suspicious of Josefina, the other girls plotted to attack Heidnik with the broken glass and lengths of pipe that littered the floor of the basement. Heidnik discovered the plan and beat them viciously. They assumed Josefina had betrayed them.

Heidnik became paranoid about the women listening to him moving around the house. He tried to drown out the sounds of his movements by playing loud music. But later, he took more drastic action. He tied the girls to a beam and punctured their eardrums with a screwdriver. Only Josefina was spared. The other girls resented her more. But Josefina did not care. She had a plan.

Although her children had in reality been adopted long ago, she had said that she had three children at home when she had first come to Heidnik's house, as an excuse to get the sex over with. On 24 March, four months after she had first been taken captive by Heidnik, she persuaded him to let her go home and visit these phantom children. In exchange, Josefina promised to return with a fresh woman for Heidnik's harem.

Heidnik drove her downtown and dropped her off near her home. He was confident that she would return. If she did not, it did not matter much. She was a simple-minded black whore. If she went to the police, no one would listen to her wild accusations.

When he dropped her off, they agreed to meet at Girard and Sixth Street, around midnight. Again she promised that she would have a new woman for him.

As Heidnik drove off, Josefina was seized with fear and panic. She ran back to the apartment she used to live in with her boyfriend, Vincent Nelson. The night before Thanksgiving, when she had gone out to pick up her deadly trick, they had had a terrible row. She had been missing for four months now. What must Vincent be thinking? It did not matter. There was nowhere else to go.

She beat on his door. When he opened it and saw her, he was angry. Where the hell had she been? She began babbling. None of what she said made any sense. He dragged her in. Her sheer terror impressed him. Plainly, she needed help.

After a couple of hours, he realised that, whatever she was talking about, this Heidnik guy was responsible for giving her a hard time. He promised to sort him out. At midnight, he went with her down to Girard and Sixth. But on the way he began to get cold feet. What if some of the things Josefina had said about chains, torture and murder were true. This freak could be dangerous.

Just one block short of the gas station, Vincent stopped at a call box and phoned the police. He put Josefina on the line. The desk sergeant found her story hard to believe, but he said that he would send out a patrol car anyway.

The car picked them up at the phone booth. Vincent ran through Josefina's story of girls chained in the basement, being raped, being fed dead bodies. He said that he himself did not believe it. Nor did the cops. But they took her to the precinct. It was only when she showed them the scars and bruises on her body, and the shackle marks around her ankles, that they began to concede that there might be something to her story.

A patrol car was sent over to the gas station at Girard and Sixth. Just as Josefina had said there would be, there was a white and grey Cadillac waiting there. The officers pulled their guns as they walked over to it. Heidnik was not alarmed when the police ordered him out of the car at gun point. He asked whether they were arresting him for non-payment of child maintenance. But why the guns? They handcuffed him and took him downtown for questioning.

Meanwhile, a police team was sent to North Marshall Street. They banged on the door. No one answered. They had no search warrant, so they just had to sit there and wait – until someone got one.

Over four hours later, the warrant came. The police crowbarred open the metal door. In the front room, they found a huge collection of pornographic video tapes and erotic books. They all contained pictures of naked black women.

In the basement, they found two naked black women huddled under a blanket. They screamed as the police came, but they were shackled and chained, and could not get away.

Once the police had calmed them, they pointed to large sacks in the middle of the floor. The police team had heard Josefina's stories and feared that they may contain a dismembered body. The girls quickly indicated that they should shift the bags. Under them were boards. When the police lifted them, they found a shallow pit with another naked black girl squatting in it. She had her arms handcuffed behind her and was chained and shackled.

All three were starving and filthy. An ambulance was called to tend them and take them to hospital. Then officer David Savidge looked in the fridge. He found a human rib.

Heidnik was charged with indecent exposure, simple assault, aggravated assault, issuing terrorist threats, reckless endangerment, unlawful restraint, false imprisonment, criminal solicitation, indecent assault, rape, involuntary deviant sexual intercourse, murder and the possession and abuse of a corpse.

In court, his defence made what it could of the antagonism between the surviving victims. The other three girls still did not trust Josefina who, they thought, had sided with Heidnik against them. And in her three-hour testimony, Josefina was almost sympathetic to Heidnik because 'the city was always taking his babies away'. Of course, the same thing had happened to her.

Jacquelyn Askins was so small that Heidnik had used handcuffs to shackle her ankles. Much was made of the fact that she was given extra long chains on her manacles. Was she not the one who was given special favours?

'He did that so I could open my legs for sex,' she said. And she sobbed while she described the beatings and the deviant group sex that the girls had been forced into.

She and the other surviving victims expressed their distrust of Josefina and her motives. But this squabbling made little difference to the jury. They found Heidnik guilty of the first-degree murder of Sandra Lindsay and Deborah Dudley. And he was found guilty of all the other charges except for involuntary deviate sexual intercourse with Josefina Rivera.

Heidnik was sentenced to two death sentences. The victims were awarded $34,000 each. Mrs Heidnik – aka Betty Disto – and her son received $30,000.

When Heidnik's father heard that his son was a sex murderer, he was typically sympathetic.

'I hope he gets the chair,' he said. 'I'll even pull the switch.'

Throughout the whole ordeal Josefina Rivera had been

extraordinarily resourceful. After it was over she was stoical. She said later: 'It's something that happened. I won't forget it. But I don't dwell on it.'

Chapter 10

Gay Killers

Houston's 'candy man' killer Dean Corll did not know he was homosexual until he was drafted into the army at the age of twenty-five. After eleven months, he was released and went back to work with his mother in their sweet factory.

Although he was late recognising the true nature of his sexuality, he quickly learnt how to exploit his situation to indulge his sexual urges. He began giving sweets away to the local boys. Corll had hired boys he fancied. But when one made complaints about his sexual advances, Corll's mother, always extremely protective of her son, simply sacked the boy. The other teenagers who worked soon made sure they were never left alone with Corll.

Around that time, Corll met a twelve-year-old called David Brooks. Brooks was from a deeply insecure background. He liked Corll, and considered him good and generous. He would pay Brooks $5 a time for oral sex.

By the time he was fifteen, Brooks was using Corll's apartment as his second home. Corll committed his first murder around that time. A Texas University student, 21-year-old

Jeffrey Konen, disappeared while hitchhiking. It seems likely that Corll picked him up and took him home. Konen's body was found three years later on High Island beach, one of Corll's favourite dumping grounds. It was so badly decomposed that forensic experts were unable to determine the cause of death, but the body was found bound hand and foot.

Corll lived in the run-down Heights area of Houston, where children were always short of money and often high on drugs. This made things easy for a predatory homosexual like Corll. Even after the candy factory closed down, Corll was known in the area as the kind man who gave sweets away to children. Other boys also knew that he gave money away too, in return for oral sex.

In 1970, Brooks visited Corll's apartment to find two naked boys strapped to a board. They were dead. Corll, who was also naked, explained that he had killed the boys during sex and offered Brooks a car if he kept quiet. Brooks was soon seen driving around in a green Corvette.

From then on Brooks was Corll's active accomplice. He would help lure boys back to Corll's apartment where Corll would rape and kill them while Brooks looked on. Brooks found the whole business highly lucrative – Corll seemed to have an insatiable desire for young boys. He penetrated them anally before strangling them.

'He killed them because he wanted to have sex and they didn't want to,' Brooks explained later.

Corll also developed a taste for double murders. In December 1970, he picked up fourteen-year-old James Glass and fifteen-year-old Danny Yates on their way back from church. Glass already knew and liked Corll and had visited his flat before. This time he and his friend ended up raped and strangled on the board.

Six weeks later the same fate befell seventeen-year-old Donald Waldrop and his brother Jerry, who was four years younger. Then on 29 May 1971, thirteen-year-old David

Hilligiest and George Winkle, aged sixteen, vanished on their way to the swimming pool. They had been seen getting into Corll's white van together.

Their disappearance was reported, but the police showed no interest in following these cases. They listed the two missing boys, like the others who had disappeared, as runaways.

This was not good enough for David Hilligiest's parents. They had posters printed up offering a $1,000 reward for information. One of the boys who distributed them was a lifelong friend of David Hilligiest. His name was Wayne Henley.

Later that summer, the Hilligiest's younger son, eleven-year-old Greg, revealed that he had once played an exciting game called poker with David, Wayne Henley and David Brooks, who had once worked at the neighbourhood sweet factory. David Hilligiest had gone missing once before, his parents recalled. On that occasion, they had found his bike outside the candy factory. David had been inside with the manager Dean Corll, a nice man who gave him free sweets. Still they did not put two and two together.

Sometime before David Hilligiest went missing, David Brooks had taken Wayne Henley along to meet Dean Corll, as a potential victim. But Corll quickly realised that Henley was a popular boy – and also that he would do anything for money. He soon began delivering his friends to Corll for $200 a time.

Henley would also sit in the car while Corll cruised the district. Corll would offer young boys a lift. As there was one teenager in the car already, they felt safe getting in. They would then be driven back to Corll's apartment to be raped and killed.

Henley soon took over from Brooks as Corll's major source of supply. Henley admitted being present at the murder of at least nine boys and confessed to killing one himself. He shot the boy in the head, but his victim did not die immediately. When he looked up at Henley and said: 'Wayne, why did you shoot me?' Henley pointed the gun and shot him again.

Henley also played an active role in the murder of eighteen-year-old Scott Mark, who was no pushover like the younger boys. Mark grabbed a knife and tried to stab Corll, but Corll disarmed him. Henley then grabbed Corll's pistol and held it on Mark as Corll strangled him.

Henley and Brooks continued to supply Corll with victims aged between nine and twenty. Corll continued to rape and kill the boys singly and in pairs. Sometimes he also castrated his victims.

Local people became more and more concerned about their missing children, but still the police did nothing. The killing spree only came to an end when Henley made a near-fatal mistake. He brought Corll a girl instead of a boy. Henley had comforted fourteen-year-old Rhonda Williams after her boyfriend, eighteen-year-old Frank Aguirre, had gone missing – another victim of Corll.

She soon considered herself Henley's girlfriend and the two of them planned to run away together. This suited Corll who was getting tired of killing and planned to go 'straight'. He now had a regular boyfriend, Guy, who he had picked up in a public lavatory. Corll had taken him back to his apartment and they had become lovers. Guy expressed interest in a locked room in the flat. Corll promised he would never take Guy into it. No more was said.

Corll also had a girlfriend called Betty Hawkins, who he had been dating on and off for five years. She had two children who called Corll 'Daddy'. Corll said that he was going to give up Guy and he and Betty then planned to move to Colorado together.

The arrangement was that Rhonda would leave home on 17 August and they would all head off together. But Rhonda could not wait and left nine days early on the 8th. That night, Henley had invited a friend named Tim Kerley to a paint-sniffing party at Corll's apartment. He had no choice but to take Rhonda along with him. Corll was furious. 'You weren't supposed to bring a girl,' yelled Corll.

But he calmed down and soon they began to get high sniffing acrylic paint sprayed into a paper bag.

Within an hour, they had all passed out. When Henley awoke he found that he had been handcuffed and bound. The other two youngsters were tied up too, and Kerley was naked. Corll was mad again.

'I'm going to kill you,' he told Henley. 'But first I am going to have my fun.'

He dragged Henley into the kitchen holding a .22 pistol against his stomach. This was the moment Henley had long been fearing. He had always thought Corll would kill him one day, in order to get his hands on Henley's fourteen-year-old brother Ronnie.

But after procuring victims for two years for him, Henley knew Corll well. He knew how to sweet-talk him. Henley said that he would be willing to join in the rape and murder of the other two. Henley would rape Rhonda while Corll would have Kerley. Corll agreed and released Henley.

They carried their bound victims into the bedroom, where Corll turned up the radio to drown any screams. He gave Henley a knife and ordered him to cut away Rhonda's clothing. Then Corll set about raping Kerley and Kerley began to struggle.

'Why don't you let me take her out of here?' Henley asked Corll, registering Rhonda's distress. 'She doesn't want to see that.'

But Corll ignored him. Henley grabbed Corll's pistol and told him to back off. 'Go on Wayne, kill me, why don't you?' taunted Corll.

Henley pulled the trigger, hitting Corll in the head. He

146

staggered forward a few paces. Henley fired again. Corll fell out through the bedroom door and Henley emptied the pistol in his back.

He untied the other two victims and they called the police. Henley admitted to killing Corll and the other two vouched for him. He had done it to save them, they believed. But a chance remark of Henley's alerted the police to the true story. He had told Kerley that, if he hadn't been his friend, he would have got $1,500 for him.

The police found a 17-inch dildo in Corll's apartment along with other tools of the sadistic trade. Inside his white Ford van, they also found rings, hooks and lengths of rope.

When questioned about all this, Henley admitted that he had taken money from Corll to procure boys for him. He said that he had shot Corll because Corll had admitted that they had killed boys before and that there were a lot of them buried in a nearby boat shed.

Three years earlier, Corll had hired a boat shed on Hiram Court Road. Henley took the police there. Inside there were some of the possessions of the missing boys and bags of lime. They started digging up the floor. They found the naked bodies of seventeen boys there. They were bound and gagged. Sometimes their genitals were buried separately. There were also other body parts that did not belong to any of the 17.

Henley then told the police that more bodies were buried around Lake Sam Rayburn and to the south at High Island. Twenty-three bodies were found in all. Henley said that two more bodies were buried on the beach, but they were never located.

Brooks was brought in by his father. When Henley saw him, he told him he had confessed – and that if Brooks did not confess too, he would recant and blame it all on him. Brooks admitted everything.

Twenty-seven bodies had been discovered by the time the

police gave up looking. The spare parts and the frequency of killing indicated that there were at least six or seven more. Altogether forty-two boys were missing from the district, although some of them may have been genuine runaways.

The trial of Wayne Henley and David Brooks took place in San Antonio, Texas, in June 1974. Their insanity plea was rejected. Henley was found guilty of nine murders – not including that of Dean Corll – and was sentenced to 594 years imprisonment. Brooks was found guilty on just one count and got life.

Corll, Henley and Brooks were only outdone in their death toll – at least in the number of corpses found – by John Wayne Gacy Jnr. Like Corll, Gacy discovered that he was a homosexual relatively late in life. Gacy was married when, in 1968, he lured a youth into the backroom of the fast-food franchise he was operating. He handcuffed him and tried to bribe him into performing oral sex. When he refused, Gacy tried to penetrate the youth anally, but his victim escaped.

The young man reported Gacy to the police. Gacy was arrested and sentenced to ten years' imprisonment. He was a model prisoner and, because he had no history of serious crime, was released after eighteen months. He moved to Chicago where he started a construction firm.

Within a year of his release, Gacy had picked up another youth and tried to force him to have sex. He was arrested, but the case was dropped when the youth did not appear in court. Gacy pulled a gun on another youth who had come to him for work, threatening to shoot him if he did not consent to sex. The youth called his bluff, even though Gacy said that he had killed people before. It was true, but the youth managed to leave unmolested.

Gacy had already taken a number of teenage boys back to his home, holding them captive and sexually abusing them over a number of days. When he tired of them, he murdered them.

In 1977, Gacy was accused of sexually abusing a youth at gunpoint. Gacy admitted brutal sex with the boy, but claimed that the youth was a willing participant and was trying to blackmail him. Gacy was released with a caution.

By this time, Gacy was a successful contractor and a leading light in the local Democratic Party. And he entertained at children's parties, dressing up as a down. He also hung out at notorious gay bars. In 1978, he met 27-year-old Jeffrey Rignall at one of these hangouts. He invited the young man to share a pint in his car. Once inside the sleek Oldsmobile, Gacy held a rag soaked with chloroform over Rignall's face.

Rignall awoke naked in Gacy's basement, strapped to a device like a pillory. Gacy was also naked and showed Rignall a number of whips and more sinister sexual devices, and explained how he intended to use them. Gacy also told Rignall that he was a policeman and would shoot him if he raised any objection.

The abuse and torture went on for hours. At times, it was so painful that Rignall begged to die. Gacy would chloroform him again, then wait sadistically until he came round before he began again. Eventually, Rignall said that he would leave town, telling no one what had happened to him. He blacked out again, and woke up fully dressed in Chicago's Lincoln Park. There was money in his pocket but his driving licence was missing.

In hospital, it was discovered that he was bleeding from the anus, and his face and liver were damaged by the chloroform. The police were sympathetic, but had nothing to go on. Rignall could not give them a name, address or licence plate number. But Rignall was determined. He rented a car and drove the route he thought Gacy had taken him, which he vaguely remembered through a haze of chloroform. He found the expressway turn-off Gacy had taken. He waited there – and struck lucky. Gacy's black Oldsmobile swept by. He

149

noted down the licence plate number and followed the car. It parked in the driveway of 8213 West Summerdale Avenue. Rignall even checked the land registry and found that the house belonged to John Wayne Gacy. He took everything he had found to the police.

When they followed up on his leads, the Chicago Police Department found that Gacy's suburban home was just outside their jurisdiction. They could not press felony charges against Gacy. Gacy agreed to give Rignall £3,000 towards his medical bills and the matter was dropped.

Later that year, Mrs Elizabeth Piest reported to the local police that her fifteen-year-old son Robert was missing. He was looking for a summer job and had said that he was going to visit a contractor who lived nearby. The local pharmacist said that the contractor concerned must be John Gacy, who had recently given him an estimate for the refurbishment of his shop.

The local police phoned Gacy but he denied all knowledge of the missing boy. Robert Piest was, in fact, lying dead on Gacy's bed as they spoke. Checking the records, the police discovered Gacy's earlier conviction for sodomy. They went to see him, but Gacy refused to come down to the precinct to discuss the matter and the police realised that they had no charge on which to hold him.

They put Gacy's house under 24-hour surveillance. Nevertheless Gacy managed to put Piest's body in a trunk and smuggle it out to his car. He jumped behind the wheel and raced off at high speed, leaving the police standing. Having lost his tail, Gacy drove down to the nearby Des Plaines River and dropped Piest's body in it.

The police finally managed to get a search warrant – quite a feat as there was so little evidence to go on. But in the house the only thing they found was a receipt from the chemist made out to Robert Piest. It wasn't much, but it was enough to justify continuing the surveillance.

Gacy was getting cocky though. One morning, he invited two of the cops stationed outside his house in for breakfast. As they sat down to eat, the policemen noticed a peculiar smell. Gacy had inadvertently switched off the pump that drained the basement. Water flowing under the house disturbed the soil where Gacy had buried twenty-one of his victims over the years. Armed with another warrant the police disinterred them.

Another four bodies – including Robert Piest's – were found in the Des Plaines River. The youngest of his victims was nine, the oldest were full grown men. John Wayne Gacy was tried for mass murder in 1980 and sentenced to life imprisonment.

In jail, despite his known homosexuality, Gacy receives fan mail from women who say they admire him because he is a deviant and that they loved the excitement of a wild fight.

Kenneth Halliwell beat in the head of his gay lover, playwright Joe Orton, before committing suicide. He was jealous of Orton's success, but Orton's copious infidelity and his endless sexual taunts drove Halliwell over the edge.

The two of them had met at the Royal Academy of Dramatic Art in 1951. Orton was just eighteen, from a working class background. Halliwell was twenty-five, well-educated and had money. His parents had died and he had inherited their house and his father's savings. He introduced Orton to good food, fine wines, books, art and the world of the intellect. Soon they were sharing a bed.

After graduating from RADA, they moved into a flat in Hampstead and started writing together. Nothing they wrote together was published, though one leading publisher was impressed with their novel *The Lost Days of Sodom*. After that, they started to work independently. Demoralised by rejection letters, Orton began to invent spoof characters who wrote letters of complaint to the newspapers and leading companies. These were the genesis of some of the characters in his plays.

Halliwell began to run out of money. They went to work in the Cadbury's factory until they had earned enough money to buy a tiny 16-by-12 foot bedsit in Islington. Frustrated by their lack of success, they began defacing books in Islington public library. Halliwell would cut the plates from art books to decorate the walls of their flat with huge collages. Sometimes they used to alter the covers of popular books, often to obscene effect. On an illustration of First World War heroine Edith Cavell, a classical male torso was added. The courageous nurse, who died in front of a German firing squad, seemed to be contemplating a set of outsize marble male genitals. The caption remained unaltered. It read: 'I was working from dawn to dusk to serve the many sailors, soldiers and airmen. American GIs came in shoals to my surgery and some had very peculiar orders for me.'

They were arrested and sentenced to six months in jail each. Halliwell had a bad time in prison. He freely admitted to a prison psychiatrist that he was a homosexual – homosexuality was still an offence then. When Orton was told this, he feigned surprise. He used his time in jail to read and think.

'Before prison I had been vaguely conscious of something rotten somewhere,' he wrote later. 'Prison crystallised this. The old whore society really lifted up her skirts and the stench was pretty foul.'

Within a year of their release, Halliwell had tried to commit suicide and Orton had sold his first play. It was produced by BBC radio and Orton's career took off; his diaries also show that he became increasingly promiscuous.

His plays *Entertaining Mr Sloane* and *Loot* were produced in London and New York. He even produced a film script called *Up Against It* for the Beatles, which implied overt homosexual relationships between Britain's lovable moptops. The Beatles' manager, Brian Epstein – himself a homosexual – decided that this was not the image his clean-living protégés were trying to put over and so he rejected it. Meanwhile Orton worked out and posed for nude studies. He aimed to be the 'most perfectly developed of modern playwrights'.

Although Orton acknowledged in private his debt to Halliwell, who continued to help and guide his work, in public he would not mention him. This was partly because his homosexuality could not be admitted publicly and partly because he increasingly wanted to move on, leaving Halliwell brooding in the shadows.

To cheer his old friend up, Orton took Halliwell and their mutual friend Kenneth Willliams on a holiday to Tangier. There they gorged themselves on hash cakes and sex – though rarely with each other. Orton voraciously consumed the willing young Moroccan boys who made themselves available for a price. Halliwell tried in vain to keep up. But he was more fastidious than Orton, preferring masturbation to full anal intercourse. From then on Orton flaunted his prowess, taunting Halliwell as an 'old queen'.

The holiday was not entirely a success. They argued over just how far the local boys would go. Orton jeered so scornfully that Halliwell attacked him.

Back in London, things did not improve. While Halliwell skulked around the flat, Orton went cottaging – hanging out in public lavatories for casual sex. Halliwell was still wheeled out for parties occasionally, but he increasingly looked like the old wife of a successful man who was now intent on finding younger, more attractive mistresses.

Halliwell implored Orton to be faithful, while Orton craved more and more conquests. Finally, Orton wanted rid of his old lover altogether. But Halliwell could not stand the rejection.

On 9 August 1967, movie producer Oscar Lewenstein sent a limousine around to their Islington flat to collect Orton. He was to have lunch with director Dick Lester. Lewenstein and Lester had bought the rights to *Up Against It*, the rejected Beatles' script.

153

Lewenstein's chauffeur, Derek Taylor, knocked on the door. There was no reply. When he opened the letterbox and peered through, he saw the top of someone's head lying on the floor.

Taylor called the police and they broke down the door. Inside, they found Orton on his bed. His head had been stoved in with a hammer, which lay beside him. Blood and brains were splattered up the walls. The hammer came from a tool box that sat on a shelf above the bed.

On the floor beside him, Halliwell was spread-eagled naked. He had swallowed twenty-two barbiturate tablets – which would have killed him within 30 seconds. He had died first. Orton could only be identified by the swallow tattooed on his chest. But despite the massive damage to his head, when the police broke the door down, his body was still warm.

The police treated the incident as a case of murder, but no third party was sought. The two men had separate funerals, and were cremated separately, but their ashes were later mingled and scattered over the Garden of Remembrance in Golders Green.

Although the loss of Orton was tragic, Halliwell's achievement as a murderer was small beer. The homosexual Fritz Haarmann was executed in Hanover in 1952, after confessing to the murder of fifty boys, twenty-eight of whom were named on the indictment

Before he was arrested for murder, Haarmann had served sentences hr theft, burglary and child molesting. Then in 1918, he went into business as a black-market meat supplier with Hans Grans, another homosexual. They would lure boys back to their rooms, where Haarmann would kill them by biting their throats out. He and Grans would then strip the meat from their corpses and sell it. They dumped what was left over in the river.

Haarmann managed to continue his grisly trade for six

years, covering up his activities by working as a police informer. But when he was eventually arrested on an indecency charge, clothing from the missing boys was hanging in his flat.

Haarmann went to the gallows, but his accomplice Grans only served twelve years.

Chapter 11

Killing for Company:
Dennis Nilsen and Friends

Dennis Nilsen was born in the Fraserburgh, a small town on the bleak north-east coast of Scotland, on 23 November 1945. His father was a Norwegian soldier who had escaped to Scotland after the German invasion of his homeland in 1940, and had married Betty Whyte, a local girl, in 1942. The marriage did not work out and Betty continued to live with her parents. A few years later, the marriage ended in divorce.

Dennis grew up with his mother, elder brother and younger sister, but the strongest influence on his young life were his stern and pious grandparents. Their faith was so strict that they banned alcohol from the house. The radio and the cinema were instruments of the Devil. Nilsen's grandmother would not even cook on the Lord's day and their Sunday dinner had to be prepared the day before.

The young Dennis Nilsen was sullen and intensely withdrawn. The only person who could penetrate his private world was his grandfather, Andrew Whyte. A fisherman, he

156

was Nilsen's hero. He would regale the little boy with tales of the sea and his ancestors lost beneath its churning waves.

When Andrew Whyte died of a heart attack at sea in 1951, he was brought home and laid out on the dining room table. Dennis was invited to come and see his granddad's body. At the age of six, he got his first glimpse of a corpse. From that moment, the images of death and love fused in his mind.

He left school at fifteen and went into the army. After basic training he was sent to the catering corps. There he was taught how to sharpen knives – and how to dissect a carcass. During his life in the army, Nilsen only had one close friend. He would persuade him to pose for photographs, sprawled on the ground as if he had just been killed in battle.

One night in Aden, Nilsen was drunk and fell asleep in the back of a cab. He found himself naked, locked in the boot. When the cab driver returned, Nilsen played dead. Then as the Arab man-handled him out of the boot, Nilsen grabbed a jack handle and beat him around the head. Nilsen never knew whether he had killed the man or not. But the incident had a profound effect on him. Afterwards he had nightmares of being raped, tortured and mutilated.

After eleven years, Nilsen left the army and joined the police force instead. Part of his training included a visit to a mortuary, where recently qualified constables were initiated in the gruesome habit of seeing death. The partially dissected corpses fascinated Nilsen. He did well in the police, but his private life was gradually disintegrating. Death became an obsession. He would pretend to be a corpse himself, masturbating in front of a mirror with blue paint smeared on his lips and his skin whitened with talcum powder.

Eleven months after he joined the police, he was on the beat when he caught two men committing an act of gross indecency in a parked car. He could not bring himself to arrest them and he decided to resign.

He went to work interviewing applicants at the Jobcentre

157

in London's Charing Cross Road. He became branch secretary of the civil service union and developed increasingly radical political views. Nevertheless his work was good enough to earn him promotion to executive officer at the Jobcentre in Kentish Town, north London.

Despite his professional progress, Nilsen was lonely and yearned for a lasting relationship. Since his teens, he had been aware of his attraction towards other men, but in the army and in the police force he had somehow managed to repress it. In 1975, he met a young man called David Gallichen outside a pub. They moved into a flat at 195 Melrose Avenue together, with a cat and a dog called Bleep. Gallichen, or Twinkle as Nilsen called him, stayed at home and decorated the flat while Nilsen went to work. They made home movies together and spent a lot of time drinking and talking. But the relationship was not destined to last. Gallichen moved out in 1977 and Nilsen was plunged back into a life of loneliness.

On New Year's Eve 1978, Nilsen met a teenage Irish boy in a pub and invited him back to Melrose Avenue. They had been too drunk to have sex. When Nilsen woke in the morning, the boy was lying fast asleep beside him. He was afraid when the boy woke up he would leave – and Nilsen wanted him to stay.

Their clothes were thrown together in a heap on the floor. Nilsen lent over and grabbed his tie. Then he put the tie around the boy's neck and pulled. The boy woke immediately and began to struggle. They rolled onto the floor, but Nilsen kept pulling on the tie.

After about a minute, the boy's body went limp but he was still breathing. Nilsen went to the kitchen and filled a bucket with water. He brought the bucket back and held the boy's head under water until he drowned. Now he had to stay.

Nilsen carried the dead boy into the bathroom and gave him a bath. He dried the corpse lovingly, then dressed it in

158

clean socks and underpants. For a while, he just lay in bed holding the dead boy, then he put him on the floor and he went to sleep.

The following day, he planned to hide the body under the floor, but rigor mortis had stiffened the joints, making it hard to handle. So he left the body out while he went to work. When the corpse had loosened up, Nilsen undressed it again and washed it. This time he masturbated beside it and found he could not stop playing with it and admiring it.

All the time Nilsen was playing with the corpse, he expected to be arrested at any moment. But no one came. It seemed no one had missed the dead boy. After a week living happily with the corpse, Nilsen hid it under the floorboards. Seven months later he cut the body up and burnt it in the garden.

Nilsen's first experience of murder frightened him. He was determined it would not happen again and decided to give up drinking. But Nilsen was lonely. He liked to go to pubs to meet people and talk to them. Soon he slipped off the wagon.

Nearly a year later, on 3 December 1979, Nilsen met Kenneth Ockenden, a Canadian tourist, in a pub in Soho. Nilsen had taken leave from work that afternoon and took Ockenden on a sight-seeing tour of London. Ockenden agreed to go back to Nilsen's flat for something to eat. After a visit to the off-licence, they sat in front of the television eating ham, eggs and chips and drinking beer, whisky and rum.

As the evening wore on, disturbing feelings began to grow inside Nilsen. He liked Ockenden, but realised that he would soon be leaving and going back to Canada. A feeling of desolation crept over him. It was the same feeling he had had when he killed the Irish boy.

Late that night, when they were both very drunk, Ockenden was listening to music through earphones. Nilsen put the flex of the earphones around Ockenden's neck and dragged him struggling across the floor. When he was dead, Nilsen took the earphones off ant put them on himself. He poured himself another drink and listened to records.

In the early hours, he stripped the corpse and carried it over his shoulder into the bathroom. When the body was clean and dry, he put it on the bed and went to sleep next to it.

In the morning, he put the body in a cupboard and went to work. That evening, he took the body out and dressed it in clean socks, underpants and vest. He took some photographs of it, then lay it next to him on the bed. For the next two weeks, Nilsen would watch TV in the evening with Ockenden's body propped up in an armchair next to him. Last thing at night, he would undress it, wrap it in the curtains and place the body under the floorboards.

As Ockenden had gone missing from a hotel, his disappearance made the news for a few days. Again Nilsen was convinced that he was about to be arrested at any moment. Several people in the pub, on the bus, at the sights they had visited and even in the local off-licence had seen them together. But still there was no knock on the door. From then on Nilsen felt that he could pursue his murderous hobby unfettered.

Although plenty of people visited the flat in Melrose Avenue and emerged alive, Nilsen now began to deliberately seek out victims. He would go to pubs where lonely young homosexuals hung out. He would buy them drinks, offer advice and invite them back to his flat for something to eat. Many accepted.

One of them was Martin Duffey. After a disturbed childhood, he ran away from home and ended up in London, sleeping in railway stations. He went back to Nilsen's and, after two cans of beer, crawled into bed. When he was asleep, Nilsen strangled him. While he was still barely alive, Nilsen dragged his unconscious body into the kitchen, filled the sink with water and held his head under for four minutes.

Nilsen went through the standard procedure of stripping and bathing the corpse, then he took it to bed. He talked to it, complimenting Duffey on his body. He kissed it all over and masturbated over it. Nilsen kept the body in a cupboard for a few days. When it started to swell up, he put it under the floorboards.

Twenty-seven-year old Billy Sutherland died because he was a nuisance. Nilsen didn't fancy him, but after meeting him on a pub crawl Sutherland followed him home. Nilsen vaguely remembered strangling him. There was certainly a dead body in the flat in the morning.

Nilsen did not even know some of his victims by name. He was not much interested in them – only their bodies, their dead bodies. The murder routine was always much the same. That part was mechanical. But once they were dead, they really turned him on. Touching the corpse would give him an erection.

Nilsen would never think of his victims' bodies lying around his flat while he was out at work. But when he got home, in the evening, he could not help playing with them. He was thrilled to own their beautiful bodies and was fascinated by the mystery of death. He would hold the corpse in a passionate embrace and talk to it, and when he was finished with it he would stuff it under the floorboards.

Some of his murders were terrifyingly casual. Nilsen found one victim, a 24-year-old Malcolm Barlow, collapsed on the pavement in Melrose Avenue. Barlow was an epileptic and said that the pills he was taking made his legs give way. Nilsen carried him home and called an ambulance. When he was released from hospital the next day, Barlow returned to Nilsen's flat. Nilsen prepared a meal. Barlow began drinking, even though Nilsen warned him not to mix alcohol with the new pills he had been prescribed. When Barlow collapsed, Nilsen could not be bothered to call the ambulance again and strangled him, then carried on drinking until bedtime. It was full of corpses under the floorboards, so the next morning Nilsen stuffed Barlow's body in the cupboard under the sink. Now that he had completely run out of storage space, Nilsen decided it was time to move.

There were six corpses under the floor, and several others had been dissected and stored in suitcases. After a stiff drink, Nilsen pulled up the floorboards and began cutting up the corpses. He put the internal organs in plastic bags, emptying them out in the garden. Birds and rats did the rest. The other body parts were wrapped in carpet and put on a bonfire in the garden. A car tyre was put on top to disguise the smell.

Nilsen moved to an attic flat at 23 Cranley Gardens. This was a deliberate attempt to stop his murderous career. He could not kill people, he thought, if he had no floorboards to hide them under and no garden to burn them in. He had several casual encounters at his new flat, picking men up at night and letting them go in the morning, unmolested. This made him elated. He had finally broken the cycle.

But then John Howlett, or Guardsman John as Nilsen called him, came back to Cranley Gardens with him and Nilsen could not help himself. He strangled Howlett with a strap and drowned him. A few days later, he strangled Graham Allen while he was eating an omelette.

The death of his final victim, Stephen Sinclair, upset Nilsen. Sinclair was a drifter and a drug addict. When they met, Nilsen felt sorry for him and bought him a hamburger. Back at Cranley Gardens, he slumped in a chair in a stupor and Nilsen decided to relieve him of the pain of his miserable life. He got a piece of string from the kitchen, but it was not long enough. Then he got his one and only remaining tie and choked the life out of his unconscious victim.

Killing in Cranley Gardens presented Nilsen with a problem. He was forced to dispose of the bodies by dissecting them, boiling the flesh from the bones, dicing up the remains and flushing them down the toilet. Unfortunately, the drains in Muswell Hill were not built to handle bodies.

The drains at 23 Cranley Gardens had been blocked for five days on 8 February 1983 when Dyno-rod sent Michael Cattran to investigate. He quickly determined that the problem was not inside, but outside the house. At the side of the house, he found the manhole that led to the sewers. He removed the cover and climbed in.

At the bottom of the access shaft, he found a glutinous grey sludge. The smell was awful. As he examined it, more sludge came out of the pipe that led from the house. He called his manager and told him that he thought the substance he had found was human flesh.

Next morning, Cattran and his boss returned to the manhole, but the sludge had vanished. No amount of rainfall could have flushed it through. Someone had been down there and removed it.

Cattran put his hand inside the pipe that connected to the house and pulled out some more meat and four small bones. One of the tenants in the house said that they had heard footsteps on the stairs in the night and suspected that the man who lived in the attic flat had been down to the manhole. They called the police.

Detective Chief Inspector Peter Jay took the flesh and bones to Charing Cross Hospital. A pathologist there confirmed that the flesh was, indeed, human.

The tenant of the attic flat was out at work when Jay got back to Cranley Gardens. At 5.40 pm that day, Nilsen returned. Inspector Jay met him at the front door and introduced himself. He said he had come about the drains. Nilsen remarked that it was odd that the police should be interested in drains.

In Nilsen's flat, Jay said that the drains contained human remains.

'Good grief! How awful,' Nilsen exclaimed.

Jay told him to stop messing about.

'Where's the rest of the body?' Jay asked.

After a short pause, Nilsen said: 'In two plastic bags in the wardrobe next door. I'll show you.'

He showed Inspector Jay the wardrobe. The smell coming from it confirmed what he was saying.

'I'll tell you everything,' Nilsen said. 'I want to get it off my chest, not here but at the police station.'

The police could scarcely believe their ears when Nilsen admitted killing fifteen or sixteen men. But in the wardrobe in Nilsen's flat, they found two large black bin-liners. In one, they found a shopping bag containing the left side of a man's chest, including the arm. A second bag contained the right side of a chest and arm. In a third, there was a torso with no arms, legs or head. A fourth was full of human offal. The unbearable stench indicated that the bags had evidently been closed for some time.

In the second bin-liner, there were two heads – one with the flesh boiled away, the other largely intact – and another torso. The arms were still attached, but the hands were missing. One of the heads belonged to Stephen Sinclair. Nilsen had severed it only four days earlier and had started simmering it in a pot on the kitchen stove.

Under a drawer in the bathroom, the police found Sinclair's pelvis and legs. In a tea chest in Nilsen's bedroom, there was another torso, a skull and more bones.

The police also examined the gardens at 195 Melrose Avenue. They found human ash and enough fragments of bone to determine that at least eight people, probably more, had been cremated there.

Nilsen was eventually charged with six counts of murder and three of attempted murder. His solicitor had one simple question for Nilsen: 'Why?'

'I'm hoping you will tell me that,' Nilsen said.

Nilsen intended to plead guilty, sparing the jury and the

victims' families the details of the horrendous crimes. Instead, his solicitor persuaded him to claim 'diminished responsibility'.

One of the most extraordinary witnesses at the trial was Carl Stottor. Nilsen had tried to strangle him three times, but his frail body had clung to life. Nilsen had then dragged him to the bath and held him under water. Somehow Stottor had found the strength to push himself up three times and beg for mercy. But Nilsen pushed him down again. Thinking he was dead, Nilsen took Stottor's body back into the bedroom and smoked a cigarette. Then Bleep, Nilsen's dog, began to lick Stottor's face and the young man began to revive. Nilsen could easily have snuffed out his life then and there. Instead, he rubbed Stottor's legs to stimulate his circulation. He wrapped him with blankets and nursed him back to life. When he was well again, Nilsen walked him to the tube station and wished him luck.

Nilsen had left another survivor to testify against him. Paul Nobbs had slept at Cranley Gardens one night and woke at 2 am, with a splitting headache. When he woke again in the morning, he found red marks around his neck. Nilsen advised him to see a doctor. At the hospital, Nobbs was told that he had been half strangled. He assumed that his attacker had been Nilsen, but did not report the assault to the police, assuming they would dismiss the attack as a homosexual squabble.

Nilsen was convicted of the attempted murder of Stottor and Nobbs, plus the actual murder of six others. He was sentenced to life imprisonment with the recommendation that he serve at least twenty-five years.

He says he does not lose sleep over what he has done, or have nightmares about it. Nor does he have any tears for his victims or their relatives.

Like Nilsen, Milwaukee mass murderer Jeffrey Dahmer kept the corpses of his victims around his home. But he wanted to possess them even more completely. So he ended up eating their flesh. That way they would be a part of him and stay with him forever.

Dahmer began his murderous career at eighteen. At that time, his parents were going through an acrimonious divorce. Dahmer's father had already left and his mother was away on a vacation. Dahmer was alone in the house and feeling very neglected. So he went out looking for company. He picked up a hitchhiker, a nineteen-year-old white youth named Stephen Hicks who had spent the day at a rock concert. They got on well and Dahmer took Hicks back to his parents' house. They had a few beers and talked about their lives. Then Hicks said that he had to go. Dahmer begged him to stay, but Hicks was insistent. So Dahmer made him stay. He picked up a heavy dumbbell, clubbed him around the head and strangled him.

Dahmer dragged Hicks's body into the crawlspace under the house and dismembered it with a hunting knife. He had had plenty of practice. His childhood hobby had been dissecting animals. He wrapped the parts in plastic bags and stashed them there. But the stench of rotting flesh soon permeated the house. That night, Dahmer took the body parts and buried them in a nearby wood. But soon he became afraid that local children would discover the grave, so he dug up the body parts, stripped the flesh and pulverised the bones with a sledgehammer. Then he scattered the pieces around his garden and the neighbouring property. It was ten years before Dahmer killed again.

Dahmer moved to Milwaukee to live with his grand-mother. He was a loner. He would hang out in gay bars. If he did strike up a conversation with another customer, he would slip drugs into their drink. Often they would end up in a coma. Dahmer made no attempt to rape them, he was simply experimenting. But when the owner of the Club Bar ended up unconscious in hospital, Dahmer was barred.

In 1986, Dahmer was sentenced to a year's probation for

exposing himself and masturbating publicly in front of two twelve-year-old boys. He claimed he was urinating and promised the judge that it wouldn't happen again.

Six days after the end of his probation, he picked up 24-year-old Stephen Tuomi in a gay club. They went to the Ambassador Hotel to have sex. When Dahmer awoke, he found Tuomi dead. There was blood around his mouth and bruising around his neck.

Dahmer had been drunk the night before and realised that he must have strangled Tuomi. Now he was alone in a hotel room with a corpse and any minute the porter would be checking whether the room had been vacated. He rushed out and bought a large suitcase. He stuffed Tuomi's body into it and took a taxi back to his grandmother's house. The taxi driver even helped him drag the heavy case inside. Dahmer then cut up the body and put the bits into plastic bags which he put out for the garbage collectors. He performed this task so well that he left no traces at all. When the police called around to ask him about the disappearance of Tuomi, there was no sign of the body. Dahmer found that he had gotten away with his second murder.

Sex, companionship and death were now inextricably linked in Dahmer's mind. Four months later, he picked up a young male prostitute. They went back to Dahmer's grand-mother's house to have sex in the basement. Dahmer gave the boy a drink laced with a powerful sedative. When the young man was unconscious, he strangled him. He dismembered the corpse, stripped off the flesh, pulverised the bones and scattered the pieces.

Two months later, Dahmer met a 22-year-old homosexual who was broke. Dahmer offered him money to perform in a video. He had oral sex with Dahmer, in his grandmother's basement. When it was over, Dahmer offered him a drink, drugged him, strangled him and disposed of the corpse.

Dahmer's grandmother began to complain of the smell

167

that persisted even after the garbage had been collected. She found a patch of blood in the garage. Dahmer said that he had been skinning animals out there. She accepted this excuse, but made it clear that she wanted him to move out.

Dahmer found himself a small apartment in a run-down predominantly black area. On his first night there, he lured Keison Sinthasomphone, a thirteen-year-old Laotian boy back to the flat and drugged him. The boy, whose older brother later perished at Dahmer's hands, somehow managed to escape. Dahmer was arrested and charged with sexual assault and enticing a minor for immoral purposes. He spent a week in jail, then was released on bail.

Dahmer could not contain his compulsion to kill. While out on bail, he picked up handsome 26-year-old black bisexual Anthony Sears. Fearing that the police were watching his apartment, he took Sears back to his grandmother's basement. They had sex, then Dahmer drugged him and dismembered his body. He disposed of Sears' corpse in the garbage, but kept the skull as a souvenir.

Back in court, the District Attorney pushed for five years imprisonment for his assault on thirteen-year-old Keison Sinthasomphone. Dahmer's attorney argued that the attack was a one-off offence. His client was a homosexual and a heavy drinker, and needed psychiatric help, not punishment. Dahmer got five years on probation and a year on a correction programme.

It did not help. Dahmer was now set in his murderous ways. He picked up a young black stranger in a club and offered him money to pose for nude photographs. Back in Dahmer's flat, the youth accepted a drink. It was drugged. When he lapsed into unconsciousness, Dahmer strangled him, stripped him and performed oral sex with the corpse. Then he dismembered the corpse, again keeping the skull, which he painted grey.

He picked up another notorious homosexual known as 'the

Sheikh' and did the same to him – only this time he had oral sex before he drugged and strangled his victim.

The next victim, a fifteen-year-old Hispanic, was luckier. Dahmer offered him $200 to pose nude. He undressed but Dahmer neglected to drug him before attacking him with a rubber mallet. Dahmer tried to strangle him, but he fought back. Eventually Dahmer calmed down. The boy promised not to inform the police and Dahmer let him go. Dahmer even called him a taxi.

Next day, when he went to hospital for treatment, the boy broke his promise and spoke to the police. But he begged them not to let his foster parents find out that he was a homosexual and the police dropped the matter altogether.

The next time Dahmer picked up a victim, a few weeks later, he craved more than the usual sex, murder and grisly dismemberment. He decided to keep the skeleton and bleached it with acid. He dissolved most of the flesh in acid, but kept the biceps intact in the fridge.

When neighbours began to complain of the smell of putrefying flesh coming from Dahmer's flat, Dahmer apologised. He said that the fridge was broken and he was waiting to get it fixed.

Dahmer's next victim, 23-year-old David Thomas, was not gay. He had a girlfriend and a three year-old daughter but accepted Dahmer's offer to come back to his apartment for money. After drugging him, Dahmer realised that he did not really fancy his latest pick-up anyway. But fearing that Thomas might make trouble when he woke up, he killed him. This time he took more pleasure in the dismemberment, photographing it step by step.

Nineteen-year-old aspiring model Curtis Straughter was engaged in oral sex with Dahmer when the sleeping potion took effect. Dahmer strangled him and, again, photographed the dismemberment. Once again his skull was kept as a trophy.

Nineteen-year-old Errol Lindsey's murder proceeded along exactly the same lines. Dahmer offered him money to pose for nude photographs, drugged, strangled and dismembered him. The grisly process was recorded photographically and his skull was added to Dahmer's collection.

Thirty-one-year old deaf mute, Tony Hughes, also accepted $50 to pose nude. But by this time, Dahmer had become so blasé about the whole procedure that he kept Hughes' body in his bedroom for several days before he cut it up.

Dahmer's next victim was Keison Sinthasomphone's older brother, fourteen-year-old Konerak. Again things went badly wrong. Dahmer drugged the boy, stripped him and raped him but then, instead of strangling him, Dahmer went out to buy some beer. On his way back to the apartment, Dahmer saw Konerak out on the street. He was naked, bleeding and talking to two black girls. When Dahmer grabbed him, the girls hung on to him. One of them had called the police and two patrol cars arrived.

The police wanted to know what all the trouble was about Dahmer said that he and Konerak had had a lover's tiff. He managed to convince them that 14-year-old Konerak was really nineteen and, back at his apartment, showed them Polaroids of Konerak in his underwear which seemed to back up his story that they were lovers. The police did not realise that the pictures had been taken earlier that day, while Konerak was drugged.

Throughout all this Konerak sat passively on the sofa, thinking his ordeal was over. In fact, it had only just begun. The police accepted Dahmer's story and left. Konerak was strangled immediately and then dismembered. The three policemen responsible were later dismissed.

Dahmer attended Gay Pride Day in Chicago and on the way back picked up another would-be model, Matt Turner. Back at Dahmer's apartment, he was also strangled and dismembered.

When Dahmer picked up 23-year-old Jeremiah Weinberger

in a gay club, Weinberger asked his former roommate whether he should go with him. The roommate said: 'Sure, he looks okay.'

Dahmer seems to have liked Weinberger. They spent the whole of the next day together having sex. Then Weinberger looked at the clock and said it was time to go – and Dahmer said he should stay for just one more drink. His head ended up next to Matt Turner's in the freezer.

When Dahmer lost his job, he knew only one thing would make him feel better. He picked up a 24-year-old black man called Oliver Lacy, took him back to his apartment, strangled him and sodomised his dead body.

Four days later, 25-year-old Joseph Bradeholt – who was married with two children – accepted Dahmer's offer of money for nude photographs and willingly joined in oral sex with him. His dismembered torso was left to soak in a dustbin filled with acid.

By the time Dahmer had killed seventeen men, all in much the same way, he was getting so casual that it was inevitable that he would get caught. On 22 June 1991, Dahmer met Tracy Edwards, a young black man who had just arrived from Mississippi. He was with a number of friends. Dahmer invited them all back to his apartment for a party. He and Edwards would go ahead in a taxi and organise some beers. The others would follow later. Edwards went along with this plan. What he did not know was the Dahmer was giving his friends the wrong address.

Edwards did not like Dahmer's apartment. It smelt funny. There was a fish tank, where Dahmer kept some Siamese fighting fish. Dahmer told lurid tales about the fish fighting to the death and Edwards glanced nervously at the clock as he sipped his cold beer.

When the beer was finished, Dahmer gave Edwards a rum and coke. It was drugged. Edwards became drowsy. Dahmer put his arms around him and whispered about going to bed.

171

Instantly, Edwards was wide awake. It was all a mistake. He had to be going, he said.

Before he knew it, his hands were handcuffed and Dahmer was poking a butcher's knife in his chest, ordering him to get undressed Edwards realised the seriousness of his situation. He knew he had to humour the man, make him relax. Slowly, he unbuttoned his shirt.

Dahmer suggested that they go through into the bedroom and escorted Edwards there at knifepoint. The room was decorated with Polaroid pictures of young men posing naked. There were other pictures of dismembered bodies and chunks of meat. The smell in the room was sickening. The putrid aroma seemed to be coming from a plastic dustbin under the window. Edwards could guess the rest.

Dahmer wanted to watch a video with his captive friend. They sat on the bed and watched *The Exorcist*. The gruesome movie made Dahmer relax and Edwards thought of ways to escape.

If Edwards did not comply with his requests, Dahmer said, he would strip out his heart and eat it. Then he told Edwards to strip so that he could photograph him nude. As Dahmer reached for the camera, Edwards seized his opportunity. He punched him in the side of the head. As Dahmer went down, Edwards kicked him in the stomach and ran for the door.

Dahmer caught up with him and offered to unlock the handcuffs, but Edwards ignored him. He wrenched open the door and ran for his life.

Halfway down 25th Street, Edwards spotted a police car. He ran over to it yelling help. In the car he explained to the officer that a maniac had tried to kill him and he directed them back to Dahmer's apartment.

The door was answered by a well-groomed white man who seemed calm and composed. The police began to have second thoughts about the story Edwards had told them – until they noticed the strange smell.

Dahmer admitted that he had threatened Edwards. He looked contrite and explained that he had just lost his job and been drinking. But when the police asked for the key to the handcuffs, he refused to hand it over and grew violent. The policemen pushed him back into the flat and, in moments, had him face down on the floor. They read him his rights. Then they began looking around the flat. One of them opened the fridge door.

'Oh my God,' he said, 'there's a goddamn head in here.'

Dahmer began to scream like an animal. The police rushed out to get some shackles. Then they began their search of the apartment in earnest.

The refrigerator contained meat, including a human heart, in plastic bags. There were three human heads in the freezer. A filing cabinet contained grotesque photographs, three human skulls and a collection of bones. Two more skulls were found in a pot on the stove. Another pot contained male genital organs and severed hands and there were the remains of three male torsos in the dustbin in the bedroom.

In the precinct, Dahmer seemed almost relieved that his murder spree was over. He made a detailed confession and admitted that he had now reached the stage where he was cooking and eating his victims' bodies.

Dahmer's cannibalism and his necrophilia were the cornerstones of his insanity plea. But the District Attorney pointed out to the jury that if Dahmer were found insane and sent to a mental hospital, his case would be reviewed in two years and if he was then found sane he could be out on the streets again. The jury found Jeffrey Dahmer guilty of the fifteen murders he was charged with and he was given fifteen life sentences. The state of Wisconsin has no death penalty. He could have faced the death penalty in Ohio for the murders that took place in his grandmother's house. As it was, he was beaten to death by a fellow inmate in 1994.

Chapter 12

Love of Death

Using corpses for sexual pleasure is not confined to the terrifying world of homosexuals like Dennis Nilsen and Jeffrey Dahmer. There are also heterosexual men who get their satisfaction by murdering women and abusing their corpses.

John Reginald Christie was born on 8 April 1898 in Black Boy House, Halifax. His father, Ernest, was a pillar of the society. A designer for Crossley Carpets, he was also a founder member of the Halifax Conservative Party and a leader of the Primrose League, an organisation promoting purity among the working classes.

One of seven children, Christie was terrified of his disciplinarian father. 'We almost had to ask if we could speak to him,' he wrote later. But Christie had other problems in the family. He found himself completely dominated by his older sisters.

Christie was good at school and sang in the choir. After school hours, he was a Boy Scout and later became an assistant Scout Master. When he was eight, his maternal grandfather died. Christie felt the trembling sensation of both fascination and pleasure at seeing the body.

174

After leaving school, Christie started work at the Gem Cinema in Halifax. One day, he and some friends went down the local lovers' lane known as the Monkey Run. They paired off. Christie found himself with a girl much more experienced than himself. Intimidated by her, he could not perform. Word got around and his friends started taunting him as 'Reggie-No-Dick' or 'Can't-do-it-Reggie'.

At seventeen, Christie was caught stealing and was sacked. His father banned him from the house. He had to sleep on the allotment and his mother would take him food.

He drifted from job to job until he was called up for service in World War I. Sent to France, he was gassed and was sent home with a disability pension.

On 20 May 1920, he married the long-suffering Ethel Waddington. The following year, working as a postman, he was caught stealing money out of letters and was jailed for nine months. Two years later, he was bound over for posing as an ex-officer and the court put him on probation for violence. Probation did not help. The following year, he served another nine months for theft. His wife left him.

In 1929, he was sentenced to six months' hard labour for attacking a prostitute. After yet another spell in prison for stealing a car from a Roman Catholic priest who befriended him, Christie wrote to Ethel, asking her to have him back. Foolishly, she did.

They moved to London. When they visited Ethel's family in Leeds, Christie spoke of his 'big house in London' with servants. But he never earned over £8 a week, the going rate for a junior clerk. They lived in a shabby little flat in North Kensington and there were no servants.

Just before the war broke out in 1939, Christie became a Special Constable. He seemed to be a reformed character. But he was never popular. Locals feared his petty mindedness. Christie and another Special were known as 'the rat and the weasel'.

Although he was losing his hair, Christie still saw himself as a charmer, but his basic hatred of women was plain. 'Women who give you the come-on wouldn't look nearly so saucy if they were helpless and dead,' he would think. Christie took pride in concealing his violent intentions from the women he took back to 10 Rillington Place, until it was too late.

His first victim was Austrian-born Ruth Fuerst. She worked in a munitions factory. But the pay was poor and she supplemented her income with a little prostitution.

Christie met her while trying to trace a man wanted for theft. She asked him to lend her ten shillings and Christie invited her home. One hot August afternoon in 1943, while Mrs Christie was away in Sheffield, she called again at 10 Rillington Place.

Christie held back from sex on this occasion, but Fuerst encouraged him. Once intercourse was over, he strangled her. Christie felt a great sense of peace after he had murdered her and was fascinated by the beauty of her corpse. He wanted to keep her, but his wife returned home unexpectedly and he had to bury her stealthily that night.

Nevertheless, he compared his first murder to an artist's first painting. 'It was thrilling because I had embarked on the career I had chosen for myself, the career of murder. But it was only the beginning,' he said later.

Christie quit the police force at the end of 1943. He went to work at the Ultra Radio Works in west London, where he met Muriel Eady. She suffered from catarrh and he said he had a remedy. One afternoon in October 1944, she came round to 10 Rillington Place and he showed her what he said was a patent inhaler. In fact, it was nothing more than a jar with perfumed water in it. There were two holes in the lid with rubber tubes attached. Unbeknownst to Muriel, one of them was connected to the gas pipe.

Christie persuaded her to inhale through the other. He was

confident that the perfume would cover the smell of gas. As she lapsed into unconsciousness he had sex with her, then strangled her. Christie was delighted with the thought that his second murder was so much cleverer than his first one. All his careful planning had paid off.

At Easter 1948, Timothy and Beryl Evans moved into the top-floor flat at 10 Rillington Place. Evans had been born in Merthyr Vale on 20 November 1924. Before he was born, his father had walked out of the house one day and was never seen or heard of again. Timothy Evans was educationally backward and had a speech impediment. In his early years, he could not pronounce his own name. His schooling was further held back by a foot injury which led to long spells in hospital.

Some years after her husband's disappearance, Timothy's mother obtained a certificate saying that he was presumed dead. In 1929, she married again and, during the Depression, the family moved to Notting Hill where, in 1947, Timothy married a local girl, Beryl Thorley.

Evans, then twenty-four, had seen the 'To Let' sign outside 10 Rillington Place while living with his mother and stepfather. Beryl was pregnant and the couple needed a place desperately, so they took the cramped attic flat.

On the floor below lived railwayman Charles Kitchener. He kept himself to himself. His eyesight was failing and he was often away in hospital. The ground floor was occupied by John and Ethel Christie.

The Evanses and the Christies got on well. Ethel was fond of the baby and looked after Geraldine when Beryl went to her part-time job.

In the summer of 1949, Beryl fell pregnant again. There was little money coming in and they were behind on the hire-purchase payments. Beryl wanted an abortion. Timothy, a Roman Catholic, forbade it. But Beryl was just nineteen and did not want to be tied to a home and family. She was adamant. She found that there was a back-street abortionist in the Edgware Road who would do the job for £1.

When Christie heard of her plans, he told Beryl that he could help her out. He could perform an abortion on her in the house. Later he approached Timothy Evans, who replied that he had not realised Christie knew anything about medical procedures. To convince him, Christie offered to show him one of his medical books. It was the first-aid manual of the St John's Ambulance Brigade. Evans, who was barely literate, knew no better. He was impressed by the pictures.

On 8 November 1949, or the day before, Evans came home to find Christie waiting for him with bad news. The operation had not been a success, Christie said. Beryl had died.

Christie begged Evans not to go to the police. He would be charged with manslaughter as Beryl had died during an illegal abortion. Evans wanted his mother to look after the baby. But Christie said he would find someone to look after her. When Evans returned from work on 10 November, Christie said that the child had been taken to a couple in East Acton who would look after her. That evening Evans helped Christie get rid of Beryl's body down the drain outside.

Christie helped Evans sell off his furniture. With £40 in his pocket, Evans headed off back to Wales. But he could not get the fate of his young wife out of his mind. As a Catholic, he should have prevented her going through with the abortion. If he had, she would still be alive. Tormented with guilt, he walked into Merthyr Vale police station and confessed.

At first, Evans thought he could take the blame without implicating his friend Christie. Evans told the police that he had been given a bottle containing something that would cause miscarriage by a man he met in a transport cafe. Although he did not mean to give it to his wife, she found it just before he went out to work. When he returned, she was dead. He opened a drain outside the front door and dropped his wife's body down it.

The Merthyr Vale police contacted the station at Notting Hill. They sent officers to 10 Rillington Place. It took three of them to lift the manhole cover. The drain was empty. Back in Merthyr, Evans's statement was challenged. A detective told him he could not possibly have lifted the manhole cover himself. Evans made a second statement, this time implicating Christie. He said that Christie had performed an illegal abortion on his wife. She had died and, together, they had disposed of the body.

Police searched Rillington Place, but not very meticulously. They did not even notice the thigh bone of Muriel Eady propped against the garden fence. But what police did find was a stolen brief-case and Evans was arrested.

Christie went to the police station and made a statement about the Evanses' domestic quarrels. Beryl, he said, had complained of her husband grabbing her by the throat. The police believed him. After all, Christie was a former policeman himself.

The house in Rillington Place was searched again. This time the police found the body of Beryl Evans wrapped in a green table-cloth behind a stack of wood. The body of baby Geraldine was found behind the door of the washroom. Both had been strangled. Beryl's right eye and upper lip were swollen and there was bruising in her vagina. To the police, this confirmed it was a simple 'domestic'.

Evans was brought back to London. He made a statement saying he had strangled Beryl with a rope and put her in the outside washhouse after the Christies had gone to bed. Two days later, he had strangled the baby and put her body in the outhouse.

He was charged with the murder of both his wife and his daughter, but the Crown only proceeded with the murder of the baby. There could be no excuse for such a crime.

The trial took place at the Old Bailey in January 1950. In the witness box, Christie denied taking part in the abortion

179

and said that he had been ill in bed on the day of Beryl's death He apologised to the judge for speaking softly, but he said this was because he had been gassed in World War I. The court was also told of his service as a Special Constable, giving the impression that he was a solid citizen and that his word was not to be doubted.

Evans gave his evidence poorly. His allegation that Beryl died during an illegal abortion performed by Christie held no water; she had been strangled. And he had no possible explanation for the death of the baby. The jury was out for only forty minutes. The verdict was guilty; the sentence – death by hanging.

To the end, Evans maintained that Christie had killed both Beryl and Geraldine and there was some public disquiet about the verdict. A petition with 1,800 signatures was sent to the Home Secretary. But he would not grant a reprieve and Evans was hanged on 9 March 1950.

On 14 December 1952, Christie said he was awakened by his wife Ethel going into convulsions. By now, she was elderly and arthritic. Christie decided it would be kindest to put her out of her misery and strangled her.

For two days he kept his wife's body in the bed, then he pulled up the floorboards of the front room and buried her under them. He claimed that her loss caused him pain. They had been married for thirty-two years.

For the next four months, Christie went on a sex and murder spree. Kathleen Maloney was lured into his flat to pose nude while he photographed her. Her body was shoved in an alcove in the kitchen. Rita Nelson had just found out that she was pregnant when she visited 10 Rillington Place on 12 January. She did not leave alive.

Christie had more trouble with Hectorina MacLennan, who was his final victim. He met her in a cafe and offered her a place to stay. But he was surprised when she turned up with her boyfriend. They stayed at Rillington Place together for three nights. On 6 March, Christie followed them to the Labour Exchange. While her boyfriend was signing on, Christie persuaded Hectorina to come back to the flat.

Christie had given her a drink and offered her a whiff of his inhaler. She did not like it. There was a struggle and he strangled her, then he had sex with her after she was dead. He bundled her body in the alcove with Kathleen Maloney, propping her in a sitting position with her bra hooked to Maloney's leg.

Beresford Brown had moved into the top flat, previously occupied by the Evanses. He was delighted when he heard the shabby, ground-floor flat was finally going to be cleaned out. Its occupant John Christie had already left.

The day before, the landlord had called to find that Christie had illegally sublet his flat to a couple called Reilly. The landlord told them to be out by the morning, and had given Brown permission to use the ground-floor kitchen.

Over the next few days, Brown cleared out the piles of clothes, rubbish and filth Christie had left behind. He put them in the tiny backyard, alongside the wash-house. Then he started to redecorate the kitchen.

He wanted to put up some brackets on the rear wall. But when he tapped on it he found it was hollow. He pulled away strips of the wallpaper and found a papered-over wooden door. He pulled open the door. Behind it, sitting on a pile of rubbish, he saw a partially clothed woman's body. He ran to fetch the police.

The police soon discovered that this was not the only body in 10 Rillington Place. Behind the first woman in the alcove there was a second woman, wrapped in a blanket. Behind that was a third woman, ankles tied together with a plastic flex. All three had been strangled. A fourth corpse had been found under some rubble in the front room. It was Ethel Christie.

Scotland Yard told the press they were looking for a John Reginald Christie and circulated the description of the slight, balding, middle-aged former tenant. Appeals were made over the loudspeaker systems at football matches and Christie's picture appeared in every national newspaper.

Digging up the tiny garden of 10 Rillington Place, the police found the skeletons of two more women. They had been there for about ten years. Both had been strangled and the skull of one woman was missing.

The day he left 10 Rillington Place, Christie had booked into Rowton House, (now the Mount Pleasant Hotel), in King's Cross Road for seven nights. But he soon moved on, wandering uneasily back and forth across London.

There were numerous reported sightings of Christie. Few were genuine. On 19 March 1953, around 11 pm, the chief crime reporter of the *News of the World*, Norman Rae, received a phone-call.

'Do you recognise my voice?' the caller asked.

Rae did. He had met Christie before, in 1950, during the murder trial of Timothy Evans.

'I can't stand any more,' Christie said. 'They're hunting me like a dog.'

In return for a meal, a smoke and a warm place to sit, he would give the *News of the World* an exclusive. Rae warned him that afterwards, he would have to call the police. Christie agreed and they arranged to meet at 1.30 am, outside Wood Green Town Hall.

Rae parked outside the Town Hall, away from the street lamps, opened the car door and waited. Christie approached. Then, purely by chance, two policemen on their beat happened by. Thinking he had been betrayed, Christie ran off.

Two days later, PC Thomas Ledger saw a man leaning over the embankment near Putney Bridge. He said he was John Waddington of 35 Westbourne Grove. But the young officer recognised him and asked him to turn out his pockets. One contained a 1950 newspaper cutting of Timothy Evans's murder trial. The hunt for Christie was over.

Christie made detailed confessions, but took care to provide separate explanations for each killing. The prostitutes had forced themselves upon him and things had got out of hand. His wife had to be put out of her misery. Muriel Eady and Beryl Evans had also been mercy killings.

At his trial, Christie pleaded not guilty by virtue of insanity. But he could not disguise the fact that he had put a lot of planning into the killing of his victims; he had constructed a special apparatus to gas four of them.

The jury found Christie guilty and the judge sentenced him to death. There was no appeal. The only problem the law had was the conviction of Timothy Evans for the murder of his wife Beryl – a murder to which Christie had now confessed. A formal inquiry was set up, which found that in 10 Rillington Place, two murderers had been operating – and that Christie had told the truth at Evans's trial but lied at his own. Christie was hanged at Pentonville Prison at 9 am on 15 July 1953.

Christie was unusual in that he liked to have sex with his victims after he had killed them. A similar case occurred in the US, thirteen years later, when Oregon State Police were baffled by the disappearance of a number of young women. On 10 May 1969, a fisherman on a bridge across the Long Tom River saw what he took to be a large parcel floating in the water. On closer examination, it was found to be the bloated body of a young woman, clad in a coat and weighed down by a car gearbox.

The body was identified as 22-year-old Linda Salee, who had vanished two weeks before. She had been in the water too long to determine whether she had been raped, but there were curious burn marks surrounding puncture wounds a few inches below her armpits.

While police frogmen were searching the area, they found another body, anchored by a cylinder head. It belonged to 19-year-old Karen Sprinkler. She had disappeared on 27 March and her body had been in the water for about two months. Although she was fully clothed, she was wearing a large black bra that did not belong to her. Both her breasts had been cut off and the ample black bra had been padded out with screwed up brown paper. Both women had been strangled.

The skeleton of another girl, sixteen-year-old Stephanie Vilcko, who had disappeared from her home in Portland the year before, had also washed up in a creek along the Long Tom. The police continued their search. They had two other missing girls on their books – nineteen-year-old encyclo-paedia salesperson Linda Slawson, who had gone missing on a sales trip in Portland, and 23-year-old Jan Whitney, whose broken-down car had been found on a nearby highway.

There was precious little to go on. Karen Sprinkler and Linda Salee's bodies had both been tied up with electrical flex – perhaps the killer was an electrician. He might also be a mechanic as both corpses had been weighed down with car parts. But Oregon was full of electricians and car mechanics.

At the Cornvallis campus of Oregon State University, where Karen Sprinkler had been a student, several of the other girls had received phone calls from a man claiming to be a Vietnam veteran and a psychic. Using various first names, he asked the girls for a date and seemed offended when they refused.

One of the college girls had met him for a date though. He had been fat and freckled. They had talked in the lounge of Callaghan Hall and the girl said that she thought there was something odd about him. He told her that she should be sad. When she asked why, he said: 'Think of those two girls whose bodies were found in the river.'

He suggested that they went for a drive. When she declined he remarked she was right to be wary. 'How do you know I wouldn't take you to the river and strangle you,' he said.

The police asked her to call them when she had arranged another date. A week later, the caller phoned again and the girl contacted the police who apprehended him as soon as he walked into the college. He gave his name as Jerry Brudos, a thirty-year-old electrician, who lived in nearby Salem.

The police had no charge to hold Brudos on, so they had to let him go. But they took the number of his car and began to check him out. Within days, they discovered that Brudos had a history of violence towards women. He had spent time in a state mental hospital for sexual deviations. And when Linda Slawson had disappeared, he had been living in the area of Portland where she had been selling encyclopaedias.

Brudos's sexual deviancy first manifested itself when he was five. He found a pair of women's patent leather shoes in a garbage dump. He took them home and tried them on. His mother was furious. She told him to take them back to the dump, but he hid them and wore them secretly. When his mother found out, she burnt them and beat him severely.

At school, he became obsessed with high-heeled shoes, even stealing a pair from his teacher. He was caught and confessed. When he was asked why he had stolen them, he ran from the room. He did not know why.

When he was sixteen, things began to get worse. He lured the girl next door to his bedroom. While he was out of the room, a masked man attacked her, threatened her with a knife and forced her to strip. Then he took pictures of her. When the masked man left, Brudos reappeared, saying that the intruder had locked him in the barn. It was a flimsy story.

A year later, Brudos had taken a seventeen-year old girl for a drive. On a deserted road, he dragged her from the car and ordered her to remove her clothes. Passers-by heard her screams and intervened. Brudos was arrested, lamely protesting that the girl had been attacked by some weirdo. The police found a box of women's shoes and underwear in his home. Although psychiatrists found that he was not mentally ill, he was sent to Oregon State Mental Hospital for observation – but discharged after nine months.

In the army, he claimed that a beautiful Korean girl sneaked into his bed every night. Returning home, he began attacking young girls and stealing their shoes. His family were convinced that he was well on his way to becoming a rapist, when he met a seventeen-year-old girl called Darcie who consented to marry him.

Eight months later, they had their first child. Married life seemed to suit Brudos well enough, but his wife became increasingly concerned about his need to photograph her in the nude – often in weird and disturbing poses. Then, while his wife was in hospital having their second child, Brudos followed a girl wearing attractive shoes back to her home, choked her unconscious and raped her.

At Brudos's home, the police found lengths of rope lying around. One was tied in the same knot used to truss the corpses. As well as being an electrician, Brudos ran a one-man car repair business from the garage of his home, near where Karen Spinkler disappeared. He had also been working in Lebanon, Oregon, close to the place where Jan Whitney's car had been found. But still none of this evidence was strong enough to make an arrest.

Then the police found that they had an eyewitness. Just two days before the disappearance of Linda Salee, a fifteen-year-old schoolgirl had been attacked in Portland by a fat, freckled man with a gun. She had screamed and fought back. The man grabbed her around the neck, but she bit his thumb. He beat her unconscious, but made off when a car approached.

The girl identified Brudos as her attacker from some photographs detectives showed her. The police were on their way to arrest Brudos when they discovered that he and his family had left Cornvallis and were driving towards Portland. When Brudos's station wagon was stopped by the Highway Patrol, his wife was driving. He was found hiding under a blanket in the back.

At the police station, Brudos was asked to change into prison overalls before being locked in his cell. Under his everyday clothes, the police found he was wearing women's underwear.

Brudos was questioned for five days before he began to loosen up. He slowly started to reveal his interest in women's shoes. He admitted to following a pretty girl home and, later, breaking in to steal her shoes. Then he talked about women's underwear he particularly enthused about a long-waist black bra he had stolen from a washing line. It was the sort of bra that had been found on the body of Karen Sprinkler.

After that the dam burst. Brudos admitted everything. In January 1968, Linda Slawson had come around selling encyclopaedias. She had been wearing attractive high-heeled shoes. His wife had visitors in the house, he said, and Brudos asked whether she would mind coming into the workshop to discuss the matter.

She was sitting on a stool going through her sales patter when he hit her with a heavy piece of wood. Then he strangled her.

His mother and two children were upstairs in the house at the time. He sent them out for dinner to a hamburger joint, then he hurried back to the garage. Much to his delight, when he undressed the corpse, he found she was wearing attractive underwear. He pulled out the box of undies that he had stolen from clothes lines and began dressing and undressing Linda's body as if she was some overgrown Barbie doll. That night, he chopped her foot off. He kept it in the freezer so he could use it to try on women's shoes. Then he threw the rest of her body in the back of the station wagon and dumped it in the river, weighing it down with a heavy cylinder head.

Ten months later, he was driving back from a job in Lebanon when he noticed a car broken down on the freeway. The driver was Jan Whitney. She was accompanied by two hitchhikers. Brudos explained that he was a car mechanic, but

187

that they would have to go back to Salem to get his toolbox.

He dropped the hitchhikers off in Salem and drove Jan back to his garage. He left the girl in the car while he went to check that his wife was not at home, then he slipped into the back seat and strangled Jan Whitney with a leather strap.

He raped her dead body anally, then started his game of dressing and undressing the body. This time he took photographs – and he repeatedly violated the corpse.

With Linda Slawson, the excitement had been over much too quickly, Brudos decided. This time he was going to prolong the pleasure. He left the body hanging from a hook and locked up the garage, and came and played with it whenever he felt the need. He cut one of her breasts off to make into a paper weight, but gave up the idea when the epoxy hardener he used refused to set

Two days after the murder, Brudos came home to discover that a car had gone out of control and knocked a hole in his garage wall. A policeman had looked in but, in the dust and gloom, he had not spotted Jan Whitney's body hanging there. That night, Brudos dumped it in the river weighed down, again, with scrap iron.

Despite this close shave, Brudos could not control his impulses. On 27 March 1969, he saw a girl in a miniskirt and high-heeled shoes while driving past a downtown department store. He quickly parked and chased after her, but he lost her in the crowd. On his way back to his car, he saw Karen Sprinkler in the parking lot. He pulled a gun and told her to come with him. Too frightened to scream, she followed him back to his station wagon. He promised not to hurt her.

Brudos's wife and children were away, so he knew he could take his pleasure without risk. Karen said that she would do anything he wanted, provided he did not kill her. He asked if she was a virgin. She said she was – and that she was having her period. It made no difference. He made her lie down on the garage floor and raped her.

Afterwards, she wanted to go to the toilet. He let her into the house to use the bathroom, then took her back into the garage where he forced her to pose in underwear and high-heeled shoes while he took pictures of her.

Finally, he tied her hands behind her back and put a rope around her neck. He asked her if it was too tight. She said it was, so he threw the end over a beam and pulled it slowly until she suffocated. Brudos recalled with relish how Karen had slowly been winched clear of the ground. 'She kicked a little and died,' he said. Brudos then violated the corpse, cut off the breasts and dumped the body in the river.

Linda Salee was buying presents for her boyfriend's birthday when Brudos approached her. He flashed a fake police ID and told her he was arresting her for shoplifting.

Linda protested her innocence but let Brudos drive her back to his garage. He parked the car inside and ordered her to follow him across the yard into the house. At this moment, Brudos's wife came out on to the porch. Brudos signalled Linda to stand still. A single scream at that moment could have saved her life. Instead Linda stood there quietly and, in the dark, Darcie could not see her.

Brudos took Linda back into the garage. He tied her up, then went into the house for dinner. When he returned, she had freed herself, but amazingly she had not picked up the telephone in the garage and called the police. 'She was just waiting for me, I guess,' Brudos told the police with a self-satisfied smile.

Suddenly, when it was too late, Linda fought back. But the petite 22-year-old was quickly overpowered by the overweight Brudos. He put a leather strap around her neck and began choking her.

'Why are you doing this to me?' she gasped.

He was in the act of raping her when she died.

Brudos decided that the girl needed to be punished. He strung her up by the neck on the hook on the ceiling. He stabbed two hypodermic syringes into her sides and ran an electric current through them. He wanted to make her dance, but all he succeeded in doing was burning her flesh.

He kept her body for another day and raped it again. He did not cut off the breasts because he did not like pink nipples, preferring brown. He made a mould of them though, and dumped the body in the Long Tom River.

In the garage, detectives found Brudos's collection of underwear and his photographs of the missing girls – hanging from the ceiling or posing in underwear. In one, Brudos had inadvertently caught his own reflection in the mirror. A female breast, hardened with epoxy, was found adorning the mantelshelf in the living room.

Brudos pleaded guilty to four counts of murder and was sentenced to life imprisonment. There, he proved to have a gift for electronics and now runs the prison's computer systems. As a reward, he is allowed to send out for mail-order catalogues showing high-heeled shoes and women modelling underwear.

It was alleged that Mrs Brudos had abetted her husband forcing women into their home. She was charged with being his accomplice in the murder of Karen Sprinkler, but was acquitted.

The body of Jan Whitney surfaced a year later. It was so badly decomposed that it had to be identified by dental records. Linda Slawson's body has never been found.

Chapter 13

Moral Crusade

Jack the Ripper has been the inspiration for many homicidal maniacs bent on a moral crusade to rid the streets of prostitutes. The name 'Jack the Ripper' was his own invention. Compared with his emulators, his death toll was low. He killed for certain just five women in a ten-week period from 31 August to 9 November in 1888, though he may have been responsible for the death of four more. All five had their throats slashed and were disembowelled and mutilated. The attacks were sexual in nature. The killer paid special attention to the destruction of the female sexual organs.

The murders all took place in the East End of London where, in 1888, there were sixty-two brothels and 233 boarding houses catering to prostitutes and their clients. Pox-ridden, middle-aged alcoholics also offered sexual favours standing up in alleyways and doorways.

On the night of 3 April 1888, 45-year-old Emma Elizabeth Smith solicited a well-dressed gentleman. Later that night, she collapsed in the arms of a constable, saying that she had been attacked by four men. They had cut off her ear and shoved a foreign object up her vagina. She died a few hours later, perhaps the first victim of the Ripper.

Martha Tabram was stabbed to death on 7 August 1888. There were thirty-nine frenzied wounds on her body, mainly around the breasts and sexual organs. The police assumed that Smith and Tabram, like the Ripper's later victims, had turned their backs in the street and hoisted their skirts for an entry from behind when they were attacked.

The first woman known to have been killed for certain by the Ripper was 42-year-old Polly Nichols. Her body was found in Buck's Row at 3.15 am on 31 August 1988. She did not cry out. The attack took place under the window of a sleeping woman who did not wake. The body revealed that she fought for her life, but was overcome by her attacker. Her throat had been slashed twice, so deeply that she had almost been decapitated. There were deep wounds around her vagina, but no organs had been removed. Pathologists examining the corpse concluded that the killer had some medical knowledge.

Polly had almost certainly turned her back on her killer for an assignation there in the street. While she was turned away from him, he pulled out a knife, put it to her throat and pushed her forward onto it as he slashed her. This explained the depth of the wound and would have meant that all the blood would have sprayed forward and not over the assailant, leaving him clean to make his escape unnoticed.

The police realised that they had on their hands a maniac motivated by a hatred of prostitutes. Detectives were sent out into the East End, searching for men who mistreated prostitutes. The name 'Leather Apron' came up several times in the investigation. A shoemaker called Pizer was picked up. He used a leather apron and sharp knives in his trade, but his family swore that he was at home on the three occasions women had been attacked.

On 8 September 1888, 47-year-old Annie Chapman was

bragging in the pubs of Whitechapel that the killer would meet his match if he ever came near her. She was wrong. Later, she was seen talking to a 'gentleman' in the street. They seemed to strike up a bargain and went off arm in arm. Half an hour later, she was found dead in an alleyway. Her head was only connected to her body by a strand of flesh. Her intestines were found thrown over her right shoulder, the flesh from her lower abdomen over her left. Her kidneys and ovaries had been removed. The killer had taken them with him. He had also left a piece of leather near the corpse. The police realised that this was all too convenient. The killer was obviously an avid reader of the newspapers and had read of the arrest of Pizer. He also left a blood soaked envelope with the crest of the Sussex Regiment on it. It had been reported that Martha Tabram had been seen in the company of a soldier shortly before her death and the newspapers said that her wounds could have been caused by a bayonet or army knife.

Three weeks after the death of Annie Chapman, the Central News Agency received a letter that gloated over the murder and the false clues. His author regretted that the letter was not written in the victim's blood, which had gone 'thick like glue', and promised to send the ear of the next victim. The letter was signed 'Jack the Ripper'.

On 30 September 1888, the Central News Agency received another letter from the Ripper, apologising that he had not enclosed an ear – but promising that he was going to do a 'double'.

At 1 am that night, 45-year-old 'Long Liz' Stride, a Swedish prostitute whose real name was Elizabeth Gustsaafadotter, was found in a pool of blood with her throat slashed. The delivery man who discovered her body heard the attacker escaping over the cobblestones.

Around that same time, 43-year-old prostitute Catherine Eddowes was being thrown out of Bishopsgate Police Station where she had been held for creating a drunken disturbance. As she walked towards Houndsditch she met Jack the Ripper. He cut her throat, slashed her face and cut her ear, though it was still attached. He removed her intestines and threw them over her shoulder. The left kidney was missing altogether.

The murder of two women in one night sent London into a panic. Queen Victoria demanded action, but the police seemed powerless. East End resident George Lusk set up the Whitechapel Vigilance Committee to patrol the streets. Two weeks later, Mr Lusk received a small package through the post. It contained half of Catherine Eddowes's kidney. The other half had been fried and eaten, according to the accompanying note which was again signed 'Jack the Ripper'.

Queen Victoria concluded that the Ripper must be a foreigner. No Englishman would behave in such a beastly way, she said. A cabinet meeting was called to discuss the matter. They ordered checks on all the ships tied up in the London docks. This proved to be a huge waste of police manpower.

The last victim that was certainly the Ripper's was unlike the others. She was young, just twenty-four, and attractive. Her name was Mary Kelly and she only turned occasionally to prostitution to pay the rent. She was killed indoors and had cried out.

On the night of 9 November 1888, she had been seen on the street soliciting a 'well-dressed gentleman'. Sometime between 3.30 and 4 am' the woman sleeping in the room above Kelly's heard Kelly scream: 'Oh, murder.' In the morning, the rent man found her mutilated corpse.

Being indoors and undisturbed, the Ripper had been able to spend more than an hour on his grisly task. Mary Kelly's clothes were found neatly folded on a chair so it is thought that she took her 'gentleman' back to her room and undressed herself ready for sex. It was then that he pulled his knife. This time, she had been facing him, saw the murder weapon and cried out. He slashed her throat, almost decapitating her, but blood splashed on his clothes, which were found burnt in the stove.

Then he set about her corpse. Both breasts were cut off and placed on the table, along with her nose and flesh from her thighs and legs. Her left arm was severed and was left hanging by the flesh. Her forehead and legs had been stripped of flesh and her abdomen had been slashed open. She was three months pregnant at the time of the attack. Her intestines and liver had, once again, been removed and her hand was shoved into the gaping hole left. There was blood around the window where the Ripper was thought to have escaped, naked except for a long cloak and boots.

Other murders followed that may have been the work of the Ripper. The headless corpse of Elizabeth Jackson, a prostitute working in the Chelsea area, was found floating in the Thames in June 1889. In July that year, Alice McKenzie, a prostitute in Whitechapel, was found with her throat cut from car to ear and her sexual organs cut out. And street walker Frances Cole, also known as 'Carroty Nell' because of her flaming red hair, was found in Whitechapel with her throat cut and with slashes around her abdomen. A policeman saw a man stooped over the body, but he ran away before the constable could get a good look at him.

The description of the Ripper that has seized the public's imagination comes from a friend of Mary Kelly's who saw her with a man that night. He was five feet six inches tall, about thirty-five, well-dressed with a gold watch chain dangling from his waistcoat pocket. Kelly was seen in conversation with him.

'You will be all right for what I have told you,' he said.

'All right my dear,' she replied, taking him by the arm.

'Come along, you will be comfortable.'

A few hours later a chestnut vendor saw a man matching that description wearing a long cloak and silk hat, his thin moustache turned up at the ends and carrying a black bag.

'Have you heard there has been another murder?' he said.

'I have,' the chestnut seller replied.

'I know more of it than you do,' said the man as he walked away. There are a huge number of theories as to the identity of the Ripper. The police had 176 suspects at the time. The most popular is the mad Russian physician Dr Alexander Pedachenko who worked under an assumed name in an East London clinic that treated several of the victims. A document naming him as the Ripper was said to have been found in the basement of Rasputin's house in St Petersburg after the mad monk's assassination in 1916. Some have pointed out that Rasputin's house did not have a basement.

A Dr Stanley is another popular suspect. He is said to have contracted syphilis from a Whitechapel prostitute and thus swore vengeance on them all. He fled to Buenos Aires where he died in 1929, after confessing all to a student.

V. Kosminski, a Polish Jew who lived in Whitechapel, threatened to slice up prostitutes. He went insane and died in an asylum. East European Jewish immigrants, who were unpopular in London at the time, were regularly blamed for the Ripper killings. It was said that the murders were ritual Jewish slaughters performed by a shochet, a butcher who kills animals according to Talmudic law. This theory was given some credence by the confused message 'The juwes are not the men that will be blamed: for nothing' that was scrawled on a wall in Whitechapel after the murder of Catherine Eddowes. 'Juwes' the Masonic spelling of 'Jews' also gave rise to the theory that the murders had been some Masonic rite. The police commissioner of Sir Charles Warren was himself a high ranking Mason. He had the graffito removed, he said, to prevent inflaming anti-Jewish feelings in the area. Sir Charles Warren resigned after the murder of Mary Kelly, admitting his utter failure to solve the case.

Another Polish immigrant, Severin Klosowich – alias

George Chapman – was also suspected. He was a barber's surgeon in Whitechapel and kept sharp knives for bloodletting and for the removal of warts and moles. He poisoned three of his mistresses and went to the gallows in 1903.

Thomas Cutbush was arrested after the murder of Frances Cole for stabbing women in the buttocks. He died too in an insane asylum. Newspaper reporter Roslyn D'Onston, a failed doctor and drug addict, was said to have killed the women to write about the murders for his paper. It is said that his stories carried details that the police never released.

The insomniac G. Wentworth Bell Smith who lived at 27 Sun Street, off Finsbury Square, was a suspect. He railed against prostitutes, saying 'They should all be drowned'.

Frederick Bailey Deeming confessed to the Ripper's murders. He had killed his wife and children in England, then fled to Australia where he killed a second wife. He was about to kill a third when he was arrested. It is thought that his confession was an attempt to delay, if not evade, the gallows in Australia.

Dr Thomas Neill Cream poisoned prostitutes in London and went on to murder more in the US. He is said to have told his hangman 'I am Jack . . .' as the trap was opened.

The police's prime suspect was Montague John Druitt, an Oxford graduate from a once-wealthy family. After failing as a barrister, Druitt became a school teacher, but he was a homosexual and was dismissed for molesting a boy. He moved to Whitechapel where he was seen wandering the streets. In December 1888, his body was fished out of the Thames. There were stones in his pockets, he had drowned himself.

Salvation Army founder William Booth's secretary was also a suspect after saying 'Carroty Nell will be the next to go' a few days before the slaying of Frances Cole. Alcoholic railway worker Thomas Salder was arrested after the murder of Alice McKenzie. He also knew Frances Cole, but was released due to lack of evidence.

Sir Arthur Conan Doyle, creator of Sherlock Holmes, believed that the Ripper was a woman. His theory was that 'Jill the Ripper' was a midwife who had gone mad after being sent to prison for performing illegal abortions.

The spiritualist William Lees staged a seance for Queen Victoria to try and discover who the Ripper was. The results frightened him so much he fled to the Continent. The Ripper, he believed, was none other than the Queen's physician Sir William Gull.

Gull's papers were examined by Dr Thomas Stowell. They named Prince Eddy, the grandson of Queen Victoria who died of syphilis before he could ascend to the throne, as the Ripper, Stowell says. Another suspect is James Kenneth Stephen, a homosexual lover of Prince Eddy. The two of them were frequent visitors to a homosexual club in Whitechapel.

The painter Frank Miles, a friend of Oscar Wilde's, has also been named. But the truth is the identity of Jack the Ripper will probably never be known.

Nearly ninety years later, Peter Sutcliffe, the Yorkshire Ripper, picked up where Jack – or Jill – left off. By the time he was caught, twenty women had been savagely attacked, thirteen brutally murdered and a whole community was virtually under siege. In a reign of terror spanning nearly six years, he managed to elude the biggest police squad that has ever assembled to catch one man.

It started on 30 October 1975 when a Leeds milkman on his rounds saw a shapeless bundle in a bleak recreation ground. With Bonfire Night just a week away, he thought it was only a Guy. But he went over to investigate anyway. He found a woman sprawled on the ground, her hair matted with blood, her body exposed. Her jacket and blouse had been torn open, her bra pulled up. Her slacks had been pulled down below her knees and in her chest and stomach there were fourteen stab wounds.

The milkman didn't see the massive wound on the back of her head that had actually caused her death. The victim had been attacked from behind. Two vicious blows had been delivered by a heavy, hammer-like implement, smashing her skull. The stab wounds were inflicted after she was dead.

The body belonged to a 28-year-old mother of three, Wilma McCann. She regularly hitchhiked home after a night on the town. She had died just 100 yards from her home, a council house in Scott Hall Avenue. Post-mortem blood tests showed that she had consumed 12 to 14 measures of spirits on the night of her death.

Although her clothes had been interfered with, her knickers were still in place and she had not been raped. There seemed to be no overt sexual motive for her murder. Her purse was missing. So, in the absence of any other motive, the police treated her killing as a callous by-product of robbery.

This changed when a second killing occurred in the area of Chapeltown, the red-light district of Leeds, three months later. Not all the women who worked there were professional prostitutes. Some housewives sold sex for a little extra cash. Others, such as 42-year-old Emily Jackson, were enthusiastic amateurs who did it primarily for fun. She lived with her husband and three children in the respectable Leeds suburb of Churwell. On 20 January 1976, Emily and her husband went to the Gaiety pub on the Roundhay Road, the venue for the Chapeltown irregulars and their prospective clientele. Emily left her husband in the main lounge and went hunting for business. An hour later, she was seen getting into a Land Rover in the car park. At closing time, her husband drank up and took a taxi home alone. His wife, he thought, had found a client who wanted her for the night.

Emily Jackson's body was found the next morning huddled under a coat on open ground. Like Wilma McCann, her breasts were exposed and her pants left on. Again, she had been killed by two massive blows to the head with a heavy hammer. Her neck, breasts and stomach had also been stabbed – this time over fifty times. Her back had been gouged with a Phillips screwdriver and the impression of a heavy ribbed Wellington boot was stamped on her right thigh.

The post mortem indicated that Emily Jackson had had sex before the attack, not necessarily with the murderer. Once again, there seemed to be no real motive. And the killer had left only one real clue: he had size seven shoes.

Over a year later, on 5 February 1977, 28-year-old part-time prostitute Irene Richardson left her tawdry rooming house in Chapeltown half-an-hour before midnight to go dancing. The following morning, a jogger in Soldier's Field, a public playing-field just a short car ride from Chapeltown, saw a body slumped on the ground and stopped to see what the matter was. It was Irene Richardson. She lay face down. Three massive blows had shattered her skull. Her skirt and tights were torn off. Her coat was draped over her buttocks and her calf-length boots had been removed from her feet and laid neatly across her thighs. Again, her neck and torso were studded with knife wounds. The post mortem indicated that she had not had sex and had died only half-an-hour after leaving her lodgings.

After the murder of Irene Richardson, the police were able to link the three cases. They were plainly the work of a serial killer and the parallel with Jack the Ripper quickly sprang into the public imagination. The murderer of Wilma McCann, Emily Jackson and Irene Richardson soon became known as the Yorkshire Ripper.

The girls of Chapeltown heeded the warning. They moved in droves to Manchester, London and Glasgow. Those who could not travel so far from home began plying their trade in nearby Bradford. But the next victim, Patricia 'Tina' Atkinson, was a Bradford girl. She lived just around the corner from the thriving red-light district in Oak Lane. On 23

April 1977, she went to her local pub, The Carlisle, for a drink with her friends. She reeled out just before closing time. When she was not seen all next day, people assumed she was at home, sleeping it off.

The following evening, friends dropped round and found the door to her flat unlocked. Inside, they found her dead on her bed covered with blankets. She had been attacked as she came into the flat. Four hammer blows had smashed into the back of her head. She had been flung on the bed and her clothes pulled off. She had been stabbed in the stomach seven times and the left side of her body had been slashed to ribbons. There was a size seven Wellington boot print on the sheet.

The man the footprint belonged to was Peter Sutcliffe. Like Jack the Ripper before him, he was on a moral crusade to rid the streets of prostitutes.

He had been a timid child and inscrutable young man, who was always regarded as being somehow different. The eldest of John and Kathleen Sutcliffe's six children, he was born in Bingley, a dour town just six miles north of Bradford. He was small and weedy. Bullied at school, he clung to his mother's skirts.

His younger brothers inherited their father's appetite for life, the opposite sex and the consumption of large quantities of beer. Peter liked none of these things. Although he took no interest in girls, he spent hours preening himself in the bathroom. He later took up body building.

Leaving school at fifteen, he took a job as a grave-digger at a cemetery in Bingley. He regularly joked about having 'thousands of people below me where I work now'. He developed a macabre sense of humour during his three years there. Once he pretended to be a corpse. He lay down on a slab, threw a shroud over himself and started making moaning noises when his workmates appeared. They called him 'Jesus' because of his beard.

At his trial Sutcliffe claimed that he had heard the voice of God while he was working at the cemetery. He said he was digging a grave when he heard a voice coming from a cross-shaped headstone. The voice told him to go out onto the streets and kill prostitutes.

Despite Peter Sutcliffe's youthful good looks, girls were not attracted to him. His first proper girlfriend, Sonia was a 16-year-old schoolgirl when he met her in the Royal Standard, his local pub. Sonia suffered the same introversion as Peter. On Sundays, they would sit in the front room, lost in their own conversation. Sonia would speak to other members of the Sutcliffe family only when it was absolutely unavoidable.

A devout Catholic, Peter was devastated when it was discovered that his mother was having an affair with a neighbour, a local policeman. His father arranged for the children, including Peter and bride-to-be Sonia, to be present at a Bingley hotel for a humiliating confrontation. His mother arrived in the bar believing she was meeting her boyfriend, only to be greeted by her husband and children. He forced her to show the family the new night-dress she had bought for the occasion. This was particularly painful for Peter who had discovered earlier that Sonia also had a secret boyfriend.

Later that year, 1969, Sutcliffe carried out his first known attack. He hit a Bradford prostitute over the head with a stone in a sock following a row over a £10 note. Psychiatrists later said that the discovery of his mother's affair triggered his psychosis.

After an eight-year courtship, Peter and Sonia married. They spent the first three years of their married life living with Sonia's parents, then they moved to a large detached house in Heaton, a middle-class suburb of Bradford, which they kept immaculate.

On the evening of Saturday, 25 June 1977, Peter Sutcliffe dropped his wife off at the Sherrington nursing home where she worked nights. With his neighbours Ronnie and Peter Barker, he went on a pub crawl around Bradford, ending up at the Dog in the Pound where an ex-sailor in drag worked behind the bar. At closing time, they went to get some fish and chips.

It was well past midnight when he dropped the Barker brothers at their front door. But instead of parking his white Ford Corsair outside his house, Sutcliffe drove off down the main road towards Leeds. At around 2 am, he saw a lone girl wearing a gingham skirt in the street light of Chapeltown Road. As she passed the Hayfield pub and turned left down Reginald Terrace, Sutcliffe parked his car, got out and began to follow her down the quiet side street.

The girl's body was found lying by a wall the next morning by a group of children on their way into the adventure playground in Reginald Terrace. She had been struck on the back of the head, then dragged 20 yards and hit twice more. She was also stabbed once in the back and repeatedly through the chest. The trademarks were unmistakable.

However, the victim was not a prostitute. Jayne McDonald was sixteen, had just left school and was working in the shoe department of a local supermarket. On the night of her death, she had been out with friends in Leeds. When she was attacked, she was on her way back to her parents' home, which was just a few hundred yards from where her body was found.

The murder of a teenage girl gave the investigation new impetus. By September, the police had interviewed almost 700 residents in the area and taken 3,500 statements, many of them from prostitutes who worked in the area.

Two weeks after the killing of Jayne McDonald, the Ripper savagely attacked Maureen Long on some waste ground near her home in Bradford. By some miracle she survived, but the description of her assailant was too hazy to help the inquiry.

The staff of the investigation was increased to 304 full-time officers who had soon interviewed 175,000 people, taken 12,500 statements and checked 10,000 vehicles. The problem was that they had no idea of the type of man they were looking for. Certainly no one would have suspected long-distance lorry driver Peter Sutcliffe. The 31-year-old was a polite and mild-mannered neighbour, a hard-working and trusted employee, a good son and a loyal husband. He was the sort of man who did jobs around the house or tinkered with his car at weekends. Nothing about him suggested that he was a mass murderer.

Those who knew him would even have been surprised if they had seen him out picking up prostitutes. But that's what he did, regularly. On Saturday, 1 October 1977, Jean Jordan climbed into Sutcliffe's new red Ford Corsair near her home in Moss Side, Manchester. She took £5 in advance and directed him to some open land two miles away that was used by prostitutes with their clients. They were a few yards away from the car when Sutcliffe smashed a hammer down onto Jean Jordan's skull. He hit her again and again, eleven times in all. He dragged her body into some bushes, but another car arrived and he had to make a quick getaway.

As he drove back to Bradford, Sutcliffe realised that he had left a vital clue on the body. The £5 note he had given Jean Jordan was brand new. It had come directly from his wage packet and could tie him to the dead girl.

For eight long days, he waited nervously. In that time, there was nothing in the press about the body being found. So he risked returning to Moss Side to find the note. Despite a frantic search, he could not find Jean Jordan's handbag. In frustration, he started attacking her body with a broken pane of glass. He even tried to cut off the head to remove his hammer blow signature. But the glass was not sharp enough to sever the spine. In the end, he gave up, kicked the body several times and drove home.

The following day, an allotment owner found Jean Jordan's naked body. The damage to her head made her unrecognisable and there was no evidence to identify her among her scattered clothing She was eventually identified from a fingerprint on a lemonade bottle she had handled before leaving home for the last time.

The police also found the £5 note. They set about tracing it. In three months they interviewed 5,000 men. One of them was Peter Sutcliffe. But after leaving Sutcliffe's well-appointed house, detectives filed a short report which left him free to go about his gruesome business.

Sutcliffe's next victim was eighteen-year-old Helen Rytka, who shared a miserable room by a flyover in Huddersfield with her twin sister Rita. The two of them worked as a pair in the red-light district around Great Northern Street. They concentrated on the car trade.

The Yorkshire Ripper murders scared them, so they had devised a system which they thought would keep them safe. They based themselves outside a public lavatory. When they were picked up separately, they took the number of the client's car. They each gave their client precisely twenty minutes and then returned to the toilet at a set time. But their system went terribly wrong.

On the snowy night of Tuesday 31 January 1978, Helen arrived back at the rendezvous five minutes early. At 9.25 pm, a bearded man in a red Ford Corsair offered her the chance of a quick £5. She thought she could perform her services quickly and make it back to the rendezvous before Rita returned. She could not. Rita never saw her again.

Helen took her client to nearby Garrard's timber yard. There were two men there, so he could not kill her straight away. Instead, Sutcliffe had to have sexual intercourse with her in the back of the car. When they were finished, the men were gone. As she got out of the back seat to return to the front of the car, Sutcliffe swung at her with his hammer. He missed and hit the door of the car. His second blow struck her on the head. Then he hit her five times more. The walls of the foreman's shed a few feet away were splattered with blood.

Sutcliffe dragged Helen's body into a woodpile and hid it there. Her bra and black polo-neck sweater were pushed up above her breasts. Her socks were left on, but the rest of her clothes were scattered over a wide area. Her black lace panties were found the next day by a lorry driver, pinned to the shed door.

Back at the lavatory, Rita was desperately worried, but fear of the police prevented her from reporting her sister's disappearance for three days. A police Alsatian found the hidden body. It had been horribly mutilated. There were three gaping wounds in the chest where she had been stabbed repeatedly.

The Ripper's latest victim had disappeared from a busy street. Over a hundred passers-by were traced, and all but three cars and one stocky, fair-haired man were eliminated. The police appealed on the radio to any wife, mother or girlfriend who suspected that they were living with the Ripper. No one came forward.

A few weeks later, a passerby spotted an arm sticking out from under an overturned sofa on wasteland in Bradford's red-light district. He thought it was a tailor's dummy but the putrid aroma sent him rushing to a telephone.

The body was that of 22-year-old Yvonne Pearson. She was a high-class prostitute, who serviced a rich businessman trade in most of Britain's cities. She had been killed two months earlier, ten days before Helen Rytka. The killing bore all the hallmarks of the Ripper. A hammer blow to the head had smashed her skull. Her bra and jumper were pulled up exposing her breasts, and her chest had been jumped on repeatedly. Her black flared slacks had been pulled down. Horsehair from the sofa was stuffed in her mouth.

Yvonne Pearson had spoken of her fear of the Ripper only

days before she disappeared. On the night of her death, she had left her two daughters with a neighbour. Soon after 9.30 pm, she was seen climbing into a car driven by a bearded man with black, piercing eyes. On the wasteland in nearby Arthington Street, he killed her with a club hammer. Then he dragged her body to the abandoned sofa and jumped on her until her ribs cracked.

Although he had hidden her body, the killer seemed concerned that it had not been found and returned to make it more visible. He tucked a copy of the *Daily Mirror*, from four weeks after her death, under her arm.

Two months after Yvonne Pearson's body was found, the Yorkshire Ripper attacked 41-year-old Vera Millward. The Spanish-born mother of seven children, Vera had come to England after the war as a domestic help. She lived with a Jamaican and had resorted to prostitution in Manchester's Moss Side to help her support her family. On the night of Tuesday, 16 May, she went out to get pain-killers from the hospital for her chronic stomach pains. She died in a well-lit part of the grounds of Manchester Royal Infirmary. Sutcliffe hit her three times on the head with a hammer and then slashed her across the stomach. Her body was discovered by a gardener the next morning on a rubbish pile in the corner of the car park.

Three months after Vera Millward's death, the police visited Sutcliffe again because his car registration number had cropped up during special checks in Leeds and Bradford. They returned to question him about the tyres on his car. They were looking for treads that matched tracks at the scene of Irene Richardson's murder, 21 months earlier.

As always, Sutcliffe was helpful and unruffled, giving them absolutely no reason to suspect him. They never even asked Sutcliffe for his blood group – the Ripper's was rare – or his shoe size which was unusually small for a man.

Suddenly the Ripper's killing spree stopped. For eleven

months he dropped out of sight. The police believed that he had committed suicide, taking his identity with him to the grave. This man was eerily similar to the disappearance of Jack the Ripper ninety years before.

But Sutcliffe was not dead. Nor could he contain his desire to murder. On the night of Wednesday, 4 April 1979, he drove to Halifax. Around midnight, he got out of his car and accosted nineteen-year-old Josephine Whitaker as she walked across Savile Park playing fields. They spoke briefly. As they moved away from the street lamps, he smashed the back of her head with a hammer and dragged her body into the shadows. Her body was found the next morning.

Like Jayne MacDonald, Josephine Whitaker was not a prostitute. She lived at home with her family and worked as a clerk in the headquarters of the Halifax Building Society. Now no woman felt safe on the streets after dark.

Two weeks before Josephine Whitaker died, a letter arrived at the police station. It was postmarked Sunderland, 23 March 1979. Handwriting experts confirmed that it came from the same person that had sent two previous letters purporting to come from the Yorkshire Ripper. This one mentioned that Vera Millward had stayed in hospital. The police believed, wrongly, that this information could only have come from Vera herself. On this basis they leapt to the conclusion that the writer of the three letters was indeed the Ripper.

The letter said that the next victim would not be in Bradford's Chapeltown district as it was 'too bloody hot there' because of the efforts of 'curserred coppers'. This odd misspelling so closely aped the original Ripper's notes that it should have rang warning bells.

Traces of engineering oil had been found on one of the letters. Similar traces were found on Josephine Whitaker's body. The police called a press conference. The public were asked to come forward with any information they had about anybody who might have been in Sunderland on the days the letters were posted. The response was overwhelming, but all it added up to was more useless information to be checked, analysed and filed.

Then, on the morning of 18 June 1979, two months after Josephine Whitaker's death, a buff-coloured envelope arrived. It was addressed in the same handwriting and contained a cassette tape. On it, there was a 257-word message in a broad Geordie accent.

A huge publicity campaign was mounted. The public could dial in and listen to the 'Geordie Ripper Tape', in the hope that someone might recognise the voice. Within a few days, more than 50,000 people had called.

Language experts confirmed the accent as genuine Wearside, and pinned it down to Castletown, a small tightly knit suburb of Sunderland. Eleven detectives were installed in a Sunderland hotel and 100 officers combed the town. Only 4,000 people lived in Castletown, but the police could not find their man – because he was a cruel hoaxer who had a cast-iron alibi. To this day, no one knows who the Geordie Ripper was.

In July 1979, Detective-Constable Laptew visited Sutcliffe again. His car had been spotted in the red-light district of Bradford on thirty-six separate occasions. This time Laptew felt suspicious of Sutcliffe but, because all eyes were focused on the Geordie tape, his report was not followed up and Sutcliffe went back to Bradford for his eleventh victim.

On Saturday, 1 September 1979, Sutcliffe cruised the streets around Little Horton, a residential area. At about 1 am, he saw Barbara Leach, a student, moving away from a group of friends outside the Mannville Arms. Just 200 yards from the pub, he attacked Barbara Leach and dragged her body into a backyard. He stabbed her eight times, stuffed her body into a dustbin and slung an old carpet over it. It was found the following afternoon.

Two high-ranking officers from Scotland Yard were sent to Yorkshire but got nowhere. A taskforce from Manchester reviewed the £5 note inquiry. They narrowed the field down to 270 suspects, but could get no further.

Like everyone else in Yorkshire, Sutcliffe spoke to family and friends about the Ripper. He would make a point of picking up Sonia from work to protect her and told a workmate: 'Whoever is doing all these murders has a lot to answer for.' Once his colleagues at the depot made a bet that he was the Ripper – but Sutcliffe just laughed and said nothing.

The Ripper took another break of nearly a year. Then on Thursday, 18 August 1980, he struck for the twelfth time. The victim was Marguerite Walls, a 47-year-old civil servant. She was working late at the Department of Education and Science in Leeds, tidying up loose ends before going on a ten-day holiday. She left at 10 pm to walk home. Her body was found two days later, under a mound of grass clippings in the garden of a magistrate's house. She had been bludgeoned and strangled, but her body had not been mutilated so the police did not realise that she was one of the Ripper's victims.

Three months later, Sutcliffe had just finished eating a chicken dinner when he saw Jacqueline Hill, a language student at the University of Leeds, get off the bus outside a Kentucky Fried Chicken outlet. His fingers were still greasy from his supper when he viciously struck her down. He dragged her body to the waste ground behind the shops and attacked it savagely. Death had struck Jacqueline so suddenly that one of her eyes had remained open. Sutcliffe stabbed it repeatedly with a rusty Phillips screw-driver specially sharpened into a fine point.

The Home Office appointed a special squad to solve the case. But six weeks after Jacqueline Hill's murder, it reached the same conclusion as the West Yorkshire force – it had no idea how to crack the case. What was needed was a little bit of luck.

On 2 January 1981, Sergeant Robert Ring and Police Constable Robert Hydes started their evening shift by cruising along Melbourne Avenue in Sheffield's red-light district. They saw Olivia Reivers climbing into a Rover V8 3500 and decided to investigate. The driver – a bearded man – identified himself as Peter Williams. He said he wanted no trouble. Then he scrambled out of the car and asked if he could relieve himself. He went over to the bushes lining the street and, while pretending to take a pee, dropped a ball-peen hammer and sharp knife which he kept in a special pocket of his car coat. The police did not notice this as Olivia Reivers was remonstrating loudly with the men who had just saved her life, complaining that they were ruining her livelihood.

But by the time the man had strolled back to his car, the police had discovered that the number plates were false. He was taken to the police station where he admitted his name was Peter William Sutcliffe.

During his interview, Sutcliffe said his main worry was that the police would tell his wife that he had been picked up with a prostitute. Otherwise, he was calm and forthcoming. He readily admitted that he had stolen the number plates from a scrapyard in Dewsbury. The police even let him go to the lavatory alone, where he hid a second knife in the cistern.

There was no real reason to suspect Sutcliffe, but the police had so little to go on that, when any man was caught with a prostitute, his details had to be forwarded to the West Yorkshire Police before he could be released. Sutcliffe was locked up for the night. The next morning he was taken, unprotesting, to Dewsbury police station.

There, Sutcliffe was a chatty, eager interviewee. In passing, he mentioned that he had been interviewed by the Ripper Squad about the £5 note and that he had also visited Bradford's red-light district.

Dewsbury police called the Ripper Squad in Leeds. Detective Sergeant Des O'Boyle discovered that Sutcliffe's

211

name had come up several times in the course of the investigation. He drove to Dewsbury. When he called his boss, Detective Inspector John Boyle, in Leeds that evening, he told Boyle that Sutcliffe was blood group B – the rare blood group the police knew the Ripper had. Sutcliffe was locked in his cell for a second night.

Meanwhile, Sergeant Ring heard one of his colleagues casually mention that the man he had arrested was being interviewed by detectives from the Ripper Squad. Ring rushed back to Melbourne Avenue. Hidden in the bushes there, he found a ball-peen hammer and a knife.

Sonia Sutcliffe was questioned and the house was searched. Then, early on Sunday afternoon, Boyle told Sutcliffe that they had found a hammer and knife in Sheffield. Sutcliffe, who had been talkative up to this point, fell silent.

'I think you're in trouble, serious trouble,' said Boyle. Sutcliffe finally spoke.

'I think you are leading up to the Yorkshire Ripper,' he said.

Boyle nodded.

'Well,' Sutcliffe said, 'that's me.'

Sutcliffe's confession took almost 17 hours to complete. He said that he began killing after a Bradford prostitute cheated him out of £10 in 1969. At that time, he mentioned nothing about hearing a voice from God.

Sixteen weeks later, Sutcliffe stood trial at the Old Bailey. The Crown Prosecution, defence counsel and Attorney General Sir Michael Havers agreed that Sutcliffe was mentally ill, suffering from paranoid schizophrenia. But the judge would have none of this. He told both counsels that the jury would listen to the evidence and decide whether Sutcliffe was a murderer or a mad man.

Sutcliffe pleaded guilty to manslaughter. He was calm and self-assured, even managing a laugh when he recalled that during his questioning about the size seven Wellington-boot imprinted on Emily Jackson's thigh and Tina Atkinson's bedsheet the policeman interviewing him had not noticed he was wearing the boots. He also chimed that he had been acting on instructions from God to 'clean the streets' of prostitutes.

The jury would have none of it. They found him guilty of thirteen murders and he was sentenced to life imprisonment, with a recommendation that he should serve at least thirty years.

In 2006 in Suffolk the police thought they had another Ripper on their hands. On 2 December, the body of a young woman was found in the water of Belstead Brook at Thorpe's Hill, near Hintlesham, six miles from Ipswich. She was later identified as 25-year-old Gemma Adams and, although she was naked, she had not been sexually assaulted. She was a prostitute and heroin indict, and had last been seen outside the BMW dealers in West End Road in Ipswich on 15 November.

Six days later, on 8 December, police divers found the body of 19-year-old Tania Nicol at Copdock Mill just outside Ipswich. A friend of Gemma Adams, she had been missing since 30 October. Again she was a prostitute, she was naked and there was no evidence of sexual assault. She was addicted to heroin and cocaine.

On 10 December, a third victim was found in woodland by the A14 road near Nacton just outside Ipswich. Her naked body was laid out in the form of a cross. She was identified as 24-year-old Anneli Alderton. The post mortem established that she had been asphyxiated and was about three months pregnant when she died. Although she lived in Colchester with her mother and five-year-old son, she was known to work as a prostitute in Ipswich and the police warned women to stay away from the red light district there.

On 12 December, two more bodies were found in Nacton, near the Levington turn-off from the A1156. One belonged to

29-year-old Annette Nicholls, who had disappeared from Ipswich on 8 December. Again her naked body had been laid out in the shape of a cross and she had not been sexually assaulted. A trained beautician and mother of a young son, she had become a drug addict in the early 2000s and took to prostitution to feed her addiction.

The other body belonged to 24-year-old Paula Clennell. She had last been seen in Ipswich on 10 December. The post mortem said that she had died from 'compression of the throat'. Her three children had already been taken into care and adopted because of her drug addiction. Interviewed on television about the murders shortly before her disappearance, she said that she was a bit wary about getting into cars but continued to work as a prostitute because she needed the money.

It was clear to the police that they were dealing with a serial killer and that the women had been killed elsewhere and dumped where the bodies had been found. On 18 December, the police arrested a 37-year-old supermarket worker, but he was released without charge after four days. The following day, forklift-truck driver Steve Wright was arrested and, on 21 December, was charged with the murder of all five women.

Born in Norfolk in 1958, Wright was the son of a military policeman and, while he was growing up, the family had lived in both Malta and Singapore. Wright was the second of four children, but the marriage was rocky and, in the 1960s, his parents split up. His mother later claimed that his father was violent. She went to live in the US, leaving the children behind. But Wright and his siblings did not get on with his father's second wife, who had two more children.

Wright left school at sixteen with no qualifications. He joined the Merchant Navy as a chef on ferries sailing from Felixstowe. In 1979, he married and had a son called Michael, born in 1983. The couple separated in 1987 and

Wright became a steward on the *QE2*. During shore leave, he started using prostitutes. After he was arrested, ex-prostitute Lindi St Clair – aka Miss Whiplash who boasted of MPs among her clients – claimed that Wright had tried to throttle her in the 1980s.

On board the *QE2*, he met Diane who became his second wife. Taking work ashore, they married at the brewer's insistence when they took over the licence of the Ferry Boat Inn, a pub in the red-light district of Norwich. Within a year, they split up and Wright started another relationship with a barmaid. They had a daughter, but split before the child's first birthday. In 1992, Wright's mother flew over to England for a visit, but Wright fell out with her in a drunken rage.

By then he was a regular customer of massage parlours. His gambling plunged him deeply into debt and, missing his daughter, he tried to commit suicide by gassing himself in his car, but was revived. He was declared bankrupt and his brother noted a profound change in him. Before he had been outgoing, now he was reserved.

Wright sold his remaining possessions to fund a ten-week trip to Thailand. When he returned, he tried to kill himself again, this time with an overdose of pills. Again he survived and moved back in with his father and stepmother in Felixstowe. There he met Pamela Wright, whose surname he shared by coincidence. In 2001, they moved in together and he signed on for driving and labouring jobs with the Gateway Recruitment Agency, which was based in Levington, then moved to Nacton. This is when he became familiar with the area where the victims' bodies were later deposited.

The couple moved to Ipswich and Wright said that he gave up going to massage parlours. But after six months the urge proved too much for him. Pamela began working nights and he found that he could buy sex for as little as £20 from the drug-addict prostitutes who worked on the streets near his home, procuring a dozen in the last three months of 2006.

One woman said she had sex with Wright three days after the fifth victim was discovered, but he was a regular customer and felt safe with him. However, on the night of 18 December, he had changed.

'He pinned me down,' she said. 'He never used to do that. It did scare me when he did it because it wasn't like him. He was a bit nasty. When I heard he had been charged, I thought "Oh my God, I've been in his house. He could've done anything." I never thought it would be him. I thought it would be someone from another country, or just a maniac.'

Wright was remanded in custody and his trial began on 14 January 2008 at Ipswich Crown Court. He pleaded not guilty, although he admitted having sex with all five victims. DNA and fibre evidence also linked Wright to the victims. On 21 February 2008, he was found guilty of all five murders. He was sentenced to life imprisonment with a recommendation that he should never be released.

Since then another sex killer has sought to follow in the footsteps of the Ripper. In October 2008, 48-year-old delivery driver Derek Brown – dubbed the 'Whitechapel Ripper' – was given a double-life sentence with the recommendation that he serve at least thirty years. The court found that, in the summer of 2007, Brown had butchered 29-year-old illegal Chinese immigrant Xiao Mei Guo, who sold counterfeit DVDs on the streets of Whitechapel, and 24-year-old drug addict and prostitute Bonnie Barrett, who worked in the same area. He lured them back to his one-bedroom council flat in Rotherhithe, murdered them, then disposed of their bodies so successfully that neither was found. He refused to tell the police what he had done with them, despite the anguish of their families.

When police searched his flat, traces of blood from both victims were found spattered throughout, even though he had tried to steam clean every surface. They also found a heavy-duty bow saw, a Black and Decker power tool, a waterproof

216

sheet and roll after roll of industrial-strength clingfilm. This was enough for the jury who made legal history by returning the first guilty verdict in trial when the bodies of the victims had not been found.

Brown, who is a convicted sex offender after being jailed in 1989 for rape, is the main suspect for a third murder.

More disturbingly though, the London *Evening Standard* reported that Brown 'was also an avid reader about killers and mass murder and his library card showed that one of his favourite writers was Jack the Ripper author Nigel Cawthorne. Three weeks before he began his murderous spree he had borrowed a library copy of Cawthorne's *Killers: The Most Barbaric Murderers Of Our Time*.

You have been warned.

Chapter 14

Once Is Not Enough

As in the case of Jack the Ripper, the file on Jack the Stripper has never been closed – even though Scotland Yard are sure they know who killed six women in 1964 and left their naked bodies along the banks of the River Thames.

The first body was found under a pontoon at Hammersmith on 2 February 1964. The victim had been strangled and the remnants of her underwear had been shoved down her throat. She was small, five foot two, and apart from her stockings she was naked.

The body was identified as that of Hannah Tailford. She was thirty years old and lived with her boyfriend in West Norwood. She had a three-year-old daughter, an eighteen-month-old son and was pregnant

By day, she worked as a waitress or a cleaner. At night she supplemented her meagre wages by working as a prostitute on the streets of Bayswater. Her record showed four convictions for soliciting.

She had disappeared from her flat ten days before her body was found, though a man and his wife said they saw her on

Charing Cross Road, just two days before. She was depressed and suicidal. They tried to cheer her up.

Forensic experts concluded that she had been dead for just 24 hours when she was found, and they believed that she may have been drowned in a bath or pond before she was dumped in the river. Tide tables showed that she must have entered the Thames at Duke's Meadow in Chiswick, a popular spot for courting couples as well as for prostitutes and their clients.

By interviewing over 700 people in London's underworld of vice, the police discovered that Hannah had been a star turn at sex parties and that she often attended kinky orgies in Mayfair and Kensington. A foreign diplomat known for his perverted tastes had been one of her clients, but he had been out of the country at the time of her disappearance.

This left the police with little to go on. They believed that Hannah had been attacked and sexually assaulted. Her knickers had been shoved in her mouth to stop her screaming as she was killed. But they could not even prove that she had been murdered and the inquest recorded an open verdict.

Hannah Tailford's passing would have been mourned by those who knew her – and dismissed as one of the professional risks of being a prostitute by those who did not – if a death with eerie similarities had not occurred two months later. On 8 April 1964, the body of 26-year-old Irene Lockwood was found among the tangled weeds and branches on the river bank at Duke's Meadow. She was naked.

The pretty young redhead also worked the streets of Bayswater and Notting Hill. She, too, was small like Hannah and had attended kinky parties. She also performed in blue movies. Both girls solicited cab drivers late at night. And both were pregnant when they died.

In both cases, it was impossible to determine how they had died. Marks on the back of Irene's head showed that she could have been attacked from behind and the police believed that she had been killed elsewhere, then brought to Duke's Field.

The police also suspected that both girls were mixed up in a blackmail racket. In Hannah's flat, they found an address book and photographic equipment. Irene's flatmate Vicki Pender, who had been found battered to death a year earlier, had once been beaten up after trying to blackmail a client who had been photographed with her without his knowledge or consent.

But the most striking similarity between the two killings was that the victims were found naked. There was no sign of their clothes, which were never found.

On 24 April, another naked female body was found – this time in an alley off Swyncombe Avenue in Brentford. The victim, 22-year-old Helen Barthelemy, had been strangled, probably from behind.

Three of her front teeth had been extracted after death. It was also established that she had been stripped after her death and fresh tyre marks in the alley way indicated that she had been killed elsewhere and dumped there.

Helen was also a prostitute. Educated in a convent, she had become a stripper in Blackpool. In Liverpool, she had served a prison sentence for luring a man into a trap where he had been robbed. Then she came to London and went on the game. She was known to cater for any sort of perversions, but would often entertain local black men for free because they were more sympathetic than her kinky clientele. One Jamaican man admitted being with her on the night she disappeared, but he had a strong alibi and was quickly ruled out as a suspect.

With three similar killings, the papers caught on to the story. The victims' nudity was obviously the most sensational aspect and the Sundays quickly dubbed the mysterious murderer 'Jack the Stripper'.

Looking back in their records, Scotland Yard found another case that fitted Jack the Stripper's modus operandi. On 8 November 1963, three months before Hannah's murder, the body of 22-year-old Gwynneth Rees had been found buried in a shallow grave in an ash tip near Chiswick Bridge. She was naked except for one stocking. At first, the police thought that she had been the victim of an abortion racket. Then it was discovered that she had been the target of a sexual attack. The body had lain there since May or June and it was thought that she may have been sunbathing when she was attacked. Now, though, it looked like she was another victim of Jack the Stripper.

Kenneth Archibald, a 54-year-old caretaker, walked into Notting Hill police station and confessed to the murder of Irene Lockwood. He was already a suspect. His card had been found in Irene's flat. He said that he had met her in a pub on the night of the murder. On open land near Barnes Bridge they had quarrelled over money. He had lost his temper and put his hands around her throat so she could not scream. He had strangled her accidentally. When she was dead, he had taken her clothes off and rolled her into the river. Then he took her clothes home and burned them.

Archibald, however, said he knew nothing about the murders of Hannah Tailford, Helen Barthelemy or Gwynneth Rees. He was charged with the murder of Irene Lockwood. But when he appeared in the Old Bailey, he retracted his confession. As there was no other evidence against him the jury acquitted him.

The forensic scientists paid special attention to Helen Barthelemy's body. It had not been buried for long, unlike Gwynneth Rees's, nor had it been in contact with water. In fact, it was filthy, as if it had been stored somewhere dirty before it had been dumped.

A minute examination of her skin showed that she was covered from head to toe in tiny flecks of paint. Home Office scientists concluded that her naked body had been kept somewhere near a spray-painting shop.

It was clear that the man who had killed Helen Barthelemy

and the other victims sought the company of prostitutes in the Bayswater area. The police organised an amnesty for girls working the streets in that area and appealed for anyone to come forward who had worried about odd or eccentric clients, especially those who made them strip naked. The girls' response was overwhelming.

Police women went out on the streets, posing as prostitutes. They carried tape recorders in their handbags. The experiences they recorded were often unpleasant, but they failed to move the inquiry forward.

On 14 July 1964, another body was found. At around 5.30 am, a man driving to work down Acton Lane had to brake hard to miss a van speeding out of a cul-de-sac. The police were called. At the end of the cul-de-sac, outside a garage, they found the naked body of Mary Flemming.

Again the murdered girl was a prostitute who worked in the Bayswater area. Her body had been kept for approximately three days after her death. Once more, her clothes had been removed after death and there were tiny flecks of paint all over her naked body.

Mary had been warned of the dangers of continuing to work the streets where Jack the Stripper was on the prowl. She took to carrying a knife in her handbag. It did her no good. Like the other victims, she had been attacked from behind. And no trace of her handbag, the knife or her clothes were ever found.

Pressure on Scotland Yard, by this time, was intense. Over 8,000 people had been interviewed, 4,000 statements had been taken, but the police were still no nearer to finding the culprit. Plain-clothes policemen blanketed the area the murdered girls had worked. But on 25 November 1964, the body of 21-year-old Margaret McGowan was found on some rough ground in Kensington. The hallmarks were unmistakable. McGowan was a prostitute and an associate of society pimp Dr Stephen Ward, who stood trial during the Profumo scandal. She had been strangled and her body was left naked. Her body had lain on the open ground for at least a week, but had been stored somewhere else before being dumped there. Again her skin was covered in tiny flecks of paint.

The evening she went missing, McGowan and a friend had talked about the murders in the Warwick Castle on Portobello Road. The two of them had gone their separate ways, McGowan with a client. McGowan's friend gave a good enough description of McGowan's client for the police to issue an identikit picture of the man. But no one answering the description was found. The police also noticed that McGowan's jewellery was missing, but a check on all the pawn shops also drew a blank.

Christmas and New Year passed uneventfully, then on 16 February 1965, the naked body of 28-year-old Bridie O'Hara was found in the bracken behind a depot in Acton. Like the other victims, she was short, five foot two, and worked as a prostitute. Her clothes had disappeared along with her engagement and wedding rings. They were never found. Again, her body was covered with tiny flecks of paint. But this time there was a new clue. One of her hands was mummified. That meant it had been kept near a source of heat that had dried the flesh out.

Scotland Yard threw all their resources into the case. Every premises in an area of 24 square miles was to be searched and samples of any paint found compared to the flecks on the victims' bodies. The police also worked out that all the victims had been picked up between 11 pm and 1 am, and dumped between 5 am and 6 am. This meant that Jack the Stripper was a nightworker, probably a nightwatchman who guarded premises near a spray shop.

They also worked out that he was a man of about forty with a high libido and curious sexual tastes. The police dismissed an earlier theory that the culprit was on a crusade against prostitution. They now believed that the culprit could not satisfy his bizarre requirements at home, turning to prostitutes who would do anything for money in order to indulge his craving. Detectives now realised that, during orgasm, the man went into a frenzy which resulted in the girls' deaths. He could not help himself and had learned to accept that murder was the price he had to pay for sexual satisfaction.

All this was little enough to go on. But the police held regular press conferences saying that a list of suspects had been drawn up. They were working their way through them and the killer would soon be behind bars. In fact, the police had no list and were not nearly as confident as they pretended, but they felt that it was best to keep up pressure on the culprit.

The murders fell into a ten-week cycle and the police were determined to prevent the next one. They threw a police cordon around a 20-square mile area of central London and every vehicle entering or leaving it at night was recorded. Anyone moving in or out of the zone more than three times was tracked down.

The police would visit their home under the pretext of investigating a traffic accident – to spare the embarrassment of those who were where they were not supposed to be. The suspect was then interviewed out of the earshot of his family.

Weeks of searching paid off. A perfect match was made between paint found under a covered transformer at the rear of a spraypainting shop in the Heron Factory Estate in Acton and the paint flecks on the victims' bodies. The transformer itself generated enough heat to mummify flesh left near it.

Every car entering or leaving the estate was logged and all 7,000 people living in the vicinity were interviewed. At a specially convened press conference, the police announced that the number of suspects was being whittled down to three, then two, then one.

Despite the huge amount of man-hours put in, all Scotland Yard's detective work was a waste of time. It was these press conferences that worked.

In March 1965, as the detectives continued their meticulous search, a quiet family man living in south London killed himself. He left a suicide note saying that he could not 'stand the strain any longer'. At the time the police took little notice.

By June 1965, Jack the Stripper had not struck again. The ten-week cycle had been broken. The police wanted to know why. They began looking back at the suicides that had occurred since the murder of Bridie O'Hara in January.

This particular suicide victim worked at a security firm and his duty roster fitted the culprits. Despite an intensive search of his house and extensive interviews with his family, no evidence was ever found that directly linked him to the murders. Nevertheless, the murders stopped and the police were convinced, from the circumstantial evidence alone, that this man was Jack the Stripper.

By July 1965, the murder inquiry was scaled down. It was wound up the following year. In 1970, Scotland Yard confirmed that the South London suicide was Jack the Stripper. But they have never named him and, officially, the file on the Jack the Stripper case is still open.

A younger man's irrepressible sexual ardour terrorised a small town in Michigan for more than two years. He killed young women and mutilated their bodies for sexual pleasure. He showed no remorse and was not ashamed, or pressured, into suicide. He was caught by the slimmest of chances, and was convicted of only one murder and then only by the flimsiest of forensic evidence.

He was first seen at about nine o'clock on a warm Sunday evening in June 1967, in the small university town of Ypsilanti. Attractive brunette Mary Fleszar, a student, was walking down the street. A car pulled over and the young man leaned out to speak to her. An onlooker assumed that he was offering her a lift. She refused and the car drove off. It turned at the next corner then, moments later, sped back past the girl and into a private driveway. By this time Mary had reached her apartment block and was safe – or so she thought.

The following day, Mary's flatmate phoned her parents to say that she had not come home. They called the police who were unconcerned. Mary was nineteen, and students often stayed out all night, at parties or with boyfriends. But Mary was not that sort of girl, they protested. She was a quiet, studious girl who had never behaved that way.

The following day, the police issued a missing person's report. They found a witness who had seen the young man that had offered Mary a lift. But he was unable to give a detailed description of the youth or the car the man was driving.

Four weeks later, two boys came across a fly-covered mass of rotting meat, which they took to be a deer carcass, near a secluded lover's lane two miles north of Ypsilanti. A pathologist identified it as human flesh, a young woman who had been stabbed in the chest more than thirty times. There were fresh tyre tracks beside the body.

An extensive search of the area failed to uncover the victim's clothes. But about 50 yards from the body, searchers found one sandal. Mary Fleszar's parents identified it as their daughter's.

At the funeral home, the young man was seen again. He turned up and asked the receptionist if he could take a photograph of the body as a memento for his parents. The receptionist said that was impossible. It was only when the young man was going out of the door that she saw he was not carrying a camera.

Almost exactly a year later, 20-year-old art student Joan Schell left her apartment just three blocks from where Mary had lived. She was on her way to spend the night with a girl friend in nearby Ann Arbor. Her flatmate went with her to the bus stop. They waited three-quarters of an hour. Then a red car pulled up and a young man, wearing an East Michigan University sweat-shirt, asked if they wanted a lift. Joan was suspicious at first, but there were two other men in the back of the car and she thought she would be safe enough. As she climbed into the car, she told her flatmate she would phone later when she arrived in Ann Arbor. She never called. Five days later, Joan Schell's body was found rotting in a storm drain. Her blue miniskirt and white slip had been pulled up round her neck. She had been raped and stabbed to death. Although she had been dead for almost a week, the pathologist noted that she had been on the spot where she was found for less than a day.

Extensive enquiries revealed that Joan Schell had been seen later on the evening she went missing, walking with a young man. The witnesses could not be certain but they thought the young man was John Norman Collins. He was an all American boy – a fine football and baseball player, an honours student and a devout Catholic. But he had a troubled background. His father had run off with another woman soon after he was born. Her mother's second marriage lasted only a year. Her third husband, who adopted John and his older brother and sister, turned out to be an alcoholic who beat his wife. By the age of nine Collins had gone through a great deal of domestic strife.

Unbeknownst to the police, Collins was suspected of stealing $40 from his fraternity house, as well as other petty thefts. Although he lived directly across the street from Joan Schell, he claimed he did not know her when the police interviewed him, and they had no alternative but to let him go.

Ten months later, a thirteen-year-old schoolboy found a shopping bag in a cemetery. There was a gift inside. His mother went with him back to the spot where he had found it. Under a yellow raincoat, she found a girl's body. The skirt had been pulled up and the tights rolled down. It was 23-year-old Jane Mixer, a law student who had been reported missing a few hours earlier. The man who the press was now calling the 'Co-ed Killer' had struck again.

Four days later, the body of sixteen-year-old Maralynn Skelton was found in a patch of undergrowth. She had been brutally beaten and a tree branch had been jammed into her vagina. Plainly the urges that were driving this sexually obsessed serial killer were getting more urgent and the police feared that he would soon kill again.

Three weeks later, the body of thirteen-year-old Dawn Basom was found amongst some weeds. The youngest victim yet, she was wearing only a white blouse and a bra which had been pushed up around her neck. The rest of her clothes had been strewn over a wide area. She had been strangled with a length of electric flex and her already well-developed breasts had been slashed again and again in a frenzy. The police tried to keep the discovery of the body secret, but it was too late. A young reporter had already phoned the story through to his radio station.

The pace was now increasing. On 9 June, three teenage boys found the body of a girl in her twenties, with her clothes strewn around her, near a disused farmhouse. She had been shot in the head and repeatedly stabbed. Although the use of a gun was new, the police were convinced that this killing was the work of the same man. Pathologists said that the girl had been dead for less than a day. The police were already beginning to suspect that the murderer returned to the spot where he had dumped the corpses several times – even moving them to a new dumping ground if he had the chance.

Again the police ordered a news blackout. But again it was too late. One of the boys had called the local radio station.

The town was now in a panic. A $42,000 reward was offered and the police were heavily criticised for not catching the killer. But they still had little to go on.

On 23 July, eighteen-year-old student Karen Sue Beineman went missing. She had last been seen in a wig shop, buying a $20 hairpiece. There were two foolish things she had done in her life, she told the shop assistant – one was

228

buying a wig; the other was accepting a lift on a motorbike from a stranger. He was waiting for her outside.

The assistant agreed that accepting a lift from a stranger was stupid and took a look out of the window at the young man on the motorbike. She had to admit the young man looked decent enough.

Four days later, a doctor out for a walk near his suburban home stumbled across Karen's naked body in a gully. She had been raped and her knickers had been stuffed into her vagina. The odd thing was that there were hair clippings inside the panties.

This time the news blackout held. The police replaced Karen's mutilated body with a tailor's dummy and staked out the area. It rained heavily that night, cutting down visibility, but shortly after midnight an officer spotted a man running out of the gully. The policeman tried to summon help, but his radio had been soaked in the rain and failed to work. The man got clean away.

It was then that a young campus policeman put two and two together. The description of the young man on the motorbike that was circulating reminded him of a member of his fraternity house who had dropped out after being suspected of stealing. The young man's name was John Norman Collins and he had already been interviewed by the police.

The campus cop found a picture of Collins and both the shop assistant from the wig shop and the owner of the shop next door identified it as the man on the motorbike. The young policeman then went to interview Collins himself, expecting a confession. None was forthcoming. Collins even refused a lie-detector test. The young officer's initiative had, in fact, been counterproductive. The following night Collins emerged from his room carrying a box covered with a blanket. His flatmate glimpsed inside. It contained a handbag and women's clothing and shoes.

Police Corporal David Leik had been on holiday with this

family and had missed the latest developments in the Co-ed Killer case. When he returned home, his wife was taking some washing down to the laundry room in the basement when she noticed that the floor was covered in black spray paint. Only one person had been in the house while they had been away. Leik's nephew, John Norman Collins, had been letting himself in to feed their dog. But why would he be painting the basement floor?

Leik soon found out. He received an urgent call, asking him to report into work. When he arrived at the station house, he was told, to his surprise and disbelief, that Collins was a prime suspect in the Co-ed Killer case.

That evening, Leik scraped some of the black paint off the basement floor with a knife. Under it, there were brown stains – which Leik thought could be blood. Within two hours, lab technicians were crawling all over the basement floor. They quickly identified the brown stains as varnish stains left behind after he had painted some window shutters. But a more extensive examination of the basement floor revealed what later proved to be nine tiny blood stains. More significantly though, forensic experts found hair clippings on the floor next to the washing machine. Leik's wife used to cut the children's hair down there. Their hair matched the hair clippings found in the panties stuffed into Karen Beineman's vagina.

That afternoon, Collins was arrested. Although shaken – even moved to tears – he refused to make a confession. A search of his room revealed nothing. His box of gruesome mementoes had already been disposed of.

Collins ran four motorbikes and funded his activities by petty theft. But on closer examination, it was found that his background was even more disturbed than was thought at first. He seemed unable to express his sexual feelings in any normal way. When his girlfriend danced close with him, he condemned her for inciting lust in him.

His sister got pregnant at eighteen and married the child's father. The marriage did not last, but when Collins found her dating another man he lost control of his temper. He beat the man unconscious and hit his sister repeatedly until she bled, screaming that she was a tramp.

Later, when his defence attorney was testing to see how well Collins would stand up under cross-examination, he called Collins' mother – who had a new boyfriend but had not remarried. She was a kept woman. Collins' usually calm demeanour dissolved into apoplectic rage.

The police case was still flimsy. They began to hunt for Andrew Manuel, a former roommate of Collins who had committed a number of burglaries with him. He and Collins had also hired a caravan, under false names, for a trip and had not returned it. It had been left in the backyard of Manuel's uncle in Salinas, California. Around that time, seventeen-year-old Roxie Ann Philips disappeared from Salinas, after telling a friend that she had a date with a man called John from Michigan who was staying with a friend in a caravan. Two weeks later her body was fount in a ravine. She had been strangled and her body showed all the trademarks of the Co-ed Killer.

Manuel was found in Phoenix, Arizona. He was charged with burglary and stealing the caravan. He knew nothing about the murders, he said. However, he did admit leaving Ypsilanti when he heard that the police suspected Collins. He was sentenced to five years probation.

Collins went to trial charged only with the murder of Karen Beineman. The prosecution case centred on the identification of Collins by the staff of the wig shop and the hair clippings in Karen Beineman's panties. Defence counsel questioned the wig shop attendant's eyesight and contended that the comparison of sixty-one hairs from the panties and fifty-nine from the basement floor was insufficient evidence to convict a man of murder.

After long deliberations, the jury brought in a unanimous verdict of guilty and Collins was sentenced to twenty-years-to-life.

As in the case of Jack the Stripper, no one was ever prosecuted for the murders committed by the Boston Strangler. But, again, police are convinced they know who he was. But, unlike Scotland Yard, the Boston Police Department named their suspect. His name was Albert DeSalvo.

DeSalvo was the son of a vicious drunk. When he was 11, DeSalvo watched his father knock his mother's teeth out then bend her fingers back until they snapped. This was nothing unusual in the DeSalvo household.

When they were just children, DeSalvo and his two sisters were sold to a farmer in Maine for $9. After he got back home, his father taught him how to shoplift, taking him to the store and showing him what to take. His father would also bring prostitutes back to the apartment and make the children watch while he had sex with them.

Soon young DeSalvo had a lively interest in sex, making many early conquests among the neighbourhood girls, as well as earning a healthy living from the local gay community who would pay him for his services. In the army, DeSalvo continued his sexual adventuring, until he met Irmgaard, the daughter of a respectable Catholic family in Frankfurt. They married and returned to the US, where DeSalvo was dishonourably discharged from the army for sexually molesting a nine-year-old girl. Civilian charges were not brought because the mother feared the publicity.

DeSalvo pursued a career of breaking and entering, but at home he was the perfect family man. However, his sexual appetite was more than his wife could cope with. He demanded sex five or six times a day. This annoyed Irmgaard and finally repelled her. So DeSalvo found an outlet as the 'Measuring Man'.

He began hanging around the student areas of Boston,

looking for apartments shared by young women. He would knock on the door with a clipboard, saying that he was the representative of a modelling agency, and ask whether he could take their measurements. Sometimes his charm succeeded in seducing the women – sometimes they would seduce him. Other times he would just take their measurements, clothed or naked, and promise that a female representative would call later. He never assaulted any of the girls. The only complaints were that no one came on a follow-up visit.

About that time, DeSalvo was caught housebreaking and sent to jail for two years. The experience left him frustrated. When he was released he started a new career, breaking into houses throughout New England and tying up and raping women. At that time, he was known as the 'Green Man' because he wore a green shirt and trousers. The police in Connecticut and Massachusetts put the number of his assault in the hundreds. DeSalvo himself claimed more than a thousand – bragging that he had tied up and raped six women in one morning.

In 1962, DeSalvo confined his activities to Boston and added murder to his repertoire. The body of 22-year-old Anna Slesters was found in her apartment. DeSalvo had left it in an obscene pose, with the cord he had used to strangle her tied in a bow around her neck. This was to become his trademark.

Two weeks later, DeSalvo murdered 85-year-old Mary Mullen, even though he said she reminded him of his grandmother. Next he raped and strangled 65-year-old nurse Helen Blake. Then he strangled Nina Nichols, though she fought back, scratching flesh from his arms. Seventy-five-year-old Ida Irga was raped and strangled on 19 August and 67-year-old Jane Sullivan was murdered by DeSalvo the next day.

By this time, the Boston police force realised that they had a serious maniac on their hands and began questioning all known sexual deviants. But DeSalvo was overlooked because

233

he only had a record for burglary and housebreaking. The only official record of his sexual deviancy was in his army file.

DeSalvo cooled off for a bit and took a long autumn break. But by his wedding anniversary on 5 December, his mind was so overheated with violent sexual images that he thought it was going to explode. He saw an attractive girl going into an apartment block. He followed her and knocked on her door. Using his usual ploy, he pretended to be a maintenance man sent by the landlord to check the pipes. She would not let him in. So he tried the next apartment. The door was opened by a tall, attractive, 25-year-old black woman called Sophie Clark. DeSalvo reverted to his Measuring Man routine. He remarked on her stunningly curvaceous body and, when she turned her back, he attacked her. Once he had subdued her, he stripped her and raped her. Then he strangled her. He left her naked body, like the others, propped up with the legs spread and the ligature he had used to strangle her tied in a bow under her chin.

Three days later, DeSalvo went back to one of the women he had previously visited as the Measuring Man, 23-year-old secretary Patricia Bissette. She invited him in for a cup of coffee and when she turned her back he grabbed her round the throat and raped her, then strangled her with her own stockings.

DeSalvo's next victim escaped. She fought back so violently, biting, scratching and screaming that the Strangler fled. This seems to have been something of a turning-point in DeSalvo's career. But she was so distraught after the attack that the description she gave was next to useless.

From then on the Boston Strangler's attacks became even more violent. On 9 March 1963, he gained access to 69 year-old Mary Brown's apartment by saying he had come to fix the stove. He carried with him a piece of lead pipe which he used to beat her head in. He raped her after he had killed her, then

234

stabbed her in the breasts with a fork which he left sticking in her flesh. He maintained his modus operandi by strangling her, but this time the victim was already dead.

Two months later, DeSalvo took a day off work. He drove out to Cambridge, Massachusetts, where he spotted a pretty girl, 23-year-old student Beverley Samans, on University Road. He followed her to her apartment. Once inside he tied her to the bedposts, stripped her, blindfolded her, gagged her and raped her repeatedly. Then he strangled her with her own stockings. But this time, it was not enough. Before he left the apartment, he pulled his penknife from his pocket and started stabbing her naked body. Once he started he could not stop. He stabbed and stabbed her. Blood flew everywhere. There were twenty-two savage wounds in her body. Once the frenzy subsided, he calmly wiped his fingerprints from the knife, dropped it in the sink and went home.

On 8 September, the Boston Strangler struck again. This time it was a straightforward rape and strangulation. The ligature was 58-year-old Evelyn Corbin's own nylons. He left them tied in a bow around her ankle. The city was in panic. The killer seemed to come and go at will. With no description of the man and no dues, the police were powerless. In desperation they brought in Dutch psychic Peter Hurkos, but he failed to identify the Strangler.

While America – and Kennedy's home state of Massachusetts particularly – was in mourning following the assassination of the president, the Boston Strangler struck again. He raped and strangled 23-year-old dress designer Joan Gaff in her own apartment, leaving her black leotard tied in a bow around her neck

DeSalvo admitted later that he did not know why he had killed Joan Gaff. 'I wasn't even excited,' he said. After he left her apartment, he went home, played with his kids and watched the report of Joan Gaff's murder on TV. Then he sat down and had dinner, without thinking of her again.

On 4 January 1964, the Boston Strangler struck for the last time. He gained access to the flat of nineteen-year-old Mary Sullivan, tied her up at knifepoint and raped her. This time he strangled her with his hands. Her body was found propped up on her bed, her buttocks on the pillow and her back against the headboard. Her head rested on her right shoulder, her eyes closed and viscose liquid was dripping from her mouth down her right breast. Her breasts and her sexual organs were exposed and there was a broom handle protruding from her vagina. More semen stains were found on her blanket. Between her toes he placed a card he found in the apartment which read 'Happy New Year'.

Later that year, a woman reported being sexually assaulted by a man using the Measuring Man routine, but otherwise all the activity of the Boston Strangler stopped. This coincided with the arrest of DeSalvo for housebreaking. Held on bail, DeSalvo's behaviour became disturbed and he was transferred to the mental hospital at Bridgewater, where he was diagnosed as schizophrenic.

Although they had him in custody, the police still had no idea that DeSalvo was the Boston Strangler. But in Bridgewater, another inmate, in for killing a petrol pump attendant and also a suspect in the Boston Strangler case himself, listened to DeSalvo's manic ramblings and began to put two and two together. He got his lawyer to interview DeSalvo.

In these taped interviews, DeSalvo revealed facts about the murders – the position of the bodies, the nature of the ligature and the wounds inflicted – that the police had not revealed. He also admitted to two murders that had not already been attributed to the Boston Strangler.

DeSalvo was a mental patient, so he was not prosecuted for the rapes and murders he confessed to. But there was no doubt that he was, indeed, the Boston Strangler. DeSalvo was transferred to Walpole State Prison. He was found dead in his cell in 1973, stabbed through the heart.

Ted Bundy also had the power to charm women. Many of them paid with their lives. His sexual impulses were so strong that there was no way that he could control them. During his first attacks he later maintained that he had to wrestle with his conscience. But soon he began to desensitise himself. He claimed not to have tortured his victims unnecessarily, but said that he had had to kill them after he had raped them to prevent them recognising him.

Bundy had been a compulsive masturbator from an early age and later became obsessed by sadistic pornography. After glimpsing a girl undressed through a window, he also became a compulsive Peeping Tom. His long-time girlfriend Meg Anders described how he would tie her up with stockings before anal sex. This sex game stopped when he almost strangled her. For years they maintained a more or less normal sexual relationship, while Bundy exercised his craving for total control with anonymous victims, whom he often strangled during the sexual act.

His attitude to sex was often ambivalent. Although he desired the bodies of attractive young women, he would leave their vaginas stuffed with twigs and dirt and sometimes sodomise them with objects such as aerosol cans.

Some of the bodies, though partly decomposed, had freshly washed hair and newly applied make-up, indicating that he had kept them for necrophilia. In only one case did he admit to deliberately terrorising his victim – or rather victims. He kidnapped two girls at once so that he could rape each of them in front of the other, before killing them.

Bundy's first victim was Sharon Clarke of Seattle. He had broken into her apartment while she was asleep and smashed her around the head with a metal rod. She suffered a shattered skull, but survived. She could not identify her attacker and no motivation for the attack has been given.

Then young women began to disappear from the University of Washington campus nearby. Six disappeared within seven months. At the Lake Sammanish resort in Washington State, a number of young women reported being approached by a young man calling himself Ted. He had his arm in a sling and asked them to help get his sailboat off his car. But in the parking lot they found that there was no boat on the car. Ted then said that they would have to go to his house to get it. Sensibly, most declined. Janice Ott seems to have agreed to go with him. She disappeared. A few hours later, Denise Naslund also disappeared from the same area. She had been seen in the company of a good-looking dark-haired young man who fitted Ted Bundy's description. The remains of Janice Ott, Denise Naslund and another unidentified young woman were later found on wasteland, where they had been eaten and scattered by animals.

Other witnesses at the University of Washington came forward, saying that they had seen a man wearing a sling. Some other bodies were found, again disposed of on waste ground.

The police had two suspects. Ex-convict Gary Taylor had been picked up by the Seattle police for abducting women under false pretexts. And park attendant Warren Forrest picked up a young woman who consented to pose for him. He took her to a secluded part of the park, tied her up and stripped her naked. He taped her mouth and fired darts at her breasts. Then he raped her, strangled her and left her for dead. But she survived and identified her attacker. Both were in custody though, and the attacks continued. Bundy's girlfriend called anonymously, giving his name, but it disappeared among the thousands of other leads the police had to follow up.

Bundy began to travel further afield. On 2 October 1974 he abducted Nancy Wilcox after she left an all-night party. He raped and strangled Melissa Smith, daughter of the local police chief. Her body was found near Salt Lake City. He took Laura Aimee from a Halloween party in Orem, Utah. Her naked body was found at the bottom of a canyon.

In Salt Lake City a week later, he approached a girl named Carol DaRonch. Bundy pretended to be a detective and asked her the licence number of her car. Someone had tried to break into it, he said. He asked her to accompany him to the precinct to see the suspect. She got into his car, but once they were in a quiet street he handcuffed her.

She began to scream. He put a gun to her head. She managed to get out of the door and Bundy chased after her with a crowbar. He took a swing at her skull, but she managed to grab the bar. A car was coming down the street. Carol jumped in front of it, forcing it to stop. She jumped in and the car drove away.

Carol gave a good description to the police, but Bundy continued undeterred. He tried to pick up a pretty young French teacher outside her high school. She declined to go with him. But Debbie Kent did. She disappeared from a school playground where a key to a pair of handcuffs was later found.

The following January in Snowmass Village, a Colorado ski resort, Dr Raymond Gadowsky found that his fiancée, Caryn Campbell, was missing from her room. A month later, her naked body was found out in the snow. She had been raped and her skull had been smashed in. Julie Cunningham vanished from nearby Vail and the remains of Susan Rancourt and Brenda Bell were also found on Taylor Mountain.

The body of Melanie Cooley was found only ten miles from her home. Unlike the other victims, she was still clothed, though her jeans had been undone, convincing the police that the motive was sexual.

The Colorado attacks continued with Nancy Baird who disappeared from a petrol station and Shelley Robertson whose naked body was found down a mine shaft.

A Salt Lake City patrol man was cruising an area of the city that had recently suffered a spate of burglaries. He noticed Bundy's car driving slowly and indicated that he

239

should pull over. Instead, Bundy sped off. The patrolman gave chase and caught up with him. In his car, they found maps and brochures of Colorado. Some coincided with the places girls had disappeared.

Forensic experts found a hair in Bundy's car that matched that of Melissa Smith. A witness also recognised Bundy from Snowmass Village. He was charged and extradited to Colorado to stand trial. However, few people could believe that such an intelligent and personable young man could be responsible for these terrible sex attacks, even though Carol DaRonch picked him out of a line-up.

Bundy was given permission to conduct his own defence. He was even allowed to use the law library to research. There he managed to give his guard the slip, jumped from a window and escaped. He was recaptured a week later.

Bundy still protested his innocence and managed to prolong the pre-trial hearings with a number of skilful legal stalling manoeuvres. In the time he gained, he lost weight and cut a small hole under the light fitting in the ceiling of his cell. He squeezed through the one-foot-square hole he had made and got clean away.

He travelled around America before settling in Tallahassee, Florida, a few blocks from the sorority houses of Florida State University. One evening, Nita Neary saw a man lurking in front of her sorority house. She was about to phone the police when a fellow student, Karen Chandler, staggered from her room with blood streaming from her head. She was screaming that she had just been attacked by a madman. Her roommate Kathy Kleiner had also been attacked. Her jaw was broken Margaret Bown had been attacked sexually and strangled with her own pantyhose. Lisa Levy had also been sexually assaulted. Bundy had bitten one of her nipples off and left teeth marks in her buttocks. Then he beat her around the head. She died on the way to hospital. In another building, Cheryl Thomas had also been viciously attacked, but she survived.

The police had only a sketchy description of the attacker. But Bundy had plainly got a taste for killing again. While making his getaway, he abducted twelve-year-old Kimberley Leach, sexually assaulted her, strangled her, mutilated her sexual organs and dumped her body in the Suwannee River Park.

Bundy was now short of money. He stole some credit cards and a car, and sneaked out of his apartment where he owed back rent. But the stolen car was a give-away. He was stopped by a motorcycle cop and arrested. At the police station, he admitted that he was Ted Bundy and that he was wanted by the Colorado police.

The Florida police began to tie him in with the Tallahassee attack. When they tried to take an impression of his teeth, he went berserk. It took six men to hold his jaw open. The impression matched the teeth marks on murdered student Lisa Levy's buttock.

Again Bundy conducted his own defence, skilfully using the law to prolong the court case and his personality to charm the jury. But the evidence of the teeth marks was too strong. He was found guilty of murder and sentenced to death. At 7 am on 24 January 1989, Bundy went to the electric chair. He is said to have died with a smile on his face. On death row, Bundy made a detailed confession. He also received sacks full of mail from young women whose letters dwelt on cruel and painful ways to make love. Even on death row he had not lost his charm.

Chapter 15

The Pig Farmer

In December 2007, Canadian pig farmer Robert William 'Willie' Pickton was convicted of the second-degree murders of six women. He has been charged with the murder of another twenty women. In court a videotape was played which showed him bragging to an undercover police officer posing as a cell mate. In it, he boasted of killing forty-nine women and rued being stopped before he had made it fifty.

'Fifty?' asked the undercover officer.

'I was going to do one more; make it an even fifty,' Pickton replied. 'So let everything die for a while . . . then do another twenty-five new ones.'

In the conversation the undercover officer suggested that throwing corpses in the sea was an effective way of disposing of them.

'I did better than that,' said Pickton. 'Rendering plant.'

It had baffled the police, he bragged.

'They never seen anything like this before,' he said, boasting he was 'bigger than the Green River.'

He was referring to the so-called Green River killer, Gary

Ridgway, who in 2003 had pleaded guilty to the murder of forty-eight prostitutes in Washington State.

Pickton was well aware that he was being videotaped. At one point, he waved at the camera in his cell and said: 'Hello!'

Despite Pickton's boast, he was anything but systematic and well organised and it is thought that he may well have killed more that the forty-nine he claimed. He rarely knew the names of his victims, picking them from the hookers and drug addicts who inhabited Vancouver's Downside Eastside. During his rampage, at least sixty-five women went missing from that area alone.

The ten blocks of Vancouver's Downtown Eastside comprise not just the poorest area in British Columbia, but the poorest in the whole of Canada. They call the neighbourhood 'Low Track'. At its centre is the intersection of Main and Hastings, called 'Pain and Wastings' by locals. Its shabby hotels, rundown bars and dilapidated pawn shops are home to between five thousand and ten thousand drifters at any one time. Crack cocaine and heroin are supplied by Asian gangs and bikers who are frequently involved in turf wars. Most of the women addicts support their habits by prostitution, giving Low Track the highest HIV infection rate in North America.

In the 2000s, Low Track became famous for its 'kiddy stroll', where prostitutes as young as eleven worked. Some underage girls walk the streets, while others are kept by pimps in special 'trick pads'. New 'twinkies' – runaways lured by the city's bright lights – arrive every day. Over eighty per cent of the prostitutes in Low Track were born and brought up outside Vancouver, while seventy-three per cent of the girls had started in the sex trade as children. The same figure were mothers with an average of three children each. Some ninety per cent of them had had their children taken into care. Most did not know where their children were.

There is an average of one death a day from drug overdoses among these women.

But over the last twenty-five years there were other dangers. In 1983, women began to go missing from Low Track. The police did not notice this for nearly fourteen years. It was hardly surprising as many of the inhabitants of Low Track are transients. Runaways change their names and addresses regularly. Some simply moved on. But by 1997, the police began to fear that more than two-dozen had been murdered. Early the next year they began to compile a list.

The first name on the list was that of twenty-three-year-old Rebecca Guno, a prostitute and drug addict last seen alive on 22 June 1983. She was reported missing three days later. The next on the list, forty-three-year-old Sherry Rail whose disappearance was not reported until three years after she was last seen in January 1984.

Elaine Auerbach, aged thirty-three, told friends she was moving to Seattle in March 1986 but she never turned up and she was reported missing in mid-April. Teressa Ann Williams, the first Aboriginal on the list, was fifteen when she was last seen alive in July 1988, but was not reported missing until March 1999. Thirty-year-old Ingrid Soet, a schizophrenic under medication, disappeared on 28 August 1989 and was reported missing on 1 October 1990. The first black woman on the list was Kathleen Dale Wattley. She was thirty-two years old when she vanished on 18 June 1992 and was reported missing eleven days later.

There was then a three-year hiatus. But in March 1995 forty-seven-year-old Catherine Gonzales, a drug user and sex-trade worker, disappeared. She was reported missing on 9 February 1996. In April 1995, thirty-two-year-old Catherine Maureen Knight went missing. Her disappearance was reported to the police on 11 November. Dorothy Spence, a thirty-three-year-old Aboriginal, vanished on 6 August 1995. Her disappearance was reported on 30 October. Then

244

twenty-two-year-old Diana Melnick disappeared two days after Christmas and was reported missing two days later.

There was another hiatus until 3 October 1996, when twenty-two-year-old drug user and prostitute Tanya Holyk disappeared. Her family knew something was wrong when she didn't come home after a night out with friends to see her son, who was about to turn one. She was reported missing on 3 November. Pickton has since been charged with her murder. Olivia Gale Williams, aged twenty-one, disappeared on 6 December 1996 and was not reported missing until 4 July the following year.

Twenty-year-old Stephanie Lane left her two-year-old son with her mother along with an uncashed welfare cheque when she went missing, though she continued to call on birthdays and holidays. On 11 March 1997, she was released from hospital after an episode of drug psychosis. She was last seen alive at the Patricia Hotel on Hastings Street later that day.

Twenty-two-year old Helen Mae Hallmark was last seen alive on 17 June 1997 and reported missing on 23 September 1998. Her sister wrote a poem to her memory.

Janet Henry, who also went missing in June 1997, came from the KwaKwaQueWak Nation in Kingcome Inlet in British Columbia, the youngest in a family of thirteen. She had a happy childhood until her mother fell ill and her father died. The children were sent to residential schools and foster homes, losing all ties to their native culture. Her sister Lavina was raped and murdered when she was nineteen. Another sibling killed himself.

A bright young woman, Janet graduated from high school, became a trained hairdresser, married and had a daughter, to whom she was devoted. But when the marriage broke up in the late 1980s, her husband gained custody of their daughter. Janet was devastated and her life went into free-fall. She moved Vancouver's Downtown Eastside and began attending parties where she exchanged sex for drugs. Before she disappeared she had already had one brush with a serial killer. In the early 1980s, she met Clifford Olson, who drugged and raped her, but was spared her life. Olson pleaded guilty to murdering eleven young women and children in 1982. All too aware of the dangers of her profession, Janet would phone her brothers and sisters frequently to let them know she was okay. But the calls stopped coming. Janet Henry was reported missing on 28 June 1997, two days after her last contact with siblings.

Marnie Lee Frey, aged twenty-seven, was last seen alive in August 1997, though she was not reported missing until 4 September 1998. She had a baby at eighteen and asked her parents to adopt the child.

'She said, "Mom, this is the only thing I can do for her. I love her dearly, but I know I can't look after her as a mom,"' her mother recalled.

Her parents pretended that the child, Brittney, was Marnie's younger sister but, in the light of the publicity surrounding the case, they were forced to tell her the truth. Subsequently, Pickton was tried and convicted of her mother's murder.

Jacqueline Murdock, aged twenty-six, was last seen alive on 14 August but was not reported missing until 30 October 1998. Thirty-three-year-old Cindy Louise Beck disappeared in September 1997 and was reported missing on 30 April 1998. Andrea Fay Borhaven, aged twenty-five, had no fixed address before she vanished sometime during 1997. Her disappearance was only reported to the police on 18 May 1999. Thirty-eight-year-old Kerry Lynn Koski disappeared in January 1998 and was reported missing on the 29th of the month.

Four more women would disappear before Vancouver police began their infamous list. Twenty-three-year-old Jacqueline Michelle McDonnell disappeared in mid-January 1998 and was reported missing on 22 February 1999, and forty-six-year-old Inga Monique Hall was last seen alive in February 1998 and reported missing on 3 March. Pickton was charged with murdering both of them.

Twenty-nine-year-old Sarah Jane deVries was last seen on the corner of Princess and Hastings in the early morning of 14 April 1998 and reported missing by friends later the same day. Ex-boyfriend Wayne Leng said Sarah underwent 'a lot of turmoil' in her twenty-nine years, particularly as an adopted child of mixed parentage in an all-white west-side family.

'This started when she was twelve,' said her mother Pat. 'She has HIV, she has hepatitis C. What I do for her now is look after her kids the best I can.'

When Sarah went missing, her children were seven and two.

'It's very hard to tell a seven-year-old that somebody is missing,' said Pat.'It's something you can't come to terms with, you can't work through, because there's never an end to it.'

Nobody has seen or heard from her since – which was unprecedented as she always called on her mother's birthday, Mother's Day and her own birthday. But as Sarah herself observed in the diary she left behind: 'I think my hate is going to be my destination, my executioner.'

Wayne Leng was so concerned about her disappearance that he put up posters around the Vancouver's Downtown Eastside carrying Sarah's picture and details of a $1,000 reward. But three phone calls he got on his pager around midnight one Saturday night left him chilled.

'Sarah's dead,' said a man's slightly slurred voice, with music pounding in the background. 'So there will be more girls like her dead. There will be more prostitutes killed. There will be one every Friday night. At the busiest time.'

The second message had the same voice and the same music playing in the background.

'You'll never find Sarah again,' the man said. 'So just stop looking for her, all right? She doesn't want to be seen and heard from again, all right? So,'bye. She's dead.'

The final message said: 'This is in regard to Sarah. I just want to let you know that you'll never find her again alive because a friend of mine killed her and I was there.'

Leng said the mystery caller knew things about Sarah deVries not known by many others. Pickton was charged with her murder.

In September 1998, an Aboriginal group sent the authorities a list of women they said had been murdered in Downtown Eastside and demanded a thorough investigation. The complaint prompted Detective Dave Dickson to draw up his own list of all the Low Track women who had simply disappeared without a trace. Soon Dickson had enough names to persuade his superiors to set up a cold-case task force.

At first they started with forty cases from all parts of Vancouver dating back to 1971. But in an effort to find a pattern, they narrowed the roster down to sixteen prostitutes from Low Track who had disappeared since 1995. By the time the task force made its first arrest the number had climbed to at least fifty-four women. Dickson's investigations were given a fresh impetus in March 1999 when Jamie Lee Hamilton, a transsexual and former prostitute who went on to become the director of a drop-in centre for sex-trade workers, called a news conference complaining of the police's lax attitude towards missing prostitutes. However, despite Dickson's growing list of names, he had yet to prove that a serial killer was at work.

One person who thought that the missing women were victims of a serial killer was Inspector Kim Rossmo, the pioneer of a 'geographic profiling'. He had developed new investigative technique, where he mapped unsolved crimes in an attempt to highlight any pattern or criminal signature overlooked by detectives working on individual cases. Most serial criminals, it seems, operate close to home. Using geographic profiling police can work out the approximate location of the offender's home by analysing the spatial patterns of the attacks. In one case it traced a serial killer to within two-fifths of a mile of his home. Rossmo based his technique on research the way that African lions hunt. This matches closely to the way serial killers work. Lions look for an animal that exhibits some indication of weakness – the old, the very young, the infirm, the vulnerable. They go to a watering hole and loiter, because they know it is a draw for their potential targets.

'We see that all the time with criminal offenders,' says Rossmo, 'they go to target-rich environments to do their hunting. Spatial patterns are produced by serial killers as they search and attack. The system analyses the geography of these, the victim encounter, the attack, the murder and body dump sites.'

In May 1999, Rossmo went to work on the disappearances in Vancouver's Downtown Eastside. However, his superiors dismissed his conclusions. Rossmo resigned. His action for wrongful dismissal failed, but geographic profiling became a respected technique used worldwide to track serial killers.

The task force were further hampered by the fact that Canada's Violent Crime Linkage System did not track missing persons unless there was some evidence of foul play – and none had been found so far. In some cases, they did not even have a date when the woman had gone missing. Prostitutes and pimps were reluctant to co-operate with officers who might put them in jail. However, in June 1999, investigators met the relatives of several missing women. They reviewed police and coroners' databases throughout Canada and the United States. They also checked drug rehabilitation facilities, hospitals, mental institutions, AIDS hospices, witness-protection programmes and cemetery records to see whether the missing women had turned up there.

Disturbing news came from Agassiz, sixty miles to the east of Vancouver, where the bodies of four prostitutes had been dumped in 1995 and 1996 – but none of them were on the list. And in Edmonton, capital of the adjoining province of Alberta, the police believe a serial killer might be connected to the bodies of twelve prostitutes found around that city since 1986. What puzzled the police was that, while prostitutes were going missing in Vancouver, no bodies were being dumped. Low Track's victims were simply disappearing.

In the last three months of 1998, while the task force was compiling old cases, four more Low Track prostitutes vanished. Thirty-one-year-old Julie Louise Young was last seen alive in October and finally reported missing on 1 June 1999. Drug-addict Angela Rebecca Jardine was twenty-eight when she went missing, but she was mentally handicapped and had the mind of a ten-year-old child. She had been working Low Track's streets since she was twenty. Last seen between 3.30 and 4 pm on 20 November 1998 at a rally of around seven hundred people in Oppenheimer Park in Vancouver's Downtown Eastside, she was reported missing on 6 December. Pickton was later charged with her murder.

Twenty-nine-year-old Michelle Gurney, a native American, disappeared in December 1998 and was reported missing on the 22nd. Twenty-year-old Marcella Helen Creison got out of jail on 27 December 1998. She was last seen at one or two o'clock the following morning around the corner from the Drake Hotel and never returned to the apartment where her mother and boyfriend were waiting with unopened Christmas presents. She was reported missing on 11 January 1999.

Some women who made the list were then discovered alive. Twenty-two-year-old Patricia Gay Perkins left Low Track and her one-year-old son in an effort to make a new life for herself. No one was concerned and it was eighteen years before she was reported missing in 1996. She then appeared on the published list of the Vancouver's missing prostitutes. On 17 December 1999, she phoned from Ontario to tell the police she was alive and drug-free.

Fifty-year-old Rose Ann Jensen was found in December 1999. She disappeared in October 1991. Reported missing soon after, she made the list in 1998. The following year, police discovered that she was alive and living in Toronto when they were scanning a national health-care database.

Linda Jean Coombes was reported missing twice – once in August 1994 and again in April 1999. However, she had died of a heroin overdose on 15 February 1994. Her body arrived in Vancouver's morgue without identification. She was so wasted that her own mother did not even recognise a photograph of her. But she was eventually identified in September 1999 by DNA and removed from the list.

Karen Anne Smith was reported missing on 27 April 1999, but was removed from the list when it was discovered that she had in fact died of heart failure in hospital in Edmonton on 13 February 1999. Twenty-four-year-old Anne Wolsey was reported missing by her mother on 1 January 1997. In March 2002, her father called from Montreal to tell police his daughter was alive and well.

Although five names were removed from the list of missing women, more were added and it became clear to the task force that some of the women must have been the victims of foul play. The police then began to look for suspects among men with a history of violence against prostitutes. Suspicion fell on thirty-six-year-old Michael Leopold, who had been arrested in 1996 for assaulting a Low Track streetwalker. He had beaten her and tried to force a rubber ball down her throat, though was scared off when a passer-by heard the girl's screams. Although he told a court-appointed psychiatrist about his fantasies of raping and murdering prostitutes, more went missing while he was being held. He was eventually absolved of any involvement in the disappearances, but was sentenced to fourteen years in prison for aggravated assault.

Another suspect was forty-three-year-old Barry Thomas Neidermier, a native of Alberta. He had been convicted of pimping a fourteen-year-old girl in 1990, which seems to have left him with a grudge against prostitutes. In April 2000, he was arrested for violent attacks on seven Downtown Eastside prostitutes. The charges against him including abduction, unlawful imprisonment, assault, sexual assault, theft and administering a noxious substance. One of Neidermier's victims appeared on the missing list and he was considered 'a person of interest'.

Then there was the unidentified rapist who attacked a thirty-eight-year-old woman outside her Low Track hotel in August 2001. During the attack, the assailant boasted that he had raped and killed other women in the Downtown Eastside. And there were others. The Downtown Eastside Youth Activities Society compiled a daily 'bad date' file, recording reports by local prostitutes of clients who attacked or threatened them.

Towards the end of 1998, thirty-seven-year-old Bill Hiscox told the police of the goings on at a pig farm in Port Coquitlam just outside Vancouver owned by David Francis and Robert 'Willie' Pickton. The brothers also owned a salvage firm in Surrey, southeast of Vancouver. Hiscox got a job there through a relative who had been a girlfriend of Robert Pickton in 1997. On several occasions, Hiscox had to go out to the pig farm to pick up his pay-cheques and described it as 'a creepy-looking place'.

After reading newspaper reports on Vancouver's missing women, Hiscox grew suspicious of the Pickton brothers, particularly Robert Pickton who was 'a pretty quiet guy' and drove a converted bus with deeply tinted windows. The brothers also ran a registered charity called the Piggy Palace Good Times Society. A non-profit society, its official mandate was to 'organise, co-ordinate, manage and operate special events, functions, dances, shows and exhibitions on behalf of service organisations, sports organisations and other worthy groups'. In fact, the Piggy Palace – a converted building at the hog farm – was a drinking club for local bikers which featured 'entertainment' provided by Low Track prostitutes.

Police were already aware of the Pickton brothers. David Pickton had been convicted of sexual assault in 1992, fined $1,000 and given thirty days' probation. Pickton attacked the victim in his trailer at the pig farm, but she managed to escape. Soon after Piggy Palace opened, the Port Coquitlam authorities sued the Pickton brothers and their sister, Linda Louise Wright, for violating local zoning laws. Their farm was zoned for agricultural use, but they had converted a farm building 'for the purpose of holding dances, concerts and other recreations' that drew as many as 1,800 persons. After a New Year's Eve party on 31 December 1998, the Picktons were serviced with an injunction banning future parties and the Piggy Palace Good Times Society was stripped of its non-profit status.

Robert Pickton had been charged with attempted murder in March 1997 after Wendy Lynn Eistetter, a drug addict and prostitute with a wild and reckless past, had been picked up on the roadside by a couple driving past the pig farm at 1.45 in the morning of the 24th. She was partially clothed, had been stabbed several times and was covered in blood.

The previous evening, Pickton had picked her up and driven her to the pig farm. According to the police report, Pickton then attempted 'to commit the murder of Wendy Lynn Eistetter, by stabbing her repeatedly with . . . a brown-handled kitchen knife. Although she has been handcuffed at the time, she had managed to grab the knife, stab Pickton and escape. He later showed up at Eagle Ridge Hospital, where he was treated for a stab wound.

A provincial court judge released Pickton on a $2,000 cash

bond with the undertaking that he stay at the farm and not have any contact with Ms Eistetter.

'You are to abstain completely from the use of alcohol and non-prescription drugs,' the judge ordered.

'I don't take them,' Pickton replied.

A trial date was set, but the charges were stayed before the matter went to court because the attorney-general's office decided 'there was no likelihood of conviction', despite the grievous wounds Wendy Eistetter suffered.

Though Pickton had walked free, the stabbing had convinced Hiscox that Pickton was responsible for the disappearance of women from Low Track. He said that Pickton 'frequents the downtown area all the time, for girls', and he told the police: 'All the purses and IDs are out there in his trailer.'

However, when the police searched the pig farm – three times according to press reports – they found nothing. While the Pickton brothers would remain 'persons of interest', their farm was not put under surveillance. Meanwhile the list of missing women grew longer. This was not just because women had continued to vanish from Low Track. Other women who had disappeared earlier were now coming to the attention of the authorities.

Forty-two-year-old Laura Mah was last seen on 1 August 1985, but was not reported missing until 3 August 1999. Mary Ann Clark – aka Nancy Greek – was twenty-three when she was last seen on the evening of 22 August 1991 in Victoria, the capital of British Columbia on Vancouver Island across the strait from the city of Vancouver itself. Concerns about Clark's well-being were raised the day after her disappearance because she had failed to return home to look after her two daughters – aged eight years and eight months – which was out of character.

'It was the birthday of her child that day, and for a sex street worker, she was a bit of a home-body. That's what was suspi-

254

cious at the start, because she would never have done that,' said Victoria Policeman Don Bland. However, he expressed doubts that she should be on the Low Track list as she had no connection to Vancouver and only worked the streets of the capital. Nevertheless Pickton was implicated in her disappearance and the investigation continues.

Elsie Sebastian, another native American, was forty when she went missing on 16 October 1992. Leigh Miner, a thirty-four-year-old heroin addict and prostitute, phoned her sister to ask for money on 17 December 1993. That was the last time anyone heard of her. She was reported missing on 24 February 1994. Seventeen-year-old Angela Mary Arsenault was last seen on 19 August 1994 and reported missing ten days later. Thirty-six-year-old Frances Ann Young was reported missing on 9 April 1996. Last seen leaving her home three days before to go for a walk, she was suffering from depression at the time of her disappearance.

Fifty-two-year-old Maria Laura Laliberte – alias Kim Keller – was last seen in Low Track on New Year's Day, but was only reported missing on 8 March 2002. Forty-two-year-old Cynthia 'Cindy' Feliks was last seen on 26 November 1997 and reported missing 8 January 2001, while Sherry Leigh Irving was last seen in April 1997 and reported missing the following year. Pickton has been charged with the murder of both Cynthia Feliks and Sherry Irving.

Ruby Anne Hardy, mother of three, disappeared at the age of thirty-three sometime in 1998, but was not reported missing until 27 March 2002. Native Americans Georgina Faith Papin and Jennifer Lynn Furminger vanished in 1999 along with Wendy Crawford, but did not make the listed until March 2000. Pickton was convicted of the murder of Georgina Papin, and charged with the murders of Jennifer Furminger and Wendy Crawford.

Thirty-year-old Brenda Ann Wolfe, who went missing on 1 February 1999, made the list a month later. Tiffany Louise

Drew was 27 when she disappeared on 31 December 1999, but she was not reported missing until 8 February 2002. Pickton was convicted of Brenda Wolfe's murder, and charged with Tiffany Drew's.

Publicity surrounding the list encouraged the reporting of missing persons. Forty-two-year-old Dawn Teresa Crey was last seen on Main and Hastings on 1 November 2000 and was reported missing on 11 December. Pickton was implicated in her disappearance. Debra Lynn Jones, aged forty-three, disappeared on 21 December 2000 and was reported missing four days later on Christmas Day. Pickton was charged with her murder. Twenty-five-year-old Patricia Rose Johnson went missing from Main and Hastings on 3 March 2001, but took three months to make the list. Heather Kathleen Bottomley, aged twenty-four, made the list the same day she was last seen – 17 April 2001 – even though the police described her as a 'violent suicide risk'. But it was Tricia Johnson's disappearance that attracted the most attention. Shortly before she disappeared she had been befriended by portrait photographer Lincoln Clarkes who was recording the lives of the drug-addicted prostitutes of Low Track for his books *Heroines*. She took time off from her revolving-door hustle for heroin and sex to talk to him about her world – how she had broken her boyfriend's heart, abandoning him and their two young children for heroin and crack cocaine.

Throughout the project Clarkes stayed close to Johnson, who was his original 'heroine'. They became friends. She tried to quit drugs for the sake of her kids. But her father's suicide had sent her into a tailspin. She had quit rehab and was repeatedly arrested for breaking and entering.

The last time Clarkes heard from Patricia Johnson was when she left a message on his home answering machine in February 2001.

'Hey, it's Tricia, Lincoln,' she said in a sing-song voice. 'Trying to get a hold of you, trying to find what's up! I wish

256

I had a number you can call me back at, but I don't. So all I can do is keep trying.'

Soon after she stopped cashing her welfare cheques, stopped phoning her family and even stopped any contact with her two children. Her mother, Marion Bryce, spoke of the terrible warning she had given her daughter who had already survived five years on the streets.

'She was here on New Year's Day,' she told reporters, 'and I told her, 'Patty, you're not even going to see twenty-five if you keep on – you'll be missing like those women down there.'''

Marion Bryce also contacted Clarkes, who gave her a photo of Patricia in shoulder-length hair, wearing a leather jacket, her lips puffy, burned by a crack pipe. Later, he brought her another portrait. Followed by a film crew, he was greeted by Bryce and her daughter Kathy.

Days after this blaze of publicity, Patricia Rose Johnson was listed as Missing Woman No. 44. Her last known possessions were recorded as 'a book (title not given), a comb, condoms, water, a spoon, cigarettes, a lighter, belt, watch, rings and a chain'.

Weeks after Johnson disappeared, the Royal Canadian Mounted Police, the federal law enforcement agency, joined the case and promptly assembled a team of investigators. But that did nothing to stem the growth of the list. Six years later, Pickton was charged with the murder of Patricia Rose Johnson and that of Heather Kathleen Bottomley.

Thirty-three-year-old Yvonne Marie Boen, who sometimes used the surname England, was listed only five days after she disappeared on 16 March 2001. Her mother, Lynn Metin, began to worry when her daughter, who had three sons, failed to show up in March 2001 for a visit with her middle son Troy, who Metin was raising.

'She was supposed to be here that Sunday to pick him up and she didn't show up,' Metin told the Vancouver *Sun* in

2004. 'She never contacted me. That just wasn't her. Every holiday, Troy's birthday, my birthday – it just wasn't like her not to phone.'

Pickton is implicated in her disappearance.

Heather Gabriel Chinnock, aged twenty-nine, vanished the following month. Pickton was charged with her murder. Then twenty-two-year-old Andrea Joesbury disappeared on 6 June 2001. Her grandfather Jack Cummer said Andrea was straightening out her life and providing a good home to her infant daughter in an East Vancouver apartment before she disappeared.

'She was working very hard, she needed a lot of things, but she was doing it all herself," Cummer told the Vancouver *Sun*. 'Andrea was worn to a frazzle, but the baby was well cared for.'

However, he said, social services received a complaint about the well-being of the girl and seized her, which sent his granddaughter into a downward spiral of drugs and prostitution.

'The thing is that she lost her whole reason to live,' Cummer said.

The child was adopted and the Cummers are not able to see her. Andrea, he said, either didn't realise or wouldn't accept the finality of the adoption, and would tell her grandparents that she was going to try to get her daughter back.

'She decided that she was going to straighten up and her prime objective was to get the baby back. I didn't have the heart to tell her that she was never going to do that,' he said.

Pickton was convicted for Andrea Joesbury's murder.

Twenty-nine-year-old Sereena Abotsway went missing on 1 August. Adopted at the age of four, she had always been in trouble.

'She was sweet and bubbly but she was very disturbed,' said her adopted mother Anna Draayers. 'She gave her teachers a headache and we tried to teach her at home but there was not much you could do. At that time we did not have a name for the condition but it is now known as foetal alcohol syndrome.'

The Draayers never lost contact with the child.

'She was our girl, and we loved her a lot,' they said. 'She phoned daily for thirteen years since she left our home at age seventeen.'

And hope was at hand.

'She had come home in July,' said Mrs Draayers, 'and she agreed to come home and celebrate her thirtieth birthday on 20 August, but she never showed up.'

Pickton was convicted of her murder.

Diane Rosemary Rock, aged thirty-four, was last seen on 19 October 2001 by the owner of the motel where she was living and was reported missing on 13 December. Diane, her husband and three children had moved to British Columbia in 1992 for a fresh start in life. But in their new home, Rock's personal problems resurfaced and she was back using drugs again. After a while her marriage fell apart and she was on her own. The last member of the family to see her was her teenage daughter. That was in June 2001 when they met her to celebrate the teenager's birthday. Pickton was charged with Diane Rock's murder.

Mona Lee Wilson, aged twenty-six, disappeared on 23 November 2001 and made the list a week later. She was the last to vanish. Her common-law husband Steve Ricks told reporters he had last seen her get into a car with two men.

'She told me many times she'd like to die,' Ricks said. 'She was sick of this hell, all the hooking and drugs.'

Pickton was charged with her murder.

By then, the disappearances had been going on for over two decades – and they were getting increasingly more frequent. In an attempt to pare down the list, detectives looked back at the earlier cases to see if other known criminals could have been responsible.

259

The elusive Green River Killer had been at large over the border in Washington State for much of the period. On 30 November 2001, fifty-two-year-old Gary Ridgway was charged with murdering four of the Green River victims. Two years later he pleaded guilty to forty-eight murders between 1982 and 1984. There were reports that Ridgway had visited Vancouver, but the police could make no connection between him and the missing women.

Dayton Leroy Rogers was abducting, torturing and killing prostitutes in Oregon in 1987. He was arrested on 7 August 1987, after murdering a prostitute in a parking lot in front of witnesses. Only then did it become clear that he was responsible for the murder of seven women whose bodies had been found in a wooded area near Molalla, twenty miles outside the city. Some had had their feet cut off, possibly while they were still alive. But Rogers was soon cleared of any involvement in the earlier Vancouver abductions.

George Waterfield Russell Jr – aka 'The Charmer', 'The Bellevue Killer' and, interestingly, 'The East Side Killer' – was also considered. He had killed three women in Bellevue, Washington in 1990. But he was discounted because he killed his victims in their own homes and then displayed them in elaborate poses, after he had raped and mutilated their corpses.

In 1995, Keith Hunter Jesperson, a British Columbian, was arrested in Washington State, for the murder of his girlfriend, forty-one-year-old Julie Winningham. He had strangled her and dumped her body at the roadside. He was a long-haul truck driver and it was then discovered that he had murdered women along his trucking routes across North America, dumping their bodies like 'piles of garbage' along the roadside. At one point he boasted 160 murders, though he has been convicted for just eight. But, again, the police could make no connection between the man the newspapers dubbed the 'Happy Face Killer' and the missing women from Low Track.

Seemingly mild-mannered US Navy veteran and father of two John Eric Armstrong was arrested in April 2000 for the murder of a number of Detroit prostitutes and promptly confessed to killing thirty women around the world during his time in the Navy. But his ship the USS *Nimitz* did not put into port near Vancouver when any of the women went missing.

Middle-aged father of five Robert Yates was convicted of killing fifteen women in Washington State in October 2000, but is thought to have killed at least eighteen, many of whom were drug addicts and prostitutes. The earliest killings he admitted to were those of two women in Walla Walla in 1975 and a woman in Skagit County in 1988. However, evidence could not place him in Vancouver at the time of any of the disappearances.

Vancouver had its own home-grown suspect in the person Ronald Richard McCauley, a twice-convicted rapist. Sentenced to seventeen years imprisonment in 1982, he was paroled in September 1994. In September 1995, he was arrested again after he picked up a prostitute at Vancouver's Astoria Hotel in July and drove her to Hemlock Valley, where she was beaten, raped and dumped from his truck. The woman reported the incident to police and McCauley was convicted of rape and attempted murder in 1996, declared a dangerous offender and jailed indefinitely.

McCauley came to the attention of the police again when the bodies of prostitutes Tracy Olajide, Tammy Lee Pipe and Victoria Younker, were found that year near Agassiz and Mission near Hemlock Valley. He was also a suspect in the murder of Mary Lidguerre whose body was found in north Vancouver two years later, and in the disappearance of Catherine Maureen Knight, Catherine Louise Gonzalez and Dorothy Anne Spence who went missing in 1995. Despite circumstantial evidence against him, he was never charged. Eventually he was cleared of the three Valley murders by

DNA evidence in 2001. He was detained indefinitely after telling a parole hearing that had he not been arrested for two rapes and attempted murders, he 'would have become a serial killer such as Clifford Olson'.

Then the police got a break. On 7 February 2002, Robert Pickton was arrested for the possession of illegal firearms. Meanwhile the task force began scouring the pig farm once again. Pickton was released on bail, but arrested again on 22 February – this time on two counts of first-degree murder. The victims were identified as Sereena Abotsway and Mona Lee Wilson. On 8 March, it was revealed that DNA recovered from the farm had been conclusively identified as Sereena's. Both had gone missing since Bill Hiscox had first reported his suspicions to the police

A month later, Pickton was charged with three more counts of murder – those of Jacqueline McDonnell, Heather Bottomley and Diane Rock. He was charged for the murder of Angela Josebury, six days later. Then on 22 May, a seventh first-degree murder charge was filed against Pickton when the remains of Brenda Wolfe were found on his farm. Again, all these women had gone missing after Hiscox first fingered Pickton.

This begged the question: If Pickton was the Low Track slayer, why had the searches of the farm in 1997 and 1998 not unearthed any evidence? And how could he have continued to abduct and murder victims afterwards, when he should have been under police surveillance?

The authorities were adamant that the evidence had been hard to come by as Pickton went to great lengths to dispose of the bodies. They were thought to have been left out in the open to decompose or be eaten by insects. Otherwise they were fed to the pigs on the farm. Forensic anthropologists spent two years and $70 million shifting through the soil on the farm in an attempt to find traces of remains. Then in March 2004, the authorities said that the victims' flesh may

262

have been ground up and mixed with pork from the farm. This pork was never sold commercially, but was handed out to friends and fed to visitors to the farm – perhaps even the prostitutes themselves. One man even said he saw Pickton hang a woman's body from a meat hook to strip the flesh from it. Pickton was charged with twenty-seven counts of first-degree murder.

Meanwhile Pickton maintained his innocence, even expressing concern, as a taxpayer, at the expense of the investigation. His trial began at the British Columbia Supreme Court on 30 January 2006. He pleaded not guilty on all counts. Before the jury was admitted, the court was closed to review the evidence. In March, one of the 27 counts was thrown out by the judge, ruling that Pickton could not be charged with the murder of a woman whose remains had been found but could not be identified. Then in August, the indictment was trimmed to just six counts. The judge argued that trying all twenty-six charges would put an unreasonable burden on the jury and, in a trial that could last up to two years, it would increase the chance of a mistrial. The remaining twenty counts have not been dismissed and Pickton can be tried for them at a later date.

During the trial, the jury heard that skulls cut in half with hands and feet stuffed inside were found on Pickton's property. The remains of one victim were found in a garbage bag stuffed in a dustbin. Her blood-stained clothes were found in Pickton's trailer, along with night-vision goggles, two pairs of faux fur-lined handcuffs, the aphrodisiac 'Spanish Fly', a syringe with three millilitres of blue liquid inside, a loaded .22 revolver with one round fired and a dildo over the barrel, and boxes of .357 Magnum handgun ammunition.

Part of another victim's jaw bone and teeth were found in the ground beside the pig-farm's slaughter house and a dildo containing both the victim's and Pickton's DNA was in his laundry room. This dildo was also attached to a .22 calibre revolver. In a videotape played to the jury, Pickton claimed to have used the dildo as a makeshift silencer.

Another videotape showed Pickton's friend Scott Chubb saying Pickton had told him a good way to kill a female heroin addict was to inject her with windshield-washer fluid. Another associate named Andrew Bellwood was filmed saying Pickton mentioned killing prostitutes by handcuffing and strangling them, then bleeding and gutting them before feeding them to pigs.

However, no eyewitness to the murders came forward, so the jury could not find him guilty of first degree murder. But they did find him guilty of second degree murder on all six counts. This also carries a life sentence and the judge ruled out any possibility of parole for twenty-five years. This is maximum punishment for second-degree murder, and equal to what he would have got for first-degree murder.

Pickton was convicted of the murder of Sereena Abotsway, Mona Lee Wilson, Andrea Joesbury, Brenda Ann Wolfe, Marnie Lee Frey and Georgina Faith Papin. He has been charge with, and may still stand trial for, the murder of Jacqueline Michelle McDonell, Dianne Rosemary Rock, Heather Kathleen Bottomley, Jennifer Lynn Furminger, Helen Mae Hallmark, Patricia Rose Johnson, Heather Chinnock, Tanya Holyk, Sherry Irving, Inga Monique Hall, Tiffany Drew, Sarah deVries, Cynthia Feliks, Angela Rebecca Jardine, Diana Melnick, Debra Lynne Jones, Wendy Crawford, Kerry Koski, Andrea Fay Borhaven and Cara Louise Ellis. Pickton has pleaded not guilty to the murder of these women, and refused to enter a plea in the case of the identified women that he had also been charged with killing.

He is also implicated in the disappearance of Mary Ann Clark (aka Nancy Greek), Yvonne Marie Boen, Dawn Teresa Crey, two unidentified women and many more missing women from Vancouver's Downside Eastside.

He has been caught on videotape boasting that he has killed nearly twice as many woman as he has been charged with. He may have killed many more – and certainly wanted to and would do so if he had the chance. The women who he picked on – though dismissed as drug addicts and prostitutes – were among the weakest and most vulnerable in society. Some were barely at the beginning of their lives.

Since his conviction, Pickton has kept up a correspondence with a journalist from his prison cell. Quoting freely from the Bible, he claims that he was put on earth to rid people of their 'evil ways'.

Chapter 16

Women Strike Back

Aileen Wuornos never made any secret of the fact that she hated men. When she hung out in The Last Resort, a Hell's Angels bar in Port Orange Florida, drinking and popping pills, she would curse all men and boasted that she would get even with this rotten masculine world.

The Hell's Angels put up with her and called her Spiderwoman for the black leather outfits she wore. She was just another outcast like them. She had certainly come from a tough background. Her first recollections were of her mother screaming while her alcoholic father dished out another brutal beating. When she was five, he abandoned his family. Her mother died when she was fourteen and, by the time she was nineteen, she was all alone in the world. Her father had died in prison after being convicted for sex offences and her only brother had died of cancer.

Aileen took to prostitution and armed robbery. She occasionally worked as a barmaid or cleaner, but her love of alcohol and drugs meant she could never hold down a job for long. She had no fixed abode and hitchhiked around the highways of Florida, sleeping outdoors on the beach or at the roadside.

The Last Resort was more of a home to her than anywhere else. She sometimes slept on the porch or in the so-called Japanese hanging gardens, where the Angels hung despised Japanese motorcycles from the trees. She was known to one and all as a foul-mouthed, ill-tempered drunk.

When Aileen was twenty-seven, she fell in love with 22-year-old Tyria Moore. It was a deeply romantic affair. Aileen believed Tyria would put an end to her loneliness, and that she would never abandon her as all the men in her life had.

She petted and pampered Ty, stealing in order to lavish her with luxuries. In September 1990, Aileen stole a car for her. But when the two women took it for a spin down a dirt road, the car went out of control and they abandoned it.

The two women had been spotted though, and their descriptions were put into the Marion County computer. It matched the two women to six murders in the area. The victims were all men. Their bodies had all been found dumped miles from their cars. Each had been shot exactly nine times and there was a condom wrapper left on the back seat of each of their cars.

Shortly after the incident with the stolen car, the unthinkable happened. Tyria left Aileen and fled to Pennsylvania. In January 1991, the police traced her there and arrested her for auto theft. Tyria broke down and blamed Aileen. She had lured her into a life of crime, Tyria said, and Aileen had murdered and robbed to buy expensive gifts for her.

Aileen was picked up, asleep on the porch of The Last Resort. She thought she was being arrested for a five-year-old firearms charge. But when the police dropped the names of the murder victims into the conversation she freely admitted killing them.

Usually she would be hitchhiking when her victim stopped in his car to offer her a lift. Or sometimes she would pretend that her car had broken down and that, as a woman, she needed help. Either way, once in the car, she would offer to have sex with the man and get him to drive to a deserted spot. After sex, she would then take her vengeance on all mankind. She would kill the son-of-a-bitch, and rob him of his money and jewellery into the bargain. Even the hardened Hell's Angels were shocked that they had been harbouring a man-slayer.

'It's scary, man,' said Cannonball, the barman at The Last Resort, 'everyone of those guys could have been one of them, and we would never have known where it was coming from . . . Mind you' I sorta think she would not have gone for a biker . . . we were her only folks . . . She was a lost soul, like most of us.'

Although she was found guilty of murder, it was never entirely clear at the trial how much Scottish housewife Sheila Garvie had planned the slaughter of her husband Max. But he was a sex fiend and she was grateful to be free of his brutal attentions.

Sheila Garvie, nee Watson, was born in Stonehaven and brought up in a turret apartment at Balmoral Castle where her father worked as an ornamental stonemason. She was a stout royalist and attended parties with the young Princesses, Margaret and Elizabeth. In her mid-teens, she took a job as a royal servant herself, rising to the heights of assistant house-keeper.

At eighteen, she left and took a job in Aberdeen. At a dance in Stonehaven, she met Max Garvie. He was tall and dark-haired, and she asked him for a dance in the 'ladies' excuse me'. Soon they began going out and the following Christmas they got engaged. They married in June 1954. The Garvies moved to West Cairnbeg in Kincardineshire, to the estate left to Max by his father. Sheila felt isolated in the rough stone farmhouse. She missed the bustle of Aberdeen and found it difficult to get on with the sombre, snobbish country people.

Soon she was pregnant with their first child. A second daughter followed a year later and their son was born in 1963. To the world, they presented a picture of rural contentment – the wealthy country gentleman with his adoring family around him. But beneath the surface, tension seethed.

Max had a reckless appetite for sex, and it was far beyond his staid young wife's capacity to fulfil it. He was a selfish lover, with little thought for his wife's satisfaction or needs. Fuelled by his interest in pornography, which he received mail-order from London, his sexual demands became, she said, 'excessive and unnatural'. In her despair, Sheila sought psychiatric advice.

It was the Sixties and Max thought what Sheila needed to do was loosen up. He took her to a nudist club near Edinburgh where she, reluctantly, stripped off. Max also organised candlelit sex parties at the farmhouse and set up his own nudist colony, which the locals knew as 'Kinky Cottage'.

In an attempt to wean her husband's attention off sex and nudism, Sheila encouraged Max to start a flying club. Light aircraft had always been one of his passions. But Max found that flying only thrilled him now if he was fired up on handfuls of 'uppers' swilled down with whisky.

Crazed with this lethal mixture, he would dive on cars and try and force them off the road. In one incident, he flew so low across the local bay that the passengers in a small boat had to leap into the water for safety. Normally, the local people tolerated the eccentricity of the laird, but this incident led to a prosecution for reckless endangerment.

Max Garvie was also passionately interested in politics. In 1967, he dragged Sheila to a rally of the Scottish Nationalist Party in Stirling. Max got drunk. On the way back, Sheila had to smile apologetically at the other passengers. They were sympathetic. One of them walked her to her car while Max reeled drunkenly along behind. His name was Brian Tevendale. At twenty-two, he was ten years her junior.

Max took to Tevendale. One night, after a drinking session in the Marine Hotel, he invited Tevendale to join them in a fish supper before turning in. At the chip shop, they left Sheila in the car. But a few moments later, Tevendale returned saying Max had sent him to 'keep her happy'. They kissed and cuddled in the back of the car. When Max heard about it, he was amused.

Brian came to visit regularly. Often he would stay for weekends at the farmhouse, sleeping in the spare room. Then in September 1967, he turned up with his sister Trudy Birse, the wife of an Aberdeen policeman.

Max was immediately attracted to Trudy. He took her for a spin in his plane. Within a week, they were lovers and Max made no secret of the fact. He urged Sheila to go to bed with Brian. She resisted, but he was insistent. One night when Brian was staying, Max practically threw her into Brian's bedroom. He told her to stay there and closed the door behind her. She was a little drunk and let her guard down. That night, she and Brian made love for the first time.

When she returned to the master bedroom, Max was in a state of high excitement. The fact that she had just come from Brian's bed turned him on tremendously and he insisted on making love right away. Sheila had no choice, but the act repelled her. She had lost all respect for Max and now felt nothing for him physically.

'From then on,' she said, 'every time we were intimate I felt as though I was being raped by a stranger.'

This strange four-way relationship was not confined to the privacy of the farmhouse. They even spent nights together in Edinburgh and Glasgow hotels.

As if things were not complicated enough, Max invited Trudy's husband Fred – a policeman – along to one of his booze and drugs parties in West Cairnbeg. He even laid on a local girl for him for the night. But the arrangements were not to Fred's taste and he drove the girl home, leaving his wife in the bed of his host.

By this time, Sheila was finding it increasingly difficult to cope. She was falling in love with Brian. Max realised the danger and in a drunken rage demanded that she choose between him and her lover. Even the local minister was called in to keep the peace. Only then did Max strike up a bargain to save his marriage, saying he would give up Trudy if she would give up Brian.

Sheila agreed. But the situation had gone too far. Deprived of his usual sexual outlet, Max's behaviour became so bizarre that Sheila thought he was going mad. In February 1968, she phoned Brian and asked him to run away with her.

They fled to Bradford in Yorkshire. But this did not resolve the situation either. Within a week, she had phoned her husband. Without telling Tevendale, she met Max at Heathrow Airport and flew home with him. Back in West Cairnbeg, Sheila faced an inquisition on what she had done with Tevendale in Bradford. Max was in a drunken rage and, unable to stand any more pressure, Sheila swallowed half a dozen tranquillisers.

Max phoned a doctor, but before the doctor arrived he turned violent. He threatened her with a broken glass and threw her against a wall. After tending her wounds, the doctor suggested she visit a psychiatric clinic.

Things were a little more settled by April, but then, entirely by accident, Sheila bumped into Brian Tevendale while out shopping in Stonehaven. Tevendale warned, darkly, that men often get rid of their unwanted wives by having them committed to mental institutions. Back at West Cairnbeg, Sheila faced another inquisition. A friend had seen her with Tevendale in Stonehaven and called Max.

On the night of his murder, Max Garvie had been out at an SNP meeting in Stonehaven. When he returned home, a

271

discussion about using the Soneryl pills that he had bought to calm their sexual appetites turned into another drunken row. According to Sheila, she went up to bed, took some sleeping tablets and changed into her short white nightie. Max followed. They made love and fell asleep.

She said that the next thing she remembered was being awoken by someone standing over her. They whispered to her to get up. It was Brian Tevendale and a friend. Brian was carrying a gun.

She was bundled into the bathroom. From the bedroom, she heard terrible thumping noises. Then there was a shot. Max had been beaten to death and then, for good measure, shot in the head. Tevendale and his accomplice, Alan Peters, carried Garvie's body downstairs to their car. They drove to a ruined castle at St Cyrus in Angus nearby and hid the body in a culvert there.

Back at the farmhouse, Sheila cleaned up as best she could, scrubbing away the bloodstains. The three children, used to bizarre goings on in the home, slept through the entire thing.

Throughout her trial, she maintained that she knew nothing of Tevendale's intentions before the murder. But afterwards she decided that she would do everything she could to protect her lover. She was convinced that he had been driven to murder through his love for her.

Next day Tevendale told his sister: 'It's done . . . Max is dead.'

Once the mattress that Max had been killed on had been replaced and all the other incriminating evidence was tidied away, Max was reported missing. His picture was circulated in the Police Gazette. The description that went along with it noted that Garvie was 'fond of female company but has strong homosexual tendencies and is often in the company of young men'. When questioned, Tevendale had told the police that Max had tried several times to seduce him.

Sheila and Brian were still very much in love and for three months they were seen out together, looking happy and carefree. The good people of Kincardineshire thought that this was not the way a wife whose husband was missing should behave. When the laird did not make his court appearance for dangerous flying, they were convinced that he was dead and the locals began a search of the area.

Sheila, Brian, Trudy and Alan Peters all tried to go on as if nothing had happened. Twenty-year-old Alan got married to his eighteen-year-old girlfriend Helen Strachan, who was pregnant. At the small reception, the bride was the only one who did not know about the murder.

Sheila and Trudy helped out during the Glasgow Fair in the pub where Tevendale worked. For two weeks, Sheila manned the bar with her lover, before they went back to Trudy's, to make love into the early hours of the morning.

Sheila began to feel the strain though. She was making love each night with the man who had killed the father of her children. She had to turn to someone and confided at least part of the story to her mother, who was at West Cairnbeg looking after the children. Mrs Watson was appalled. She banned Tevendale from the farmhouse. After a final, terrible row, Mrs Watson went to the police.

In court, Sheila Garvie claimed that she knew nothing of Tevendale's plan and was guilty only of concealing the facts to protect her lover after the murder. The local minister said that Sheila Garvie had confided in him and he was led to understand that she had been subjected to all forms of perverted intercourse.

Mrs Watson also stuck up for her daughter, saying that Max Garvie had boasted that he forced her into a threesome with Tevendale.

'He just said that he had tossed up to see who would sleep with my daughter first,' she told the packed courtroom. 'It was horrible.'

273

Trudy Birse testified that Max had told her that Sheila was frigid and did not respond to his lovemaking. He had encouraged the relationship between Sheila and her brother to make her a better lover. Trudy also recounted to a stunned court that Max had told her that 'he had more pleasure from myself in two weeks than he had ever had from her in their married life – I told him it was a very cruel thing to say to her.'

She also said that her brother had told her, the morning after the murder, that Alan Peters had struck Max with a steel bar and that he had shot Max believing that he was already dead.

Alan Peters also went into the witness box. He said that he had driven up to the farmhouse with Tevendale and that Mrs Garvie had not been surprised to see them. Once inside the house, Tevendale had taken a gun from behind the door, loaded it and gone upstairs. Max Garvie was asleep face down on the bed. Tevendale had told him to stay back while he struck Garvie several times on the back of the head. Then he picked up a pillow, covered the man's head, and shot through the pillow.

Tevendale did not go into the witness box. But in his statement to the police he said that he had been drinking with Max and Sheila. Later, Sheila had told him that Max had gone upstairs with a gun and had threatened to shoot her if she did not have anal intercourse with him. This was more than Tevendale could stand. He went up after Max. There was a struggle and Garvie was killed.

Despite his admission of being present at the murder, the jury found that the case against Alan Peters was not proven. Brian Tevendale and Sheila Garvie were found guilty of murder – though in Mrs Garvie's case the verdict was not unanimous. Although it was never established in the court that Mrs Garvie had known about Tevendale's plans before the murder, she did not appeal.

Both she and Tevendale served ten years. After their

274

release, they never spoke or met again. He met and married a 21-year-old divorced mother of two in Perth. Sheila had a short turbulent second marriage to a former Rhodesian soldier thirteen years her junior, then married a third time in 1981 to a 54-year-old drilling engineer.

French housewife Simone Webber was found not guilty of killing her second husband, though he died in mysterious circumstances, but she was sentenced to twenty years imprisonment for murdering her fickle lover and hacking his body to pieces.

Eighty-year-old Marcel Fixard, a retired army officer, was looking for a new woman in his life. Despite a housekeeper and twenty-five nieces and nephews, he was lonesome after the death of his wife of fifty years. He decided to advertise in a lonely hearts column.

He was not, he explained, looking for a young lover. He wanted a woman about his own age, with no children, to keep him company in his declining years.

In 1977, a woman responded. She said she was a retired professor of philosophy and claimed that she was in her mid-seventies. She also said her name was Monique Thuot. It was not. It was Simone Webber. She was fifty-five and she had four children.

For three months, they corresponded. Marcel said that he had been very happy throughout his first marriage and thought he could be as happy in his second with 'chere Monique'. Her letters, he said, had brought 'rays of sunshine' into his life.

Simone agreed to live with Marcel Fixard, but found his unalloyed attention cloying. Then her daughter Madeleine turned up. Webber pretended that she was her niece. Her daughter said that Simone's son Philippe had committed suicide, the second of her children to do so. Simone explained to Fixard that she had to go to her home in Strasbourg.

When Simone returned to Marcel, she found him in the

275

company of another woman and felt betrayed. All talk of marriage ceased, but Simone eventually succumbed to Marcel's blandishments and moved back in with him.

Marcel was sprightly and alert and resumed his talk of marriage, sometimes entertaining other eligible spinsters to make Simone jealous. Unbeknownst to Marcel, Simone was still married to the father of her children. The marriage had broken up because Simone was so possessive that she had had her husband followed, convinced that he was sleeping around.

Alone, Simone had struggled to survive and had run up huge debts. The fact that she had not obtained a divorce had cost her her lover shortly afterwards. Finding that he could not marry Simone, her boyfriend had wed another. Simone had gone to great lengths to try to destroy their marriage. She was not going to let the same thing happen with Marcel and, this time, she pushed through her divorce. But by the time it was granted, in November 1978, Marcel had gone off the idea.

Simone and Marcel fought and one of his nephew's persuaded him to make a will in his favour. Gradually though, Marcel was coming under the control of the irascible Simone. Despite his glowing good health, she persuaded him to let her inject him with 'tonics'. Soon his health began to deteriorate. His housekeeper also noticed that Simone carried a gun. She even found a bullet lodged in an upstairs ceiling after a particularly violent row.

But Marcel still refused to marry Simone. So she hired an actor to take Marcel's place. Actor Georges Hesling underwent the prenuptial medical examination required by French law, said 'I do' in Strasbourg Town Hall and played the part of Marcel Fixard when his will was altered, making his new wife the sole beneficiary.

Two weeks after the ceremony, Simone Webber bought two boxes of digitalis, a heart stimulant that can be fatal in large doses. Soon Marcel's speech became slurred and he became unsteady on his feet. Three weeks after his marriage – which had been kept secret even from him – he suffered a massive heart attack and died.

Simone Webber paid off her debts and lived comfortably in Marcel Fixard's house. Then she met an old friend, Bernard Hettier, who she had not seen for thirteen years. He had been the lover of one of her friends, but that relationship had broken up some time before.

Simone and Bernard became lovers and moved in together. But Bernard was a ladies' man and kept another, younger, mistress on the side. Simone grew suspicious, searched his things and found letters from his young mistress thanking Bernard for his financial support. She had him followed.

Confronted with the evidence of his infidelity, he admitted everything and agreed to curb his ways. But he did not. Simone was suspicious, even checking the mileage on the clock of his car. Eventually she threw him out.

Bernard took a new lover. Soon they were bombarded with insulting anonymous phone calls. He went on seeing Simone to try and calm her down. In response, she began stealing things from him. He even began to believe that she was trying to poison him.

On 22 June 1985, Simone Webber was waiting outside Bernard Hettier's house when he returned home. They went inside. A few minutes later, neighbours saw them come out again and walk to their cars. Bernard Hettier was never seen again.

Simone maintained that Bernard had headed off to the post office. He had agreed to come round to unblock a drain for her later, but a man called 'Robert', who she did not know, had called to say that Bernard would not be able to make it. However, Simone had persuaded her son-in-law Pascal to get a doctor's certificate saying that Bernard was unfit for work.

But when it was sent to Bernard's employers, they noticed that both the social security number and the address were wrong and they alerted the police.

Suspicion turned on Simone. She was found to be in possession of Bernard's identity card and his car, with the number plates changed. In her apartment, the police found a .22 rifle, with a silencer and a spent cartridge, and an air rifle. And in her sister's apartment, which Simone also used, they found another .22 rifle, with a silencer and spent cartridge in the chamber, and two handguns. There was another spent cartridge on the floor and three sticks of dynamite. But there was still no sign of Bernard.

Simone was arrested for the illegal possession of firearms, theft, using false number plates and murder. Marcel Fixard's body was exhumed but, unlike poisons such as arsenic which linger indefinitely in a corpse, digitalis disappears completely after a few years.

Then a torso was found in the nearby River Marne. It had been weighed down by breeze blocks. The head, arms and legs were missing. They had been severed with some kind of power tool.

The missing head and limbs were never found and forensic scientists found it impossible to prove that the torso was Bernard Hettier's. However, a hand-held circular saw that Simone Webber had rented and later reported stolen was found in one of her cars.

It was the power saw that was Simone Webber's undoing. In an attempt to show that it would be possible for a small middle-aged woman to dismember a body, Judge Thiel conducted a bizarre courtroom experiment. He used the circular saw Webber had rented to cut up a side of beef. It took moments to slice off the leg and shoulder. What's more, no blood splattered. Forensic scientists explained that blood coagulates in the body a matter of hours after death and the blade of the circular saw – which was never found – rotates so fast that it would cook the meat on either side, sealing any residual fluid in.

The trial caused a sensation in France. Webber was dubbed the 'She-Devil of Nancy'. When sentenced she said calmly: 'I shall write to President Mitterrand.'

Chapter 17

Sex and Satan

Richard Ramirez, the Night Stalker who terrorised Los Angeles for two years, was a devil worshipper. A scrawled pentagram – a satanic symbol – was his calling card and he made his rape victims declare their love of Satan before he slaughtered them.

The Night Stalker's murder career began ordinarily enough. On the night of 28 June 1984, the mutilated body of 79-year-old Jennie Vincow was found spread-eagled on the bed of her one-bedroom apartment in the Eagle Rock district of Los Angeles. She had been raped and her throat had been slashed so violently that she had almost been decapitated. There was blood on the walls of the bedroom and bathroom and her flat had been ransacked. But in LA, it was just another murder.

Nine months later he attacked again. Maria Hernandez had just parked her car in her garage in the Rosemeade suburb of Los Angeles and was walking towards her apartment, when she heard footsteps behind her. She turned to be confronted by a man with a gun. He shot her but, miraculously, the bullet ricocheted off her car keys and hit her with only a glancing blow.

Even so, the impact of the bullet was enough to knock her to the ground. The gunman stepped over her, giving her a vicious kicking, and made his way into her apartment. From inside, Maria heard a gunshot. She staggered to her feet, only to be confronted again by the gunman running from the house.

'Please don't shoot me again,' she begged. The gunman froze, then took to his heels.

Inside the apartment Maria Hernandez found her boyfriend, 34-year-old Hawaiian-born traffic manager Dayle Okazaki, lying on the kitchen floor, dead. He had been shot through the head.

There was only one clue to the murder. Maria said that the gunman had worn a baseball cap with the AC/DC logo on the front. AC/DC were an Australian heavy metal band who had recently released an album called *Highway to Hell*. On it, there was track called 'Night Prowler'. This was the nom d'assassin Ramirez preferred. He was annoyed that the newspapers insisted on calling him the Night Stalker.

That night, his lust for blood had not nearly been satisfied. Less than an hour later, on his way home, Ramirez pulled thirty-year-old Taiwanese law student Tsai Lian Yu from her car and shot her repeatedly. She died before the ambulance arrived.

Ten days later, Ramirez entered the home of Vincent and Maxine Zazzara, half a mile from the San Gabriel freeway. Maxine was a successful lawyer and Vincent had just fulfilled a lifetime ambition to open his own pizzeria. Both of them were shot at point-blank range and Maxine Zazzara's naked body was mutilated after death. Ramirez stabbed her repeatedly. The wounds made a pattern of a large ragged T. He also gouged her eyes out. The bodies were found by their son Peter, when he called in at the house the next day.

On 14 May, Ramirez broke into the home of William and Lillie Doi. He shot 66-year-old William in the head while he lay sleeping. His wife, 63-year-old Lillie who was in bed next to him, was beaten repeatedly around the head until she told the intruder where the valuables were hidden. Then he handcuffed her and ransacked the house. Later he returned to rape her.

A fortnight later, Carol Kyle was awoken in her Burbank flat by a torch shining in her eyes. A man pointed a gun at her and dragged her out of bed. In the next room, Carol's terrified 12-year-old son was handcuffed and locked in a cupboard. His mother was then raped. Even then, she was sympathetic.

'You must have had a very unhappy life to have done this to me,' she said.

Ramirez shrugged off her sympathy.

'I don't know why I'm letting you live,' he spat. 'I've killed people before.'

He ransacked the apartment for valuables. Satisfied with the jewellery he found, he went away, leaving both Carol and her son alive.

Around the same time, two elderly women, 83-year-old Mabel Bell and her 80-year-old sister Florence Long, an invalid, were attacked in their home in the suburb of Monrovia. On 1 June, Carlos Venwezala, a gardener who did chores for the sisters, dropped round. The house was unusually silent and he let himself in. He found Florence lying on her bed in a coma. There was a huge wound over her ear and a bloodstained hammer was lying on the dressing table. Mabel was lying barely conscious on her bedroom floor in a pool of her own blood. Both women had been beaten with the hammer. They had been cut and tortured. There were even signs that Ramirez had tried to rape the older sister Mabel. The police concluded that the two sisters had been left that way for two days.

The house had been ransacked but, this time, the attacker had left some clues. Along with the hammer, he had left a half-eaten banana on the dining table. He had also left what was to become his trademark – an inverted pentagram, the encircled five-point star that is used in witchcraft. One was scrawled in lipstick on Mabel's thigh. Another was drawn on Florence's bedroom wall.

Six weeks after the attack Mabel Bell died. But Florence eventually regained consciousness and survived.

Then the Night Stalker's onslaught began in earnest. On the night of 27 June 1985, Ramirez slashed the throat of 32-year-old Patty Elaine Higgins in her home in Arcadia. The same fate befell Mary Louise Cannon five days afterwards. Three days later, again in Arcadia, Ramirez savagely beat sixteen-year-old Whitney Bennett with a crowbar. She survived.

Ramirez turned his attention back to Monterey Park, where Tsai Lian Yu and the Dois had been attacked. On 7 July, 61-year-old Joyce Lucille Nelson was found beaten to death in her home and 63-year-old Sophie Dickmann was raped and robbed in her apartment

On 20 July, Ramirez murdered 66-year-old Maxson Kneiding and his 64-year-old wife Lela in their Glendale home, then went on to murder 32-year-old Chainarong Khovananth at his home in Sun Valley. After shooting him as he lay asleep in his bed, Ramirez raped and beat Chainarong's 29-year-old wife Somkid. He forced her to perform oral sex on him and stole $30,000 in cash and jewellery. Then he forced her to swear in Satan's name that she would not cry out and then raped her eight-year-old son.

The police had concluded long ago that they had a serial killer on their hands. The problem was that he had no clear modus operandi. He killed with guns, hammers and knifes. He raped orally, anally and genitally both children and women, young and old. Sometimes he mutilated the bodies after death, sometimes he didn't. The LAPD quipped that he was an equal-opportunity monster.

But some patterns were emerging. The killer stalked quiet suburbs away from the city's main centres of crime, where home-owners were less security conscious. He tended to pick houses painted in beige or pastel yellow. They were usually close to a freeway, making his escape easier.

Entry was through an open window or an unlocked door. Although burglary was one of his motives, rape and sheer brutality seemed also to figure highly. Pentagrams and other satanic symbols were also commonly left by the killer.

On the night of 5 August, postal worker Virginia Petersen was awoken by the sound of an intruder. She sat up in bed and cried out: 'Who are you? What do you want?'

The burglar laughed, then shot her in the face. The bullet entered the cheek just below her eye and went clean through the back of her head. Miraculously, she survived.

Her husband Christopher, who was lying beside her, was woken by the shot. He leapt to his wife's defence. This earned him a bullet in the temple. But Christopher Petersen was a tough guy, a truck driver. It took more than one small-calibre bullet to put him down. He dived out of bed and chased his attacker. The intruder was unprepared for this. He panicked and ran.

Christopher Petersen also survived the ordeal, though he has suffered partial memory loss and has had to live ever since with a bullet lodged in his brain. But, for the first time, the Night Stalker had been put to flight.

It did not end his violent rampage though. Three days later, he shot another 35-year-old Asian man and beat and raped his 28-year-old wife. Again she was forced to swear by Satan that she would not cry out, but this time he left their two young children unharmed, though their three year-old son Amez was tied up.

By this time, public opinion was at fever pitch in Los Angeles. In the affluent suburbs, locksmiths and burglar alarm salesmen were doing a roaring trade. Gun shops quickly sold out and local residents set up neighbourhood watch committees.

So Ramirez took a vacation. He travelled north to San Francisco. There on the night of 17 August, he attacked 66-year-old Asian accountant Peter Pan and his 64-year-old wife Barbara in their home in the suburb of Lake Merced. Both were shot through the head. An inverted pentagram was painted in lipstick on the bedroom wall, and under it, Ramirez wrote 'Jack the Knife'. At first, the police thought it was a copy-cat killing. But the bullets that he killed the couple with matched the small calibre rounds found in the Los Angeles murders.

A week later, Ramirez travelled 50 miles south of Los Angeles to the small town of Mission Viejo. He shot 29-year-old computer engineer William Carns three times in the head and raped his fiancée Inez Erickson, also twenty-nine, twice.

'You know who I am, don't you,' Ramirez said. 'I'm the one they're writing about in the newspapers and on TV.'

He also forced Inez to say 'I love Satan' during her ordeal.

William Carns survived the shooting, but suffered permanent brain damage. The couple never married. Inez managed to spot Ramirez's rusty old orange Toyota after he left the house. This proved to be the vital clue that put an end to the reign of the Night Stalker.

A sharp-eyed kid, James Romero III, had also spotted the orange Toyota as it cruised the area and had noted down its licence-plate number. The police put out an all-points bulletin. Two days later, the cab was found in a parking lot of Los Angeles' Rampart suburb.

Forensic scientists used a radical new technique when examining the car. They put a dab of Superglue in a saucer in the car and sealed the doors and window. Fumes from the Superglue would react with moisture in any fingerprints and then turn them white. The interior of the car was then scanned using a laser beam. This technique should pick up any fingerprints, including those that the culprit had tried to wipe off.

The scan yielded one finger print. It was computer matched to that of 25-year-old Ricardo Ramirez, who had been arrested three times for marijuana possession in El Paso. Soon Ramirez's photograph was on the front page of every newspaper in California.

Ramirez was quite unaware of this when he stepped down from the Greyhound bus at Los Angeles' main bus station. He had been out in Phoenix, Arizona, to score some cocaine and was high. He had killed thirteen people so far and felt good. Surely by now he must be Satan's favourite son.

He went to a drugstore to buy himself a Pepsi. Then at the checkout desk he saw his own face splashed across the Spanish language paper *La Opinion*. The checkout clerk recognised him too, so did the other customers. Ramirez made a run for it.

In the street, someone cried out: 'It's the Night Stalker.' Soon he heard the wail of police sirens behind him. He knocked on a door. Bonnie Navarro opened it. Ramirez shouted 'Help me' in Spanish. She slammed the door in his face.

On the next block, he tried to pull a woman from her car, but bystanders rushed to her rescue. Ramirez jumped a fence into a backyard where Luis Muñoz was cooking a barbecue. He hit Ramirez with his tongs. In the next garden, he tried to steal a red 1966 Mustang, but 56-year-old Faustin Pinon, who was working on the transmission, grabbed him in a headlock. Ramirez broke free, but across the street 55-year-old construction worker Jose Burgoin heard Pinon's shouts. He picked up a steel rod and hit Ramirez with it. Ramirez stumbled on but Burgoin soon caught up with him. This time he dubbed him to the ground.

In the nick of time, Deputy Sheriff Andres Ramirez pulled up in a patrol car.

'Save me!' yelled the Night Stalker.

As his namesake handcuffed him, Ramirez said: 'Thank God you came. I am the one you want. Save me before they kill me.'

Only the arrival of more police patrol cars prevented the angry mob taking the law into their own hands. Even at the police station, a crowd gathered calling for him to be lynched.

Ramirez showed no contrition. He told the police: 'I love to kill people. I love watching them die. I would shoot them in the head and they would wiggle and squirm all over the place, and then just stop. Or I would cut them with a knife and watch their faces turn real white. I love all that blood. I told one lady one time to give me all her money. She said no. So I cut her and pulled her eyes out.'

In court, Ramirez made satanic signs and even appeared with the inverted pentagram scratched in his palm. He told the judge: 'You maggots make me sick. Hypocrites one and all. You don't understand me. You are not expected to. You are not capable of it. I am beyond your experience. I am beyond good and evil.'

Ramirez was found guilty on sixty-three counts, including thirteen murders. He was sentenced to twelve death penalties and over 100 years imprisonment. Automatic appeals make it unlikely that he will go to the gas chamber this century.

But curiously, while many urge his execution, many women write to him sending provocative pictures, pledging undying love and proposing marriage. When Ramirez accepted divorcée Christine Lee over nude model Kelly Marquez, it made headlines.

Christine, a mother of two, bombarded Ramirez with pin-up pictures of herself and has visited him over 150 times. She is undaunted by the fact that her husband-to-be is a perverted killer.

'We really love each other and that's all that matters,' she says. 'From the moment I saw him in prison, I knew he was special. I couldn't believe he was the evil monster people

287

were calling him. He's always been sweet and kind to me.'

Charles Manson was another murderer who flirted with Satanism. He was born in 1934 in Cincinnati, Ohio, the illegitimate son of a teenage prostitute. Unable to support herself and her son, even through prostitution, his mother left him with her mother in McMechen, West Virginia. Later, he was sent to the famous orphans home, Boys Town in Nebraska. He was kicked out for his surly manner and constant thieving.

Manson became a drifter and was soon arrested for stealing food. He was sent to Indiana Boys School, where he escaped eighteen times. In 1951, he was arrested again for theft in Beaver City, Utah, and served four years in a federal reformatory.

In November 1954, he was released. He got married, before being arrested for transporting stolen cars across a state line and sentenced to three years in Terminal Island Federal Prison near Los Angeles.

Out again in 1958, Manson became a pimp and was arrested repeatedly under the Mann Act for transporting women across state lines for immoral purposes. He started forging cheques. When he was caught, he was sentenced to ten years in the federal penitentiary on McNeil Island in Washington state.

Being small, just five foot two, he had a hard time in prison. He was raped repeatedly by other prisoners, many of whom were black. This left him with a lifelong racial chip on his shoulder.

To survive in prison, Manson became shifty, cunning and manipulative. This set him in good stead when he was released in 1967. He soon discovered that he could use the manipulative powers he had learnt in jail on the long-haired flower children that inhabited Southern California. With his hypnotic stare, his unconventional lifestyle and the strange meaningless phrases he babbled, he was the perfect hippy

288

guru. His contempt for authority and convention made him a focus of the counter-culture and he soon developed a penchant for the fashionable middle-class girls who had dropped out of mainstream society according to the fashion.

Manson travelled with an entourage of hangers-on, known as the Family. They comprised young women – who were all his lovers – and docile males who would do anything he told them to. They numbered as many as thirty at one time.

One typical recruit was Patricia Krenwinkel. She was a former Girl Scout from a normal middle-class family. Her expensive education earned her a good job at a big insurance company in Los Angeles. She met Manson on Manhattan Beach when she was twenty-one and abandoned everything for him. She ditched her car and walked out of her job without even bothering to pick up her last paycheque. She moved in with the Family on Spahn Movie Ranch, a collection of broken-down shacks in the dusty east corner of the Simi Valley where they hung out.

Leslie Van Houten was just nineteen when she had dropped out of school. She lived on the streets on a perpetual acid trip until she met Manson. Twenty-year-old Linda Kasabian left her husband and two children and stole $5,000 from a friend to join the Family. She too began to see her seamy life through a constant haze of LSD.

The woman who brought Satanism to the Family was Susan Atkins, a 21-year-old topless dancer and barroom hustler. A practising devil worshipper, she became Manson's closest aide. But, like the others, she had to share his sexual favours. Manson quenched his insatiable sexual appetite with his female followers, one or two at a time – or even with all of them together. He knew the power of sex and drugs. When, for a short while in the 1950s, he had been a pimp, he had fallen in love with his main girl, who had dumped him. Then he had picked up two girls – Mary and Darlene – and had slept with them on a rota basis. Soon he had them in his thrall.

With the girls in the Family, he used LSD and orgies to control them. He would choreograph his sexual activities with his followers, artistically positioning their naked bodies. He also promised each girl a baby in return for their devotion, while Susan used the situation to plant her naive Satanist ideas into their receptive minds.

One of the few men in the commune was 23-year-old former highschool football star from Farmersville, Texas, Charles 'Tex' Watson. He had once been an honours student, but in Manson's hands he had become a mindless automaton.

Surrounded by these compliant sycophants, the drug-addled Manson began to enjoy huge delusions, fuelled by Susan Atkins' studies of Satanism. She convinced him that his own name, Manson, was significant. Manson, or Man-son, meant Son of Man, or Christ, in her twisted logic. He was also the devil, Susan Atkins said.

The lyrics of the Beatles' songs were also dragged into Manson's growing delusions. He was blissfully unaware that a helter skelter was a harmless British funfair ride and interpreted the track 'Helter Skelter' on the Beatles White Album as heralding the beginning of what he saw as an inevitable race war. The blacks would be wiped out, along with the pigs – the police, authority figures, the rich and the famous, and what Manson called 'movie people'.

Manson fancied himself as something of a popstar himself and took one of his feeble compositions to successful West Coast musician Gary Hinman. Manson also learned that Hinman had recently inherited $20,000. He sent Susan Atkins and Bob Beausoleil – a Family hanger-on – to steal it and to kill Hinman for refusing to put Manson at the top of the charts, where he believed he belonged. They held Hinman hostage for two days and ransacked the house. The money was not there. So out of frustration, they stabbed him to death. Then devil-worshipper Susan Atkins dipped her finger in Hinman's blood and wrote 'political piggie' on the wall.

The police found Beausoleil's fingerprints in the house and tracked him down. They found the knife that killed Hinman and a T-shirt drenched in Hinman's blood in Beausoleil's car. He was convicted of murder and went to jail – without implicating Atkins or Manson.

This loyalty impressed Manson not at all and he began to plan new acts of violence. Next he tried to get his dire composition recorded by Doris Day's son, Terry Melcher. Melcher was a big player in the music industry, but failed to see the potential in Manson's material.

Manson's followers formed a death squad. They dressed in black and trained themselves in the arts of breaking and entering abandoned buildings. These exercises were known as 'creepy crawlies'. They were told that they should kill anyone who stood in their way.

On 8 August 1969, Manson's death squad was despatched to Melcher's remote home on Cielo Drive in Benedict Canyon. Melcher no longer lived in the same house in the Hollywood Hills. This did not matter to Manson. The people he saw going into the house were 'movie types'. Their slaughter would act as a warning. Tex Watson, Susan Atkins, Patricia Krenwinkel and Linda Kasabian were sent in armed with a .22 revolver, a knife and a length of rope.

The house at the end of Cielo Drive was indeed occupied by 'movie people'. Film director Roman Polanski was away shooting a movie in London. But his wife, movie star Sharon Tate, who was eight months pregnant, was at home. Coffee heiress Abigail Folger, and her boyfriend Polish writer Voyteck Frykowski were visiting. So was Sharon Tate's friend, celebrity hairdresser Jay Sebring.

Kasabian lost her nerve at the last minute and stayed outside. Tex Watson, Susan Atkins and Patricia Krenwinkel pushed open the wrought-iron gates. They bumped into eighteen-year-old Steven Parent, who had been visiting the caretaker. He begged for his life. Watson shot him four times.

Inside the house, Manson's disciplines told Sharon Tate and her guests that the house was simply being robbed and no harm would come to them. They were to be tied up, but Jay Sebring broke free. He was shot down before he could escape. Fearing they were all going to be killed, Frykowski attacked Watson, who beat him to the ground with the pistol butt. In a sexual frenzy, the girls stabbed him to death. There were fifty-one stab wounds on his body.

Folger also made a break for it. But Krenwinkel caught up with her halfway across the lawn. She was knocked to the ground and Watson stabbed her to death.

Sharon Tate begged for the life of her unborn child. Susan Atkins showed no mercy. She stabbed her sixteen times. Tate's mutilated body was tied to Sebring's corpse. The killers spread an American flag across the couch and wrote the word 'pig' on the front door in Sharon Tate's blood. They changed their bloody clothes, collected their weapons and made their way back to the Spahn Ranch.

Manson got high on marijuana and read the reports of the murders in the newspapers as if they were reviews. To celebrate this great victory, he had an orgy with his female followers. But soon he craved more blood.

On 10 August, Manson randomly selected a house in the Silver Lake area and broke in. Forty-four-year-old grocery-store owner Leno LaBianca and his 38-year-old wife Rosemary, who ran a fashionable dress shop, awoke to find Manson holding a gun in their face. He tied them up, telling them they would not be harmed. He only intended to rob them.

He took LaBianca's wallet and went outside to the car where the rest of his followers were waiting. With them was 23-year-old Steve Grogan. Manson sent Tex Watson, Leslie Van Houten and Patricia Krenwinkel back into the LaBiancas' house. He said that he was going to the house next door to murder its occupants. Instead, he drove home.

Watson did as he was told. He dragged Leno LaBianca into the living room, stabbed him to death and left the knife sticking out of his throat Meanwhile, Van Houten and Krenwinkel stabbed the helpless Mrs LaBianca as they chanted a murderous mantra. They used their victim's blood to write more revolutionary slogans on the walls. Then the three killers took a shower together.

The killers thought of their senseless slayings as a joke. They also expected them to set off Helter Skelter, the great revolutionary race war. When it did not, they knew they were in danger and the Family began to break up.

Susan Atkins turned back to prostitution to support herself. She was arrested and, in prison, she boasted to another inmate about the killings. When the police questioned her, she blamed Manson.

On 15 October 1969, Manson was arrested and charged with murder. Basking in publicity, Manson portrayed himself as the baddest man on Earth and boasted that he had been responsible for thirty-five other murders. But at his trial he pointed out a simple truth.

'I've killed no one,' he told the jury. 'I've ordered no one to be killed. These children who come to you with their knives, they're your children. I didn't teach them – you did.'

It did not make any difference. He, Beausoleil, Atkins, Krenwinkel, Van Houten and Grogan were all sentenced to death in the gas chamber. But before the sentence could be carried out, the death penalty was abolished in California. Manson and his followers had their sentences commuted to life imprisonment and they are now eligible for parole. So far, none of them have been granted it.

The Reverend Jim Jones, who ordered over 914 people to kill themselves in the Guyanian jungle in 1978, also dominated his followers by sex.

In 1957, Jones and his wife, an ex-nurse five years his senior, established the first People's Temple in a lavishly converted synagogue on North Delaware Street, Indianapolis.

Around that time, Jones made several pilgrimages to the Peace Mission of Father Divine, the most successful ministry to the urban poor in the country. He learnt at the master's feet. The keys to Father Divine's success were his absolute insistence on his own divinity and extravagant demonstrations of the power of faith. Jones quickly learnt the lesson and began putting on his own displays of healing.

In carefully contrived theatrical settings, he got believers to spew up chicken livers claiming they were cancers. Perfectly fit young people, made up to look like paralysed ancients, were raised from their wheelchairs. He astounded his congregation with his mindreading powers. He had a photographic memory and had already begun detailed files on all his followers.

Jones also noted that Father Divine, though black with an exclusively black following, surrounded himself with an inner circle of attractive, middle-class white women.

As Jim Jones's People's Temple became more prosperous, Jones moved it out to affluent Redwood Valley, California. There, he attacked an educated white middle-class congregation, which he installed as the upper echelon to organise the church's activities.

In California, Jones met an ambitious young lawyer named Tim Stoen. He had just married his young wife Grace. Stoen had been disillusioned by the assassination of President Kennedy and was searching for a revolutionary way ahead. Jones promised just that. His multi-racial congregation and free-wheeling Christian/Marxist philosophy seemed to represent the wave of the future. Jones's growing political influence also secured Stoen the plum job of assistant district attorney in San Francisco.

The price of Stoen's participation was the body of his wife. In January 1972 she gave birth to a son, John-John. The birth certificate listed the father as Tim Stoen. But in an affidavit, he stated that he requested Jones to sire a child by his wife 'with the steadfast hope that said child will become the devoted follower of Jesus Christ and be instrumental in bringing God's kingdom here on earth, as has been his wonderful natural father'. Jim Jones, Tim Stoen said, was the 'most, compassionate, honest and courageous human being on earth.' The affidavit was witnessed by Marceline, Jones's wife. Grace Stoen's feelings were not recorded.

Jones was also using his congregation as a harem and his young women followers seemed to consider it a privilege to satisfy his sexual cravings. It was the least they could do for the great man. Jones's secretaries kept a separate appointments book for these liaisons. Jones boasted of his sexual prowess. He claimed that he had almost superhuman endurance, technique and potency. At one time he even asked for medical advice on how to bring his libido under control.

Jones used sex, not just for pleasure, but for power. It corroded the bond between couples and bound each partner closer to him and the Temple. Jones banned all sex with outsiders. Any relationship inside the congregation needed the Temple's specific approval, in advance. It was seldom forthcoming. One woman had an abortion rather than bear his child, but at least three of Jones's children were carried to term by members of the congregation.

Sex was a frequent topic of discussion at the all-important Planning Commission. This was an inner circle of around 100 members, largely the better-educated middle-class whites. Meetings would drag on to the early hours, with Jones railing against bourgeois sexual attitudes. He would force members to publicly confess their sexual fears and fantasies. Sometimes Jones would sentence those less than forthcoming to long periods of celibacy. They should follow his example, Jones said. He took no sensual pleasure in sex. For him, he said, it was a revolutionary tool. During one meeting, Jones forced one white man to perform oral sex on a black woman in front of everyone to prove he harboured no racial prejudice. Sexual candour and public urination, Jones maintained, were symbolic representations of the Temple's openness. But Jones, it seemed to some, took an unhealthy pleasure in exhibiting himself.

Jones did not just sleep with the women. The men were encouraged to have sex with him. It was, Jones contended, a revolutionary act. Again, Jones entered into the spirit of the thing with a little too much relish. In 1973, he was picked up for making flagrant homosexual overtures to an undercover policeman in the toilet of a cinema during a matinee of *Jesus Christ – Superstar*.

Jones said it was part of a police vendetta against him and the Temple. If it was, it failed. Jones had enough political influence to not only get the charges dropped but also to have the arrest record sealed by a Los Angeles judge.

But lurid tales about what was going on in the Temple began to seep out. Defectors from the church filed affidavits, charging Jones with all manner of indecent behaviour. Jones struck back at his critics by accusing them of child molesting. However, the press began to pick up on the stories and New West magazine queried the exact relationship between Jones and Grace Stoen.

Grace had run away from the Temple some time before. She began suing for the return of her son. Jones was determined she should not have him – and resettled the Temple in Guyana on Tim Stoen's advice. Stoen said it would take years to fight a custody case through the courts there.

For the members of his congregation the entry fee to Jones's jungle-based utopia in Guyana was everything they owned or earned. Many chose to pay it. Others had no choice. As many as 150 children were handed over to the Temple, along with their welfare cheques, by California's welfare agencies.

On the trip to Guyana, many of his followers found

themselves briefly free from the discipline of Jones for the first time. They got drunk in the grog shops of Georgetown. On the way up the river, one teenage girl, full of rum, had a brief fling with one of the Guyanese boatmen. Jones was furious. Once inside the jungle compound at Jonestown, iron discipline was enforced again. Casual sexual encounters were prohibited – and the Relationship Committee slapped a three month sex ban on any couple applying to have a serious relationship.

Such restrictions did not apply to Jones himself of course. He lived in one hut with two of his mistresses while his wife moved into another hut nearby. One young girl who declined the privilege of sleeping with the great leader was drugged and man-handled each night from the Jonestown hospital to Jones's hut.

Those who curried favour with Jones were given generous privileges. The Jonestown doctor who backed Jones's assertion that non-revolutionary sex caused cancer was given a succession of teenage girls. And when one young girl left, Jones confessed that her defection was his fault. She had left, he said, because he had refused to have sex with her. She wanted bourgeois sex – for pleasure! For him, sex was a political act.

Beatings were commonplace for minor offences. People could be punished simply because Jones accused them of having their 'head between their legs'. They were thinking of sex rather than the socialist work ethic. Jones was especially hard on any male who fancied a girl that he wanted for himself. Even adults were caned. Or they were forced to fight each other until 'right triumphed', or until one was beaten into bloody submission.

Children were also harshly treated. When they were beaten – as many as seventy-five times – their crimes were broadcast around the compound through the PA system. One child was buried in a metal box for 24 hours. Others were lowered down a well, where they were pulled into the water by one of Jones's assistants.

Without Jones there to coerce them, a number of the congregation of Jones's People's Temple in America had left the sect. Jones called them traitors. They had told the press bizarre tales of the goings-on in Guyana. The bisexual Jones was sexually dominating his flock they claimed. Temple members were forced into gruelling manual labour in appalling physical conditions. Disciplined in humiliating rituals, they were not allowed to leave.

The Committee of Concerned Relatives was formed. One relative, Sam Houston, accused the cult of murdering his son who had left the Temple after a violent argument with Jones. The next day he died in a grisly railroad accident.

Houston was a journalist with Associated Press and was well connected. He knew Congressman Leo Ryan and several of the Temple's members came from Ryan's congressional district in south San Francisco. Houston managed to persuade Ryan to investigate the sect.

In October 1978, the US Congress authorised Ryan to go to Guyana. As legal action was threatening to cut off Jonestown's funds, Jones had no choice but to receive him. But he tried to lay down conditions. He would not allow Ryan into Jonestown if he brought the press or any 'traitors' with him.

The feisty San Franciscan congressman was not to be dictated to. He arrived in Guyana with reporters and photographers from the San Francisco dailies, the *Washington Post*, an NBC film crew and four members of the Committee of Concerned Relatives. When Jones tried to keep him out of Jonestown, Ryan called his bluff. If he was turned away from the gates, he told Jones, it would be shown in America from coast to coast on NBC's network – and a full scale congressional investigation was bound to follow.

On the afternoon of 17 November, Congressman Ryan, a

298

planefull of journalists and the four relatives of Temple members landed at Port Kaituma, an airstrip a few miles from Jonestown. They were greeted by Johnny, one of Jones's adopted sons. Just before sunset, they arrived in Jonestown on the back of the Jonestown dump truck.

The reception was deceptively friendly. Jones had retired scowling to his hut, but the other sect members had been instructed to smile. After dinner at eight, Congressman Ryan made a speech. He studiously avoided any criticism of Jones. Instead he told the Templars that Jonestown looked like a pretty nice place to live.

'From what I have seen, there are a lot of people who believe this is the best thing that ever happened to them,' he said. There was only one thing Ryan could see that was wrong with the place – it wasn't in his congressional district so no one there could vote for him.

The Templars had been resentful, but Ryan's speech had won them round. They broke into spontaneous applause. The Jonestown band struck up and the young people took to the dance floor. The older ones clapped to the rhythm. Everyone seemed happy enough. But later that night, a young black woman passed a note to an NBC journalist. It asked him to arrange for her and a friend to leave Jonestown with Congressman Ryan the next day.

The next morning, nine sect members seized their chance to escape. An official tour of Jonestown was organised, but some journalists began poking around on their own. This almost provoked a riot. NBC interviewed Jones on camera and he freely admitted his mistresses. But he denied press reports that there was a sex ban on his followers. 'Bullshit,' Jones said, 'thirty babies have been born since the summer of 1977.'

But Jones no longer came across like the smooth polyester-suited pastor who had charmed politicians in the States. The Guyanian climate did not suit him. He was now fat, pale and sweaty. And, after only a few minutes of persistent questioning, his paranoia began to show.

'The only thing I regret is that somebody hasn't shot me,' he snivelled. 'We're a small community, we're no threat to anyone, but they won't rest until they destroy us. I wish they would just shoot me and get it over with. But I guess the media smear is what they use now – in the long run it's as good as assassination.'

Other reporters began pressing Jones about the son he had had with Grace Stoen and why he refused to return him to his mother. They asked why the Jonestown security guards carried weapons and why threats were made to those who wanted to leave.

'It's all lies,' Jones insisted.

At that moment, one of Jones's henchmen brought news that the grandmother of a family that had been planning to escape for some time had asked Ryan to take them out of Jonestown. Jones went to see them.

'I am betrayed,' he ranted. 'It never stops.'

Another twenty people seized the opportunity. They asked Ryan to take them with him. By this time, Jones was hysterical.

'I've given my life for my people,' he wailed.

His aides calmed him and persuaded him to let the people go. Even now the number of defections were small in number, especially when compared to the huge number that stayed behind. But the fanatics began to turn ugly.

As the defectors left, a young man pulled a knife and grabbed Congressman Ryan. Two of Jones's aides pulled him off. But as they fought, the knife cut the young man's arm and blood spurted over Ryan.

At the last moment, another Templar named Larry Layton shouted that he was 'pissed off with Jonestown' and joined the leaving party. The other defectors were apprehensive. Layton was known as a 'robot'. He would do anything Jones said, without question.

Before he boarded the plane at Port Kaituma, Layton was searched. But he had still managed to smuggle a gun on board the aircraft. As the plane got ready to take off, the Jonestown tractor arrived and blocked the runway. There were twenty heavily armed men in its trailer.

They started shooting, hitting three of the defectors. Inside the plane, Layton opened up, hitting a woman in the chest

Still on the runway, Congressman Ryan and three of the NBC crew were caught in the cross-fire. They were cut down and Jonestown gunmen finished them off with a shot in the head as they lay on the runway. Three other journalists were left wounded. They expected to be despatched similarly, but the Jonestown tractor and trailer pulled away, leaving them, mercifully, alive.

Back at Jonestown, Jim Jones called a big meeting for all his followers. Layton, he said, had been sent to shoot the pilot of Ryan's plane in the head. The plane would have crashed in the jungle by then. If that plan had failed, twenty gunmen had been sent to take care of the congressman.

The CIA would force the left-wing government in Georgetown to send soldiers of the Guyanese Defence Force against them, Jones said. These soldiers were their black socialist brothers, he told the Templars. It would not be right to fight them. The solution was that they should all kill themselves.

The Jonestown medical staff had prepared two fifty-gallon drums of Kool-Aid, spiked with cyanide. Jones assured his followers that they would 'meet again in another place'. Then they meekly queued up for their lethal drink. Mothers administered it to their children. Infants had cyanide squirted in their mouths with a syringe. Even Jones's own children happily took the poison.

Jones assured his followers that the poison would lead to a painless death. But the children went into convulsions and panic broke out.

301

'They are not crying out of pain,' Jones said to calm them, 'it's just a little bitter tasting.'

Nevertheless, the adults went on sipping the deadly poison from paper cups. They strolled calmly out into the fields and lay down and died. Even the armed guards took their poison without resistance.

When the entire congregation was dead, Jones blew his brains out with a pistol. Jonestown's nurse, Annie Moore, shot herself in the head with the same gun moments later.

Ghoulishly, Jones had taped the final meeting and the mass suicide as a bizarre suicide note. On the tape, Jones can be heard exhorting his followers to 'take the potion like they used to take in ancient Greece; it is a revolutionary act.'

'The world was not ready for me,' he raved. 'The best testimony we can make is to leave the goddamned world . . . I don't care how many screams you hear . . . how many anguished cries; death is a million times preferable . . . Can some people assure these children of the relaxation of stepping over into the next plane? . . .'

'We've stepped over, one thousand people who said we don't like the way the world is,' Jones's voice said on the tape. 'Nobody takes our lives from us. We laid it down. We got tired. We didn't commit suicide. We committed an act of revolutionary suicide, protesting the conditions of an inhumane world.'

However, the one thing the tape does not explain to a shocked world is how even a charismatic leader like Jim Jones could drive over 900 people to kill themselves.

The day after the massacre, Guyanese soldiers entered Jonestown. They found two survivors. Grover Davis was hard of hearing and had missed the summons to the pavilion. And Hyacinth Thrush slept through the whole thing. Later she said that she was sorry to have missed the opportunity to die with her brothers and sisters.

Surveying the corpses, the Guyanese army estimated that

there were only 600 dead. But body was piled on body. Ten days later, a US army mortuary team arrived and the death toll was finally fixed at 914.

The mortuary team also looked for signs that the cyanide had been administered forcibly to unwilling victims. Although the followers were ringed by armed guards, they did not coerce the Templars into killing themselves. The victims seemed almost eager to drink the poison. According to one witness, the first victim walked up to the platform and took the poison without even being told to. She just poured it down the baby's throat. And then she took the rest herself.

'It didn't take them right away,' the witness said. 'She had time to walk outside . . . then the next woman came up with her baby and did the same thing.'

Even those outside the compound were willing to follow Jones's instructions. When he radioed to the Temple's office in Georgetown and told them to commit suicide too, the Temple's public relations officer took her three small children into the bathroom, killed them, then slit her own wrists.

There was one final irony though. One of Jones's great achievements in life was to overcome racism within his congregation. He saw himself as a revolutionary leader in the mould of Martin Luther King and Malcolm X. But when the bodies were found, the cyanide had turned the skin of even his white followers black, while Jones, who had shot himself, had turned a deathly white.

Chapter 18

Snuff Movies

The end came quite by chance. A young Chinese man had taken a vice from a general store without paying for it. The shop assistant ran to find a policeman. The officer followed the young Asian to his car. He dumped the vice in the boot then, spotting the officer, ran off. The burly police officer gave chase, but the skinny youth was too fast for him.

When the officer returned to the car, a bald bearded man was standing beside it. He explained that it had all been a big mistake. He had now paid for the vice and he showed the officer the receipt. That should have been the end of it. But why, the policeman wondered, had the young Asian run away?

The officer thought he had better examine the car. Perhaps it was stolen. In the boot, he found a holdall. It contained a .22 pistol and a silencer. Although it is quite legal to carry a handgun in the US, adding a silencer is against the law. It indicates that the gun is likely to be used for some nefarious purpose.

The bearded man handed over his California driver's

licence as ID. It said that he was Robin Scott Stapley. He hardly knew the Chinese youth who had run away, he explained, he was just about to hire him for a job.

At the police station, the bearded man asked for paper and pencil and a glass of water. On the paper, he scribbled a few words to his wife. Then, with the aid of the water, he swallowed a pill. The pill contained cyanide. He was dead in seconds. The note read: 'Cricket, I love you. Please forgive me. I forgive you. Please tell Mama, Fern and Patty I'm sorry.'

The police discovered that the dead man in the interview room was not Robin Stapley. Stapley had gone missing five months before. A few weeks later his camper van, driven by a young Chinese man, had run into a truck. The Asian begged the truck driver not to report the accident. But as the truck driver was driving a company vehicle he had no choice.

The car the bearded man was driving was registered to a Paul Cosner. His girlfriend said that Cosner had sold it to a weird-looking man who said he would pay cash. But when Cosner drove off to deliver it, he never returned.

When forensics got their hands on the car, they found two bullet holes in the front seat and two spent rounds were lodged in the upholstery. There were also bloodstains – human blood.

In the glove compartment, they found some papers belonging to a Charles Gunnar of Wilseyville, Calavers County, 150 miles north of San Francisco. A call to the local sheriff revealed that the county police already had their eye on Gunnar and his young friend, a Chinese named Charles Ng. They were suspected of handling stolen goods – videos, TV sets, furniture and other household items. Among the items they were selling was furniture belonging to Brenda O'Connor and Lonnie Bond. Gunnar had explained that the young couple had moved to Los Angeles with their baby and left the furniture in settlement of a debt.

There had been another mysterious disappearance in the area. A young couple had simply vanished from a camp site, at nearby Schaad Lake. They left behind their tent – with the coffee pot still on the stove.

The dead man's fingerprints revealed that his name was Leonard Lake. He had been charged with grand larceny and burglary in Mendocino County and had jumped bail. Lake, it seemed, was closely associated with a number of other disappearances. His younger brother Donald had gone missing two years before, after setting out to visit Lake at a survivalist camp in Humboldt County. Charles Gunnar, the man whose identity Lake was using, had gone missing early that year after being best man at Lake's wedding.

The trail led inexorably to the small ranch on Blue Mountain Road where Gunnar – that is Lake – and Ng lived. A team of deputies came up from San Francisco to examine it. Set in three acres of wooded grounds, the ranch was an ordinary-looking two bedroomed bungalow. But inside it was far from ordinary. The master bedroom was fitted out like a medieval torture chamber. There were hooks in the ceiling and walls, and boxes full of chains and shackles that could be used to immobilise someone on the bed.

There was also a wardrobe full of flimsy night-gowns and sexy underwear, and some expensive video equipment. The serial numbers confirmed that the video gear belonged to Harvey and Deborah Dubbs. It had last been seen being carried from their apartment by a Chinese removal man, after the couple and their sixteen-month old baby had disappeared.

Lake had been a dedicated survivalist. In the garden he had built a nuclear fallout shelter. Inside there was a storeroom containing foot, water, candles and guns. In the floor there was a sinister-looking trapdoor. It led to another chamber below. This again was hung with hooks and chains. The walls were covered with pictures of frightened-looking girls posing in their underwear. All the pictures had been taken in that same room.

Next to this chamber was a tiny cell, with a one-way mirror in the wall so that the person inside was under 24-hour surveillance.

The bomb-shelter basement also contained filing cabinets. In them there were more pictures and a huge collection of video tapes. The first cassette the police slipped in the video was marked 'Kathy/Brenda'. It began with a terrified girl handcuffed to a chair being menaced by Charles Ng. Then Lake enters the frame. He removes the girl's handcuffs and shackles her feet instead, then orders the girl to strip. She undresses reluctantly – she can hardly bring herself to remove her panties but is forced to do so.

'You'll wash for us,' orders Lake, 'clean for us, fuck for us.'

Later she is shown being strapped naked to the bed. As an added twist of cruelty, Lake tells her that her boyfriend is dead.

Brenda – who is identified as Brenda O'Connor – also appears handcuffed to a chair. While Ng slowly cuts her clothes off her, she enters a chilling dialogue with Lake. First she asks where the baby is. He says that it has been placed with a family in Fresno.

'Why do you guys do this?' she asks.

'We don't like you. Do you want me to put it in writing?'

'Don't cut my bra off.'

'Nothing is yours now.'

'Give my baby back to me. I'll do anything you want.'

'You're going to do anything we want anyway.'

Other videos showed women being shackled, raped, tortured and worse. They featured all the missing women that the police already knew about, others recognised from missing persons' reports and over twenty-five more that they never identified. For two years, Leonard Lake and Charles

Ng had been making 'snuff movies'. The tapes were clearly marked 'M Ladies' – 'Murdered Ladies'. Each one ended with the death of the reluctant female lead.

The police found a bloodstained chainsaw which had been used to cut the bodies up. The pieces were then incinerated and the bones scattered across the hillside at the back of the house. Other bodies were found still whole. In a narrow trench that ran across the garden, the police found a number of bodies too decomposed to attempt to identify. Among them were the bodies of a man, woman and child – this could have been Bond, O'Connor and their baby; the Dubbs family; or any other innocent man, woman and child who had fallen into Lake's gruesome trap. Two weeks of digging produced nine full bodies and 40 lb of human bones. Identification was all but impossible, but driver's licences and other papers confirmed that Robert Stapley, Paul Cosner and the couple from the camping site were all among the victims.

Among the basement files, the police found Lake's diary. It indicated that his grisly career had begun long before he moved into the ranch on Blue Mountain Road. Leonard Lake had been born in 1946 in San Francisco. Rejected by both parents, he had been brought up with military discipline by his grandparents. Leonard's brother Donald was a sadist who tortured animals and tried to rape his sisters. Leonard protected his sisters – at a price. They had to perform certain sexual favours for him.

He also took nude pictures of them and his cousins. Later, he made pornographic films starring his wife 'Cricket' Balazs.

Vietnam changed him, though he was not a front-line hero as he later claimed. He became deeply pessimistic – though he covered this up by teaching, becoming a volunteer fire fighter and doing charity work. His pessimism led him to survivalism – and a life financed by petty theft and burglary.

His marriage broke up, though his wife still acted as a

308

fence for the credit cards and other items he stole. But slowly the idea began to grow that women were the cause of all his problems. Then, by killing his troublesome brother Donald, he found the release he sought.

He began a murder spree. A crude map of California was marked with crosses saying 'buried treasure'. These were thought to be the burial sites of his early victims, but the map is too inaccurate to check them out.

In the isolated village of Miranda in Northern California, Lake came up with the idea of what he called Operation Miranda. He planned to stockpile weapons, foot, water and kidnapped women in preparation for the coming nuclear holocaust. 'The perfect woman is totally controlled,' he wrote, 'a woman who does exactly what she is told to and nothing else. There is no sexual problem with a submissive woman. There are no frustrations – only pleasure and contentment.' And with the help of Charles Ng, he put Operation Miranda into practice.

Ng was born in 1961, the son of a wealthy Hong Kong family. Educated in a private school in North Yorkshire, he had been expelled for theft. He completed his education in San Francisco but, at eighteen, he was involved in a hit-and-run accident. To escape jail, he joined the Marines and was posted to Hawaii. But his lifelong kleptomania struck again and he was arrested for the theft of ammunition and weapons worth over $11,000.

Escaping from custody in Hawaii, he returned to San Francisco where he met Lake. He looked up to the older man and they embarked on a full-time life of crime together. They were arrested in Mendocino County for burglary. Ng went down for the earlier theft in Hawaii as well, and spent some of his sentence in Port Leavenworth. When he was paroled, he joined Lake at the ranch and helped him put his paranoid fantasies into brutal reality.

Lake's journal describes how his sex slaves were

collected. He would invite unwitting couples and families to the ranch for dinner. The men and children would be murdered straight away. The women would then be stripped, shackled, sexually abused and humiliated. They would be forced to perform menial chores around the house and kept in a Spartan cell. They would also be used as the unwilling subjects of sadism and sex videos. When a woman showed any sign of rebellion against her submissive role – or when her tormentor grew tired of her – they would kill her and film that too.

Psychological studies of Lake show that when he was arrested he was in the final phase of the serial murder syndrome. Sated with blood, he felt that he had reached the end of a cul-de-sac and there was no way back. He had caused untold misery to others and now was bringing misery to himself. The only way out was suicide.

Ng, though, was a survivor. He escaped over the Canadian border. He was caught shoplifting there and shot the security guard. After serving a four-and-a-half-year sentence for armed robbery, he was extradited back to California to face charges of mass murder.